THE
LANDING LIGHTS
OF MAGONIA

UFOs, Aliens and
the Fairy Kingdom

Nigel Graddon

Adventures Unlimited Press

The Landing Lights of Magonia

ISBN 13: 978-1-939149-97-8

Published by:
Adventures Unlimited Press
One Adventure Place
Kempton, Illinois 60946 USA

auphq@frontiernet.net

www.adventuresunlimitedpress.com

The Landing Lights of Magonia

UFOs, Aliens and the Fairy Kingdom

Other books by Nigel Graddon

Otto Rahn and the Quest for the Grail: The Amazing Life of the Real Indiana Jones

(Adventures Unlimited Press)

The Mystery of U-33: Hitler's Secret Envoy

(Adventures Unlimited Press)

The Looking Glass Ripper

(writing as Gordon Finlay, CreateSpace Independent Publishing Platform)

CONTENTS

Acknowledgements

I give a big thank you to Linda Moulton Howe for her gracious permission to quote from her studies. I am also grateful to eagle-eyed Kathleen McVay for her sterling proof-reading labours, to Andras Beno for the enchanting photo of the garden ghost, to my old pal Doc Nelson for the magical stories of the Minstrel, Raoul and Luigi, and, not least, to David Hatcher Childress for his continuing support.

Up the airy mountains,
Down the rushy glen,
We daren't go a-hunting
For fear of little men;
Wee folk, good folk,
Trooping all together;
Green jacket, red cap,
And white owl's feather

Down along the rocky shore
Some make their home,
They live on crispy pancakes
Of yellow tide foam;
Some in the reeds,
Of the black mountain lake,
With frogs for their watch-dogs,
All night awake.

— William Allingham, *The Fairies*

Introduction

"We (that indivisible divinity that functions within us) have dreamed the world. We have dreamed it as enduring, mysterious, visible, ubiquitous in space and time; but we have permitted in its architecture tenuous and eternal interstices of unreason so that we might know it is false."

— Jorge Luis Borges, *Other Inquisitions*

In their classic work about high strangeness in Wales, the fabled land of Merlin and dragons, Pugh and Holiday[1] cite the late Gordon Creighton writing for *The Flying Saucer Review*. Creighton made the astute observation that:

"beings from flying saucers are much more probably creatures who share this earth with us; regarding whom science has not a single word to say; but about whom our own written and oral traditions, in all our civilisations, speak volumes."

"Creatures who share this earth with us…"—this statement requires some thought. According to folklore the world over, humankind has been sharing the earth with supernatural beings since time immemorial. Up to the pre-industrial period our traditions referred to these beings collectively as fairy folk, recondite life forms intimately connected with the natural world.

Men and women used to live their lives much closer to nature than has been the practice over the past two hundred and fifty years, a blink of an eye compared to the length of time that humankind has been living on this planet. Consequently, unusual life forms if glimpsed or experienced in former times were readily associated with the natural

---

[1] Pugh, R.J., and Holiday F.W., *The Dyfed Enigma*, Faber and Faber, London and Boston, 1979

world and invariably described and stories told of them in terms of the earth's basic elemental makeup.

Countless tales were told about the fairy folk and their supposed origins because it is the nature of men to seek to explain and rationalise the unexplainable. Then came the Industrial Revolution, the age of the machine. Those among the strata of society that for millennia had traditionally toiled on the land moved to towns and cities to find work in the new age "dark Satanic Mills." The minds of men and women were then inculcated with new mental archetypes: the spinning jenny replacing that of the plough, the navvy's spade turning to the task of digging canals, and the new-fangled railways supplanting the harvest scythe.

The rapid switch from farm to factory inevitably generated a sense of doubt and fear and a feeling of deep loss for a bucolic past. This emotional upheaval elicited a whole host of social and political challenges. Later, C.G. Jung reflected deeply on this phenomenon. He readily understood that the fear factor caused by rapid and fundamental social change had led humankind to look to the skies for help because it could no longer be found on the green and pleasant earth with which it was innately familiar, hence the appearance of signs in the heavens. What once had been routinely described as fairy visitations took on a technological connotation and revealed themselves to percipients as flying disks or other like symbols.

The sixteenth century villagers of Merionethshire were terrified of entering Coed-y-Dugoed Mawr (the Great Dark Wood) for fear of encountering the Red Fairies who lived in dens in the ground, had fiery red hair and long strong arms and stole sheep and cattle by night. Such was their fear that locals kept scythes in their chimneys to repel these terrible beings. Three hundred years later, November 1896, in Stockton, California, Colonel H.G. Shaw encountered three slender, 7-feet tall beings that tried to force him into their spacecraft. This episode has been described as one of the earliest attempts at alien abduction.

There are countless tales both of fairies and little green men. Growing evidence suggests that there is little or no difference between them and that the intrinsic nature of these accounts and the entities described is one and the same. By removing the cultural, social and temporal factors that separate these narratives we see them for what they are: encounters with non-human entities (NHEs), although *not* necessarily non-human like. It is the memes and tropes of successive epochs that seek to label these phenomena which, in essence, are simply brushes with energy forms that exist in what Jung described as "a yet unknown substrate possessing material and, at the same time, psychic qualities."[2] In *The Landing Lights of Magonia* we will examine in depth the possible nature of Jung's substrate and, in so doing, reach for insights into the vexed question: whence they came?

In the following pages I will seek to demonstrate that humans label little green men in accordance with their time, truth, tradition, belief and societal mores. One man's goblin is another's grey. No matter how we have described them in human history, one fact remains: NHEs do not originate in a galaxy far, far away. They have always been among us, are among us now and in the corner of our eye may be glimpsed by the flickering light of a candlestick if Jack be nimble, Jack be quick.

What lies behind the cracks in our world remains a mystery but for those that have a hunger to know all is not lost. Myth, legend, fairytales, sci-fi stories and, praise be to the gods, Frost and Lynch, each tell us something about the "Man from Another Place"; while cutting edge thinkers in quantum physics are beginning to reveal how the existence of "Another Place" is even possible.

In the field of traditional folklore our journey in *The Landing Lights of Magonia* will be guided by the work and insights of outstanding figures such as Reverend Robert Kirk, Walter Evans-Wentz, Edwin Hartland and Grace Cooke in our quest to understand the nature and origins of NHEs. On the subject of modern-day UFO studies, a review of the pioneering work of researchers of the calibre of Linda Moulton Howe, John Keel, Jacques Vallée, Anthony Roberts, Geoff Gilbertson, John Michell and Carl Jung and the like will further help us arrive at a deeper understanding of a great mystery.

This work will also draw inspiration from an in-depth examination of the latest ideas from the science community on the nature of physical existence and the case for multiple dimensions. This analysis will be greatly enhanced by incorporating the key principles identified by the late Professor David Bohm in his mindblowing reflections on what precisely is reality. Can it truly be the case that man's collective conscious is the engine of divine creation that makes and maintains the physical universe moment by moment?

In our study of the Wee Folk and UFOlk, *The Landing Lights of Magonia* will focus on five distinct dimensions: Earth—the base point for our investigations; Magonia—the land of the fairy folk and other curiosities of the Celtic Otherworld; "Infernia"—a term of mine to

---

[2] Jung, C.J., *Flying Saucers: A Modern Myth of Things Seen in the Skies*, ARK edition, London, 1977

denote a dimension of reality distinguished by its ultra-negative qualities; the Elemental dimension, home to the Nature Spirits and the circle makers; and Tír Na nÓg—the "heaven world," home to cosmic energies of which we know little but whose presence we may at times be privileged to feel, glimpse, even see.

Do NHEs constitute a threat to humankind? Do they perceive our military and environmentally destructive actions as an existential threat to the structural integrity of the earth and its invisible but no less real interconnecting and complementary worlds and their inhabitants? Do the worst among them regard the overall chaotic outpourings of our emotional selves as a vampiric Smörgåsbord of delights, food for the Dark Gods who relish a gift that just keeps on giving?

Conversely, in the midst of seemingly irreversible chaos, do we also begin to detect the building of a new energy, one founded on the qualities of hope, grace, inspiration, positive belief and love for nature and humanity? In the circles in the fields are we seeing, as many astute thinkers and visionaries believe, the construction of a New Jerusalem, an opportunity for individuals to develop a state of mind for a new world taking shape around us, unseen but sensed by those whose power to dream is undiminished?

In *The Landing Lights of Magonia* I will avoid conflating my ideas to encompass the various classes of "nuts and bolts" craft seen in the skies such as the mysterious giant Flying Triangles. The degree of probability that these and similar craft possess a human origin is sufficiently high to put them outside the scope of this present work. That being said, there are many who believe that advanced technological accomplishments such as these are only made possible through the exploitation of NHE knowledge and know-how, either freely given or gained as prizes after crash events such as at Roswell in the USA and in the Berwyn Mountains of North Wales.

Earlier, I was careful in my choice of words when I said that NHEs "do not originate in a galaxy far, far away." Having reflected on the matter, I am of the opinion that there *is* a specific category of space visitor that hails not from a dimensional source but from a nearby planet, the odds-on favourite being Mars. I believe that twentieth century events and the recovery of NHE personnel both dead and alive provide convincing evidence of humanlike visitors whose forbears were exiled from our own earth prior to a great cataclysm we know as the Flood. *The Landing Lights of Magonia* will examine the evidence for this and for corresponding acts of collusion between global governments and NHE representatives, posing questions on what might be the motivating factors that bind the parties in uneasy alliance.

The more one delves into the data the more one gets the feeling that the last people who are intended to benefit from these unholy tête-à-têtes are the billions of ordinary citizens in this world. But those in power should be ever wary of getting into cahoots with unknown forces:

> *"And oftentimes, to win us to our harm,*
> *The instruments of darkness tell us truths,*
> *Win us with honest trifles, to betray's*
> *In deepest consequence."*

William Shakespeare, Macbeth

Let us now step into the fairy circle and allow ourselves to make a respectful acquaintance with the Wee Folk. We begin our quest with a 1967 case study, "The Little Blue Man of Studham," an account perhaps not well known outside of Britain but one that shines a revealing light on the exciting pathway before us.

Photo taken in 2017 by a friend of a friend in their
garden in Wales. Can you make out the form of the
little bearded old man?

Chapter 1

The Little Blue Man of Studham

"Fairytales can come true, it can happen to you
If you're young at heart.
For it's hard, you will find, to be narrow of mind
If you're young at heart."

—Carolyn Leigh, 1953

On 28 January 1967, the day Lennon and McCartney agreed to compose music for London's Roundhouse Theatre where new sensation The Jimi Hendrix Experience was to perform, seven male pupils at Studham School in Bedfordshire, England, witnessed a remarkable occurrence. Even today, fifty years on, the event carries a powerful resonance and continues to exert a profound significance upon the ongoing debate on the nature of NHE phenomena.

On a thundery winter's day Tony Banks (11), Alex Butler (10), Colin Lonsdale (10), Kerry Gahill (11), David Inglis (10), Andrew Hoar (11) and John Mickleburgh (10) were playing on the local common while heading for afternoon school near an area known locally as the Dell. The Dell is a shallow valley thick with gorse, bracken and hawthorn, in those days cluttered with car tyres and other detritus.

In preceding years children and animals had created a warren of passages that criss-crossed the entire area. These passages connected dens that had been fashioned beneath the larger of the Dell's bushes. In the middle of the area was a small open space. The nearest houses were one hundred and fifty yards away, while Studham School lay fifty yards further on.

The parish of Studham, a village lying six hundred feet up in a dip on the wooded south-facing slope of the Chiltern Hills, lies east and south of the Hertfordshire and Buckinghamshire borders respectively. It is isolated by the boundary fence of Whipsnade Park Zoo close to the northwest and by a deepish valley to the south.

The rain, thunder and lightning had not long ceased. The sky was clear. From the top of the Dell's northern bank Alex, a little way ahead of the others, was scanning the terrain when he saw "a little blue man with a tall hat and beard" standing twenty yards away in front of the bushes by the opposite bank. Alex stared in bewilderment for a few seconds before calling out a breathless description to his pals and exhorting them to see for themselves. At first sceptical, the six friends ran to join him and, stunned, confirmed Alex's view of the amazing spectacle. As a body the seven boys began running towards the figure but as they neared its position a whirring cloud of yellow-blue mist moved towards them and the little blue man vanished. Soon they spotted him again, this time to their left on the top of the bank. He was standing facing them at a range of twenty yards. Once more they approached but he repeated his vanishing trick.

The third time the little blue man appeared he was back at the bottom of the Dell close to his original position. As they peered at him through the leafless wintry scrub the boys became aware of "voices" that seemed to emanate from a nearby point in the bushes down the slope to the right of their position. Afterwards, they likened the "voices" to deep-toned unintelligible babble. Were there more of these strange little men in the bushes, they wondered?

Concerned lest the little blue man had confederates with whom he was communicating, the boys adopted stealth mode and did not move forwards like before. Instead, the boys continued to circle the Dell until, eventually, they saw the little blue man for the fourth and final time. As on the previous three occasions, it stood silent and motionless. They were uncertain as to what to do, a period of indecision that was curtailed by the sound of the school whistle summoning pupils into afternoon lessons. Straightaway, the lads dashed off to school in great excitement to report to their class teacher, Miss Newcomb, what had happened. The boys prefaced their account by telling Miss Newcomb that she would not believe their story.

To Miss Newcomb's credit she chose to accept that her pupils were speaking the truth. She then separated the boys to ensure there was no copying or conferring and asked them to write down individual accounts in their own words. The accounts tallied in every respect.

Two weeks later Miss Newcomb asked the boys to re-visit their accounts purely to tidy up punctuation and spelling because they were to be pasted into a school scrapbook entitled "The Little Blue Man on Studham Common."

Alex Butler at the spot where the little blue man stood

The boys described the man as being three feet tall. It wore a tall, brimless bowler hat with a rounded top. The lads spoke of seeing a line, which they felt was either a fringe of hair or the lower edge of the bowler. The little man had two round eyes and a small flat triangle instead of a nose. Its arms were short, held at the sides, and did not appear to move at any time during the sightings.

> Brownies are small men about three feet in height…they have no noses, only holes for nostrils.[3]

The dwarf's blue beard was forked, the two parts trailing down each side of his chest. He wore a one-piece suit of glowing blue and a broad black belt. Attached to the front of the buckle was a black box about six-inches square. The boys remarked that the little man was "horrid."

Some commentators have suggested that the event was a classic UFO encounter. In this scenario the figure's grey-bluish silhouette made difficult a clear perception of details and contours, while the bowler hat imprinted a representative image into the boys' minds to describe an NHE's space helmet. In this archetypal context of imagery

---

[3] Briggs, K., *A Dictionary of Fairies*, Penguin Books, London, 1977

10

the entity's belt may have been a receiver of some kind, while the forked beard could have served as a type of breathing apparatus. The theory that it was a UFO encounter is enhanced by the blue man's posture in which its indistinct legs and feet and its arms stuck at the sides are at odds with the traditional fairytale image of a merry, scampering dwarf making playful gestures.

> In 1977 Seattle shipyard worker "Steve Bismarck" saw "a little old man" about 4-feet tall. The pale brown skinned, fair complexioned figure resembled a Filipino man but its scars gave it the appearance of having been in a fire. The figure was very thin but well muscled. It wore a metallic sparkly-blue uniform and carried under its right arm a helmet of clear plastic with white colouration at the back.[4]

No UFO sightings were reported in the Studham area at the time of the little blue man event but *were* reported as appearing over the surrounding countryside in the following months. Sources told of two subsequent "UFO landings" at the Dell but nothing precise was reported and no dates were provided. All very tenuous. Others were convinced that the boys experienced a fairy encounter. The story was reported in the Dunstable Gazette. A reader observed that: "the incident resembles the old legends and folk tales of earth fairies and elementals." With this in mind consider these descriptions:

> The Blue Burches is a harmless hobgoblin from the Blackdown Hills in Somerset. He was a little old man in baggy blue burches (breeches).[5]

> A woman from Barra in Scotland's Outer Hebrides described the fairies she saw in the 1860s as wearing bell-helmets of blue silk, garments of green satin and sandals of yellow membrane. Their heavy brown hair streamed down to their waist with lustre of the fair golden summer sun. Their skin was white as the swan and their voice was as melodious as the mavis (*song thrush*) of the wood. Their step was light and stately.[6]

So, what do we have here? From the descriptions given by the boys in comparison to past accounts of UFO and fairy sightings, the Little Blue Man of Studham Common fits both categories broadly equally. It

---

[4] Howe, L.M. *Glimpses of Other Realities, Volume II: High Strangeness*, Paper Chase Press, New Orleans, 1998, p145-146
[5] Briggs, K. *A Dictionary of Fairies*
[6] Evans-Wentz, W., *The Fairy Faith in Celtic Countries*, Henry Frowde, 1911

is impossible either for sci-fi buffs or fairy lore enthusiasts to compartmentalise the encounter to suit a mutually satisfying genre.

Pre-teen children have been observed again and again to exhibit a far higher degree of sensitivity to invisible energies than those who have subconsciously lost these abilities so that they may conform to the mass conscious rules and requirements necessary for living as "responsible" adults in the rational world.

One might wonder what an adult would have seen had one been present in the Dell that early January afternoon—quite possibly nothing at all. Grown-up minds, for the most part, record only what is perceived by the five senses.

The ability to see or sense what lies behind the veil is beyond and above the parameters of what is accessible through the physical sensate experience. To access these worlds requires that we use deeper faculties of consciousness and awareness, which, for the most part, lie dormant in the mass of humanity. Knowing this, Jung remarked with great insight that dwarfs are the "guardians of the threshold of the unconscious."

Fairy country in rural Studham

Consider for a moment a scenario in which the Little Blue Man did not actively *come* to Studham but that the seven boys saw him in *his* world as if through a window. The physical nature of Magonia varies in folklore but some tales speak of its celestial nature, a description that parallels the theory that UFOs have an extraterrestrial origin.

Others hold that Magonia is a parallel universe that coexists with our own, made visible and tangible to selected people, and the doors between them are at tangential points known only to its citizens, in this instance the Little Blue Man. Doubtless, he knew he was under observation, hence his babbling to companions invisible to the onlookers. What might it have been saying? Perhaps something along the lines of, "These earth boys can see me, what must I do?"

Here we have a circumstance in which seven humans see a dwarf, an interesting reverse twist on the classic fairy-tale narrative. It was as if on this occasion the mirror on the wall was not reflecting the apparent beauty of the onlooker but was turned inward to reveal a world which humans are not ordinarily permitted to see. Perhaps the significance of the event only became apparent to the Studham percipients later in life; maybe they are waiting still to discover why they were allowed an extraordinary glimpse behind the veil.

The boys' story is theirs alone. The important thing that we as non-participants can take from this narrative is to understand that the experience of living on this planet is one that is vastly more complex than can possibly be imagined. The earth beneath our feet, the air we breathe, the life-giving water, the warming fire—in the basic elemental sense these powers protect, feed and nurture us during our time in this beautiful world. At a much deeper level of Nature consciousness, it is my conviction that the elements are super-intelligent forces that provide thresholds to countless life forms in numberless worlds about "whom science has not a single word to say; but about whom our own written and oral traditions…speak volumes."

Let us now make a more intimate acquaintance with the Wee Folk.

Chapter 2

Wee Folk

*"To know human life one must go deep beneath its sunny
exterior; and to know that summer-sea which is the Fairy
Faith one must put on a suit of armour and dive beneath its
waves and behold the rare corals and moving sea-palms
and all the brilliant creatures who move in and out among
those corals and sea-palms, and the horrible and awful
creatures too, creatures which would devour the man were
his armour not of steel—for they all mingle together in the
depths of that sea...hidden from our view as we sail over the
surface of its sun-lit waters only."*

—Walter Evans-Wentz

The large number of documented sightings of UFOs and their
occupants has facilitated efforts to arrive at a formalised approach to
classification. The same cannot be said for fairy folk. That is not to say
there is an absence of classification data regarding types or descriptions
for the genre, but by virtue of its mythological and folklorist nature the
taxonomy is understandably less well populated.

Evans-Wentz's intensive research into the Fairy Faith[7] led him to
conclude that there had never been a time in human history when there
was not a belief in an unseen world peopled by invisible beings.
Ancient man called them gods, genii, shades and daemons (the latter
not regarded as evil but as allies of man); Christians spoke of angels,
saints, souls and (evil) demons; Celts spoke of gods and fairies of many
kinds.

The scriptures tell many stories of encounters with unworldly
beings. Ezekiel described angels in human form called cherubim
(Hebrew: "full of knowledge"):

---

[7] ibid

"their appearance like burning coals of fire, and the appearance of lamps: it went up and down among the living creatures: the fire was bright, and out of the fire went forth lightning."

Enoch dreamed of:

"two men, very tall, such as I have never seen on earth. And their faces shone like the sun, and their eyes were like burning lamps."

These men took Enoch into the sky and conducted him on a tour of "seven heavens."

Daniel saw "wheels as burning fire" and encountered an entity that came down from a "throne" in the sky, dressed in a white robe with a gold belt and had a luminous face with two bright glowing eyes.

Daniel's vision of the wheels of fire

Ufologist John Keel read the Bible many times. He concluded that in light of present day knowledge about UFOs, many Biblical accounts take on new meanings. In olden times those who saw strange objects in the sky sought help from their priest who said God was showing us signs. Nowadays, we ask questions of the airforce, astronomers and quantum physicists.

The civilizations of Greece, Rome, Egypt, China and India believed implicitly in satyrs, sprites, and goblins. They peopled the sea with mermaids, the rivers and fountains with nymphs, the air with fairies, the household and its warming fire with the gods Lares and Penates, and the earth with fauns, dryads, and hamadryads. These inhabitants of nature's finer realms were held in high esteem and were propitiated with appropriate offerings. Occasionally, as the result of atmospheric conditions or the devotee's gift of second sight, the nature spirits became visible.

The Hebrews called these beings between Angels and Man *Sadaim*; the Greeks, transposing the letters and adding a syllable called them Daimonas. The Philosophers believed them to be the Aerial Race that ruled over the Elements.

The founder of Christian monasticism, the Egyptian St. Anthony, met a tiny being in the desert. It was a "manikin with hoofed snout, horned forehead, and extremities like goat's feet." On being asked what it was, the manikin said,

> *"I am a mortal being...that the Gentiles...worship under the names of Fauns, Satyrs and Incubi. We (my tribe) entreat the favour of your Lord, and ours, who...came once to save the world, and whose sound has gone forth in all the earth."*

The Welsh Bard, Taliesin, wrote that during Britain's Dark Ages King Arthur and his Knights invaded an unearthly country to seize the oracular cauldron of Annwn, a magical vessel fired by the breath of nine maidens. Its rim was studded with pearls, suggestive of the onyx wheel of the ancient sky gods and latterly with UFO portholes.

Servant boy Gwion was stirring the contents of the cauldron when drops of it bubbled up and burned his thumb. He put it into his mouth and was immediately inspired. Just as many of today's contactees speak of receiving knowledge and insights from space visitors, the Annwn's cauldron told Gwion about the patterns of the universe and of the language of birds.

The peasants of mediaeval rural France believed in the existence of a strange country called Magonia. There, the Magonians rode about in "cloud ships" and frequently made sorties from their realm to steal the peasants' crops and livestock. One of these Magonian ships was recorded by Agobard, Archbishop of Lyons, to have fallen from the sky around A.D. 840: "I saw...four persons in bonds: three men and a woman who...had fallen from these same ships." Angry farmers stoned all four to death.

There are no absolute factors that compel one to deny the existence of things that cannot be seen with the naked eye. Belief in such matters is wholly relative to the degree of trust we place upon our instincts. Many townsfolk may never see a kingfisher or a dormouse throughout their lives but that does not make the bird or mammal any less real. On a more abstract level, we cannot see the wind but we are reminded of its presence each and every day. Why cannot the same principles of faith and intuition sustain a belief in the Wee Folk?

Evans-Wentz understood this paradigm and accepted as fact that lying deep within the human psyche is a powerful atavistic recognition that separate races of beings inhabit an invisible world or worlds contiguous with our own. What we see in myths, legends and fairytales is a reflection of man's continuing struggle to explain in human terms this unseen world, its inhabitants and laws and mankind's relation to it.

In Gaeldom, the regions in which Gaelic is spoken (Ireland, Scotland and the Isle of Man), this invisible race is known as the "Shee" or, more precisely, the *Sluagh Sidhe*—the hosts or people of the mounds. The Irish call the world of the Shee the Middle Kingdom, its inhabitants for the most part recognisably human-like, just as Tolkien portrayed the majority of folk in Middle Earth. Native Americans believe, too, that humans are but one race inhabiting the earth. Others held in reverence by them include the Standing People (the trees), the Stone People (the rocks), the Four-Legged People (the animals), the Plant People (all that grows), the Feathered People (the birds) and the Crawling People (insects).

A painted 'elf door' in Selfoss, Iceland – photo by Bob Strong/Corbis

The belief of the Icelandic people in fairies is so deeply engrained in their culture that its government introduced in 1990 an Act under which conservation projects may only proceed if they are not prejudicial to the wellbeing and security of the country's *álagablettir*—

enchanted spots—and their elven inhabitants. The Icelandic Road and Coastal Administration is so used to dealing with enquiries it now has a standard response to journalists:

"It cannot be denied that belief in the supernatural is occasionally the reason for local concerns and these opinions are taken into account just as anybody else's would be."

In the past, it adds, "issues have been settled by delaying construction projects so that the elves can, at a certain point, move on." By any measure of what constitutes modern day progressive governmental thinking, the Icelanders are way out in front in making and vigorously enforcing this remarkable piece of legislation.

Evans-Wentz's Irish mystic said that there are three great worlds that we can see while we are still in the body: the earth-world, mid-world and heaven-world. He explained that the Sidhe are divided into two great classes: those that are shining and occupy the mid-world and those that are opalescent and seem lit up by a light within themselves. This latter class resides in the heaven-world and its inhabitants are more rarely seen. Its members hold the positions of great chiefs or princes among the tribes of Dana. The opalescent beings, approximately 14-feet tall, appear as a dazzle of light. Through their bodies runs a radiant, electrical fire and around their heads are flaming wing-like auras.

The mystic explained that among the shining orders there does not seem to be any individualized life, thus if one raises his hands all raise hands and if one drinks from a fountain all do. It was the mystic's understanding that the shining beings seem to move and to have their real existence in a being higher than themselves, to which they are a kind of body. Theirs is a collective life.

He had observed that some of the tribes of shining beings seem to be little more than one being manifesting itself in many beautiful forms. Among the opalescent beings in the heaven-world there is an even closer spiritual unity but also a greater individuality. The mystic believed that the members of this higher class seem capable of creating new elemental forms by breathing forth beings out of themselves. In the chapter, "High Spirits," we will study the Elemental nature spirits. These little balls of light that at times one might be priviliged to see are the guardians and caretakers of nature. The ancients taught that without their ceaseless toil all life on Earth would quickly wither and die.

Isle of Man resident John Davis told Evans-Wentz that he believed fairies are the lost souls of those who died in Noah's Flood, adding his conviction that there are as many kinds of fairies as there are populations here on Earth. Davis was surely correct. Nineteenth century folklorist Michael Denham listed 198 different types of fairies and Otherworldly forms in his two-volume work.[8] Here is an extract:

> *What a happiness this must have been...when the whole earth was overrun with ghosts, boggles, bloody-bones, spirits, demons, ignis fatui, brownies, bugbears, black dogs, spectres, shellycoats, scarecrows, witches, wizards, barguests, Robin-Goodfellows, hags, night-bats, scrags, breaknecks, fantasms, hobgoblins, hobhoulards, boggy-boes, dobbies, hobthrusts, fetches, kelpies, mum-pokers, Jemmy-burties, satyrs, pans, fauns, tritons, centaurs, calcars, imps, spoorns, men-in-the-oak, hell-wains, fire-drakes, kit-a-can-sticks, Tom-tumblers, melch-dicks, larrs, kitty-witches, hobby-lanthorns, Dick-a-Tuesdays, Elf-fires, Gyl-burnt-tails, knockers, elves, raw-heads, Meg-with-the-wads, old-shocks, ouphs, pad-fooits, pictrees, giants, dwarfs, tutgots, tantarrabobs...*

To this, Thomas Keightley from his studies added: Bull-beggars, Jack-wi'-the-Lanthorn, Calcars, Coujurors, the Spoorn, the Irish Cluricaun, the Mare, the Highlands Urisk, the Puckle, the hairy brownie-like Phynnodderee of the Isle of Man, and the mischievous English Portune. Keightley described the latter as no more than half an inch tall with the appearance of a very old man in a patched coat. For sport it will tease horsemen by invisibly taking the reins and leading the horse into a bog before running off laughing.[9]

If one uses Katherine Biggs' dictionary as a starting point and extrapolates accordingly, the figures increase exponentially. Briggs, focusing exclusively on Britain, listed hundreds of different fairy types, sub-types and variations. She was deterred from expanding the scope of her work to include Europe's fairies in face of the many additional years of enormous effort required to meet the task. Europe has scores more distinct ethnic groupings than Britain, while globally some estimate them to exceed twenty thousand.

If we stand back and consider the numbers we may conclude that in terms of comparable scope and scale, the fairies' invisible home may be visualised as a world just like our own, with at least as many residents of all shapes, sizes, temperament, and social and cultural variations. The fact that we cannot readily see this world is irrelevant. Whether it is a ball spinning in another kind of space or an environment

[8] Denham, M., *The Denham Tracts,* The Folklore Society, London, 1895
[9] Keightley, T., *Fairy Mythology, vol. 2*, VAMzzz Publishing, Amsterdam, 2015

unimaginable to our senses is a subject for a conversation that we will develop in the coming pages.

Interestingly, Evans-Wentz believed that people who inhabit the Celtic regions are more in tune with their subconscious self and so better equipped psychically to feel and perceive invisible influences. He believed that through this enhanced faculty the Celts enjoy an innate ability to respond to nature's rhythms and, correspondingly, can feel the essence of this Otherworld more keenly than most.

Being part Celtic on his mother's side, Evans-Wentz firmly believed in the existence of invisible life forms, describing them as being as much a part of nature as is visible life in this world. Consequently, he decried the use of the term "supernatural" to describe these beings on the basis that, logically, nothing in existence can be supernatural.

What precisely is a fairy? In seeking to answer this question, it is important to understand that "fairy" per se is no more than a relatively late etymological construct. The word does not appear prior to the mediaeval period and its initial use referred specifically to mortal women with mooted magical powers (as personified, for example, by the Arthurian figure of Morgan le Fay—in fact, "fairy" can also mean a spell for a fay). "Fai" is derived from the Italian "fatae," the otherworldly women who visited a child at birth to determine its future as in the mythological role of the Three Fates. "Fai" was extended into "fai-erie" then conjoined as "faerie" to indicate a state of enchantment, while the French "fée" described a woman skilled in the healing arts and in the corresponding magical use of herbs, potions and minerals.

Thereafter, the evolving use of the word "fairy" to refer to unseen beings in a narrow sense, excluding gnomes and goblins and the like, became a distinctly English development. Folklorists trace this to a conflation of the ancient German tradition of elves and dwarfs (*huldra* or *hudufólk*—hidden people) with Celtic influences. In turn, this led to the groundless formulation of an image of fairy folk as a largely diminutive race in contradiction to folklore in which fairies are depicted in every shape and size. By the time of the Victorians and their love of twee children's stories, fairies were being portrayed as mischievous but essentially good-natured, tiny winged creatures.

This contrasts sharply with King James VI of Scotland's 1597 description of fairies in his "Daemonologie" as demonic entities that consort with and carry off individuals. William Shakespeare is believed to have drawn inspiration from James' book in creating the three witches for Macbeth, thus perpetuating the stereotypical attitude of the day that wise women were supernatural figures to be feared and punished. Seen in this perspective, one can readily appreciate that an objective student of "fairies" cannot begin their journey without firstly confronting a stiff reality check. They must face the fact that there is neither consensus on how a distinctly human mediaeval village healer became transmogrified over time into a winged Wendy figure, nor on the word's relevance and meaning in the twenty-first century. This internal dialogue might conclude that seeking to apply a label to something of such flimsy provenance is to neglect far wider possibilities of discovery and learning.

Armed with fresh insight, the student may come to understand that if he continues down an increasingly narrow "fairy" path he will become ill-equipped to deal with other creatures that might jump out from the bushes like gnomes and goblins and other truly bizarre entities such as the It, the Boneless and that weird hotchpotch of present day tricksters collectively termed Road Ghosts. This is our intrepid investigator's Eureka moment. In a flash, he sees that what he is actually seeking to understand are, purely and simply, non-human entities that defy categorisation and description.

In *Indiana Jones and the Crystal Skull* Indy asks John Hurt's character, Oxley, about the NHEs' startling mode of departure. "Where did they go? Space?" Oxley who had it figured all along replies, "Not into space. Into the space between spaces." Our student is thus rewarded with Oxley's insight, having arrived at the understanding that "fairies" is a catch-all composite term to encompass all those beings, entities, energies and life forms that occupy dimensions outside (or in "the space between spaces") of our physical universe.

Seventeenth century Scottish minister Robert Kirk was the Oxley of his day. Transcending the ignorant belief of the time that fairies were witches or midwives, Kirk said in his classic work[10] that fairies are of a middle nature between man and angels, varying in size, powers, lifespan and moral behaviour. Mentally and, it was said, physically (Kirk was reputed to have the gift of second sight) he saw a canvas populated by spirit forms that occupy invisible realms between this universe and the heavenly spheres. In Kirk's vision evil species such as monsters, hags, hobgoblins and bogies had no place in these higher worlds.

In the daunting task of defining fairies, folklorists often defer to Kirk's categorisation. In his acclaimed work[11] John Gregorson Campbell took up Kirk's line of thinking in saying that fairies are counterparts of mankind. Although the concept of dimensions that interconnect with Earth was not a hot topic of conversation in the late Victorian era, Campbell's statement indicates that, presciently, he visualised parallel worlds inhabited by beings perhaps much like us but with greater variation, type and appearance.

Welsh myth, too, proceeds along broadly similar lines in suggesting that fairies are a real race of invisible or spiritual human-like beings, rarely seen, who inhabit a world of their own. The ancient Celts went further, believing that fairies could be embodied as members of the human race, echoing, for example, our present day concept of the "walk-in."

"A belief in the existence of a class of beings, not human but belonging to the world of man, seems to be universal."

Professor Reidar Thoralf Christiansen

Shakespeare was the first writer to describe fairies in their later form as unsubstantiated, picturesque descendants of nature spirits equipped with tiny wings. The true fairy tradition refers to fairies as

---

[10] *Secret Commonwealth OR, a Treatise displaying the Chief Curiosities as they are in Use among the Diverse People of Scotland to this Day; SINGULARITIES for the most Part peculiar to that nation*, published after the author's death in 1692.

[11] Campbell, J., *The Gaelic Otherworld*, James Maclehose and Sons, Glasgow, 1900

looking very much like humans, only rather smaller which makes it easier for them to infiltrate our communities unnoticed. John Michell[12] observed that this characteristic of fairies has engendered the fear that persists to the present day that there are those among us who are decidedly not human such as the "walk-in."

According to Janet Bord,[13] one of the traditional tests of the fairy nature is the ability for fairies and humans to intermarry and produce children. Bord explains that the "Little People" were so-called because, as far as one could judge, they were naturally formed people small in stature, whose distinct mode of dress set them apart from normal human convention and made them conspicuous.

Others hold that fairies are descended from a primitive earth dwelling race that was driven into hiding in the far distant past by invaders. While others believe that fairies are variously fallen angels, the souls of the dead, the descendants of the Greek and Hindu gods, the elementals of the mediaeval mystics, astral or elemental spirits, once mortal beings of flesh and blood before withdrawing into the Otherworld or vestiges of pre-Christian religious teachings.

Evans-Wentz echoed this last opinion, suggesting that a belief in fairies has the same origin as all religions and mythologies. His extensive research revealed that fairy faith grew out of a pre-Celtic belief, probably among the more learned members of society, and paralleled the sophisticated Eastern systems of metaphysical science and esoteric philosophies.

Katherine Briggs found merit in all of these ideas, including Jung's psychological theory (to be discussed in Chapter 9) but counselled against accepting one over another. She wrote, "On the whole we may say that it is unwise to commit oneself blindfold to any solitary theory of the origins of fairy belief, but that it is most probable that these are all strands in a tightly twisted cord." In compiling her dictionary, Briggs gave credence to Kirk's specific categorisation but extended her work to cover the whole of the supernatural order while excluding angels, devils, phantoms and the like.

Irrespective of favouring one definition over another, it is mutually accepted among folklorists and mythographers that fairy folk find humans objectionable and dislike the use of the term "fairy," which is why people tend to speak of them euphemistically using terms like the Good Neighbours, the Wee Folk, the Gentry, the People of Peace, the

---

[12] Michell, J., *The Flying Saucer Vision*, Abacus, London, 1974
[13] Bord, J., *Real Encounters with Little People*, Michael O'Mara Books, London, 1997

Seelie Court, and Scotland's "Grey Neighbours" (grey-clad goblins) so as not to get on their wrong side (because wherever we are they can always hear what we are saying).

We can thank Evans-Wentz for the fact that we are not limited to "once upon a time" accounts of fairy encounters and can applaud folklorists of the calibre of Katherine Briggs for her encyclopaedic opus. However, before we explore what these and other twentieth century authorities revealed we should first turn to that folklore luminary of seventeenth century Scotland, the Reverend Robert Kirk and his extraordinary observations concerning fairies. Kirk stands apart among folklorists. Not only did he provide stories of unparalleled insight as if from personal experience but he also was the subject of a fairy story. Many in his day believed that Kirk did, in fact, commune with fairies and that, finally, they carried him away into their underground world.

Born in Aberfoyle, Scotland, in 1644 Robert was the seventh and youngest son of James Kirk, minister at Aberfoyle in the county of Perthshire. After a course of study at St Andrews, Kirk received his master's degree in theology at Edinburgh in 1661, becoming minister of Balquhidder three years later and of Aberfoyle on his father's death in 1685. In 1670 he married Isobel, daughter of Sir Colin Campbell of Mochaster. From this union came a son, Colin. When Isobel died on Christmas Day 1680 Kirk cut out an epithet with his own hands. Later he married Margaret, daughter of Campbell of Fordy, who after her husband's death in 1692 bore a second son, Robert, later minister at Dornoch in Sutherlandshire.

Robert Kirk Sr. was a renowned Gaelic scholar. Among his chief accomplishments were the first metrical translation of the psalms into Gaelic and his participation in the printing of a Gaelic Bible (An Biobla Naomhtha), a project funded by Robert Boyle of the Royal Society. Boyle was fascinated by Kirk's gifts as a man of the Second Sight and made efforts to pursue enquiries of his own.

As a folklorist Kirk is universally known for the Secret Commonwealth, a treatise on fairy folklore, witchcraft, ghosts and second sight, written in 1692 but not printed until 1815. In its Foreward, Kirk described the work as *"An Essay of the nature and actions of the subterranean (and, for the most part) invisible people, heretofore going under the name of ELVES, FAUNES, and Fairies, or the like, among the low-country Scots, as they are described by those who have the second sight; and now, to occasion further enquiry, collected and compared, by a circumspect inquirer residing among the Scottish-Irish in Scotland.*" His study is objective and impartial but its overall empathetic tone indicates that he believed absolutely in the existence of fairy-folk.

Kirk enjoyed visiting at night a fairy knowe (knoll) beside the manse, his minister's residence. He would roam around in his nightgown before turning in. On 14 May 1692 he was found lying unconscious on the knowe (in Scottish Gaelic *sith bhruaich* and in Irish

A fairy knoll

Mullach na Sidhe). He died without regaining consciousness and was buried in the Aberfoyle churchyard. His grave bears the inscription, Robertus Kirk, A.M., Linguæ Hiberniæ Lumen.

There are many who believe that what lies in the tomb are ashes, stones or even a fairy-made doppelganger. Many of Kirk's parishioners held that he had broken the taboo against spying on the fairies and as a punishment the body was replaced by a stock, a rough resemblance of a person fashioned by the fairies from wood. The fairies impregnate the stock with "Glamour" to imbue it with a temporary appearance of life, which soon fades. Often the fairy changeling would be a baby (known in Scotland as the "wee diel") but occasionally the fairies would take an older person they were glad to be well rid of.

Others said that Kirk "went to his own herd" and was serving as "Chaplain to the Fairy Queen." Some even said that Kirk had been a changeling since birth, placed by the fairies on earth to serve as their ambassador from the Secret Commonwealth to acquaint lesser mortals with their ways and customs.

It is claimed that after Robert Kirk's funeral he appeared to his relative, Grahame of Duchray, and said that he was not dead but had been carried off under the fairy knowe at Aberfoyle. He said that he had one chance of escape. He explained to Grahame that his child had just been born. He said that if his child was christened in the manse then he could exert his power beyond the confines of the fairy knowe and appear in the church. Grahame must at that moment draw his dirk and throw it over his apparition. The fairies, unable to counter the magical power of iron, would then have no choice but to disenchant him and set him free. Come the day, Grahame was so transfixed by the sight of Kirk's appearance in the church that he failed to draw his dirk. Kirk's image then disappeared and his imprisonment continued.

However, legend had it that a second chance would one day become available. During the Second World War the chance arose. An officer's wife, a tenant of Aberfoyle Manse, was expecting a child. She was told that if during the christening someone stuck a dirk into Kirk's favourite armchair his soul would be released. For whatever reason this act of mercy never took place and Kirk's Otherworldly fate was sealed forever.

In his essay Kirk said that the good people, the *sleagh maith*, are of a middle nature between man and angel as were daemons of old. He described them as intelligent studious spirits with light, astral changeable bodies akin to a condensed cloud. Some, he said, have bodies so spongy, thin and pure that they feed only by ingesting fine spirituous liquors that pierce like pure air and oil.

Others feed more grossly on foison (harvest produce), including corn, which fairies steal away, partly invisibly and partly preying on the grain in the manner of crows and mice. This description is closely analogous with that of category EBE Type 1 NHE entities, which feed on plant material and use photosynthesis to convert the food to energy. We will review NHE descriptions in the next chapter.

In 1705 Kirk's contemporary, John Beaumont, published his *Treatise of Spirits* in which he told of his encounters with fairies. He once saw them dancing in a ring. They were 3-feet tall with brown complexions, wore black, loose, netting-style gowns tied with a black sash within which was a golden garment with somewhat of a light striking through it. Adorning their heads were white linen caps with lace on them covered with a black network hood. Beaumont asked them what they were. They said that they were an order of creatures, superior to mankind and could influence our thoughts and that their habitation was in the air.

Kirk said that fairy-folk are not subject to human ailments but dwindle and decay after a certain period. He suggested that their sad disposition is a reflection of their uncertainty about what will become of them on the Day of Judgement. He said that every element and different state of being has animals resembling those of another element. He added that the Romans' invention of good and bad daemons and guardian angels and assigning them names was an ignorant mistake sprung only from their observance of this original. Eventually, this copy, echo or living picture expires and goes to its own herd.

Kirk remarked that fairies' bodies are fashioned from congealed air and are sometimes carried aloft; otherwise they grovel in different shapes and enter their dwellings through any cranny or cleft in the earth, it being full of cavities and cells. Their dwellings are lit by continual lamps and fires in the Rosicrucian style with no apparent fuel to sustain them. In them food is served by pleasant children who act like enchanted puppets. The fairies can sometimes be heard baking bread and striking hammers. Kirk described fairy speech as "whistling, clear, not rough." In their relaxation periods fairies prefer books on arcane subjects, again in the Rosicrucian manner.

Some fairies, known as Brownies, enter human dwellings at night and busy themselves with tidying the kitchen and washing pots and pans. The country folk in Ireland's county of Munster are afraid of a type of Brownie known as the "Fear Dearg": the Red Man. The Fear Dearg is a little old man with dark, hairy skin, a long snout and skinny tail. It wears a red coat and a sugar-loaf hat. The Fear Deargs are also known as Rat Boys as they are said to be rather fat,

Kirk believed that there is no place or creature on Earth that does not have other animals, greater or lesser, living in or upon it as inhabitants. He said that fairies are distributed in tribes and orders and, like humans, have children, nurses, marriages, deaths and burials, except for those times they do so for mock show or to make prognostications among us.

They live far, far longer than humans before they vanish into the element from which they are composed, following this cycle in accordance with an important tenet. Fairies, Kirk said, hold that nothing perishes but as with the sun and year everything proceeds in a circle and is renewed and refreshed in its revolutions; that nothing moves but has another animal moving on it and so on to the smallest corpuscle capable of being a receptacle for life.

Loathe staying in one place for too long, fairies change lodgings every quarter. They love to travel abroad, their chameleon-like bodies swimming in the air near the earth with bags and baggage. It is at these times that those with the second sight have encounters with fairies.

Those with the sight may only see a fairy between two blinks of an eye.

Kirk is describing here the "trooping fairies," the gregarious type that live in communal groups, usually under mounds or hills. Their social structure closely imitates that of humans, ordered according to rank with aristocrats (the kings, knights, ladies and royal courts of the Heroic Fairies) at the top of the chain, followed by the gentlemen and then the rustic, peasant folk.

Troopers enjoy undertaking *rades*, solemn processions on foot or on horseback; and the Heroics have a particular fondness for hunts, battles, sporting games, feasts and balls. Processions of trooper fairies may be seen on the night of a full moon at a spot where four roads cross.

The Gentry class are working fairies, not as sophisticated as the aristocrats but more refined than the peasants. When men and women meet a fairy it is more likely to be one of the Gentry. Kirk observed that many among this class have human ancestry, some even being half-human.

Humans with second sight see fairies at banquets and burials. The wee folk have even been seen to carry a coffin to the graveside. On these occasions some claim to have seen a double-man or the shape of a man occupying two places at once. Men call this double the reflex-man or co-walker, in every atom of detail identical to the man it replicates.

The Scottish fairies' graveside tradition is echoed in Welsh folklore, which describes instances where fairies have been seen in churches participating in phantom funerals called "toeli." In Wales the will-o'-the-wisp lights are known as *canwyll corfe*—corpse candles: harbingers of pending death.

Kirk contrasted the trooping fairies with the solitary kind, the Unseelie Court, populated, it is said, by the unblessed dead and those expelled from the Seelie Court. Their appearance is likened to a great black cloud that passes ominously overhead in the breeze at night. For the most part, the Unseelie Court keep their own company but will on occasion come together to have meetings or hold fairs. On the whole, the solitary fairies are far less kindly disposed to humans but according to Kirk only a handful are truly inimical.

The fairies' travel habits may be likened to the phenomena of UFO waves during which UFOs are seen in successive locations, each ripple of a wave being separated by a relatively short period of time. Such, for example, was the pattern of sightings in Wales in the recent past, a series of extraordinary phenomena that will be explored in Chapter 6 (The Welsh Triangle).

Walter Yeeling Evans-Wentz made an outstanding contribution to fairy lore. An American anthropologist and writer, Evans-Wentz is most famously known for publishing an early English translation of *The Tibetan Book of the Dead*. Born in Trenton, New Jersey from a German father and an Irish mother, Evans-Wentz read Madame Blavatsky's *Isis Unveiled* and *The Secret Doctrine* in his teenage years and went on to develop his interests in Theosophy and the occult. At Stanford University he read religion, philosophy and history, moving to Jesus College Oxford in 1907 to study for his doctorate in Celtic mythology and folklore. For these studies Evans-Wentz undertook very considerable fieldwork, collecting fairy folklore in Wales, Scotland, Ireland, Cornwall, Brittany and the Isle of Man.

He was not alone among contemporary creative figures in believing in the reality of the fairy faith. W.B. Yeats wrote to Evans-Wentz saying that "I am certain that the (Fairy Folk Kingdom) exists and will some day be studied as it was by Kirk."

In Evans-Wentz's day the growing influence of psychology and the public's fascination with psychic phenomena forced researchers to address the possibility of invisible intelligences and entities able to interact with and influence man. This new line of thinking was known as the Psychological Theory of the existence of fairy-folk. Evans-Wentz was a leading proponent, believing that a greater age is rapidly approaching when all the ancient mysteries will be carefully studied and the Celtic mythologies in particular will be held in very high esteem.

Evans-Wentz's understanding was that the heaven world of the Celts is not to be found in planetary space but here on Earth. He said that the rational mind of the twentieth century businessman denies him the possibility of seeing fairies because their whole world is subconscious and materially orientated, completely closed to nature's energies and influences. In contradistinction, the Celtic mystic believed that the universe comprises two interpenetrating parts: the visible world and the invisible realm of the fairies, which are intelligent beings residing in the Otherworld occupying all orders of society and hierarchy.

This magical world is a subterranean region invisible to humans except under special circumstance. Through secret passages and beneath mountains, raths, moats and dolmens the Otherworld was once inhabited by the Partholon, the megalith builders of ancient Ireland. They were succeeded by the aristocratic and humanesque Tuatha dé Dannan who retired long ago after their defeat by the Sons of Mil into Ireland's emerald hills together with the leprechauns, pixies, dwarfs and knockers (miners) of the fairy folk.

The Tuatha dé Dannan were the tall, beautiful Good People (*Daoine Maithe*), a highly cultured and refined race much like us who lived in the hills, married, bore children, toiled and feasted. They were extremely gifted in the fields of architecture, science, mathematics and engineering. They exercised command over the power of sound to lift and move massive weights. Over time, the Dannan, born from the "waters of heaven or space," a representation of the goddess Anu (later Christianised as Brigit), became known as the fairy folk (later the Sidhe of folklore).

In the Mabinogian Don means "the wizard children." The enemies of the Dannan, the Fomorians, were children of the goddess Domnu, meaning an abyss or deep sea. Legend speaks of the Fomorians as a race of hideous giants (the Nefilim). In a description mindful of a Tolkien tale, the Fomorians were defeated on the Plain of Towers by a cataclysmic Flood generated by the Dagda Mor.

Anu's wizard children include those that make fairytale witches appear sweet and tender. Black Annis is a cannibal hag with a blue face, long white teeth and iron claws. She lives in a cave in Leicestershire that she dug out with her own nails. Her blue-faced sister hag in the Highlands is Cailleach Bheur. Personifying winter, Cailleach Bheur is an analog of the Greek goddess Artemis.

Irish manuscripts refer to the Celts' Otherworld as Hy-Brasil, a land once situated in the midst of the western ocean as though it were old Atlantis or its double. The Piri Reis map locates the island of Hy-Brasil 200 miles west of Ireland. Curiously, among the documents in the possession of Deputy Führer Rudolf Hess when he parachuted into Scotland in 1941 was a map depicting Hy-Brasil.

Myth has it that Hy-Brasil appears to human sight every seven years. In 1908 at the beginning of Evan-Wentz's Celtic odyssey Hy Brasil was seen by too many people for its existence to be dismissed as fantasy. Hy-Brasil's ruler is Manannan Mac Lir, the Son of the Sea, foster father of Lugh, God of Light. He ferried the dying Arthur to Avalon. Manannan Mac Lir travels his domain in a magic chariot (so very reminiscent of UFO sightings). Fairy women would venture forth from this enchanted region, sprinkle mortal men with Glamour and entice them into their keeping.

Thousands of years after the fall of Atlantis Christians evolved their concept of Hell from this dark and fearful notion of the Celtic Otherworld. To those who perceived the Otherworld as a place of joy and happiness it was known variously as Tír Na nÓg, Land of Youth;

Tir-Innambeoi, Land of the Living; Tir Tairngire, Land of Promise; Mag Mar, the Great Plain; and Mag Mell, The Happy Plain. To the ancient Greeks, it was the Elysian Fields.

Intelligent and perceptive observers recognised that Tír Na nÓg interpenetrates our earth and has no limits other than that of the universe itself. They understood that, in essence, Tir N-aill, the Otherworld, is a composite term that encompasses all dimensions, which interpenetrate the physical earth experience.

Evans-Wentz recounted the legend that to enter the Otherworld before the appointed hour requires the seeker to secure a passport, often a silver branch of the sacred apple-tree or simply just the apple. Often the apple branch produces music so soothing that mortals forget their plight when they are taken by the fairies to Tir N-aill. The Silver Bough of the Celts is synonymous with the Golden Bough and Golden Fleece of old. It is the Silver Cord that binds the astral body to its human host when journeying out of the body. The branch is the magic wand of the fairies, the caduceus of Hermes, and the staff with which Moses struck the rock to release pure water.

> *A branch the apple-tree from Emain*
> *I bring, like those one knows;*
> *Twigs of white silver are on it,*
> *Crystal brows with blossoms.*
> *There is a distant isle,*
> *Around which sea-horse glisten:*
> *A fair course against the white-swelling surge,*
> *Four feet uphold it.*

From the *Voyage of Bran, Son of Febal*

Evans-Wentz (pictured) invested a great deal of time and energy into his investigations, interviewing hundreds of Celtic folk who related stories handed down or, in some cases, described personal experiences of seeing fairies. He recognised that people native to Celtic regions are born with an unusual power to know and to feel invisible psychic influences. His observations were later echoed by the late Grace Cooke, an acclaimed British medium who in a series of books wrote of the wisdom of a spirit energy known as White Eagle. White Eagle described to Cooke the ancient paradise realm of Hyperborea and its inhabitants, the God-Men, who came as guardians of a young human race. White Eagle said that in Britain's isles, once a part of Hyperborea and, later, Atlantis, the very stones are impregnated with the light of the God-Men. Because of this tremendous power many ancient people journeyed to Britain after the Flood and established mystery centres of great light and wisdom. Such, said White Eagle, were the beginnings of these isles' noble and learned Celtic races. In these esoteric observations of a period far back in the vast reaches of human life on Earth, one begins to get a sense of the true origins of Yeats's *"conscious beings, who are not of heaven but of the earth, who have no inherent form, but change according to their whim, or the mind that sees them."*

Across the Irish Sea in the Isle of Man fairies are known variously as the Little People (*Mooinjer veggey*), "Themselves," "Little Boys" (*Guillyn veggey*) or "Little Fellas." They are the men of the Middle World. On the Isle of Man's Dalby mountain folk used to put their ears to the ground to hear the Sounds of Infinity (*Sheean-ny-Feaynid*), murmuring sounds that came from space, believed by Manx folk to be filled with invisible beings.

This piece of folklore echoes Kirk's Welsh story. He referred to the legend that Merlin enchanted the fairy folk to forge arms for Arthur and his Britons until their future return. Kirk said that ever since Merlin cast his spell one can stoop down on the rocks on Barry Island in the South Wales County of the Vale of Glamorgan and hear the fairies at work: the striking of hammers, blowing of bellows, clashing of armour and the filing of irons. The fairies are compelled to continue with their toil because as Merlin was killed in battle he cannot return to loose the knot that ties the Tylwyth Teg to their perpetual labours.

In England one form of house fairy is the charming "lob-lie-by-the-fire." In Wales the same spirit is known as *bwbach*, brown and usually hairy. In Cornwall the Pobel Vean are known by names such as the Small People, Spriggans and Piskies, while the Buccas or Bockles are a deity not a fairy. The piskies are tricksters that delight in leading humans in circles and using the power of Glamour to seize them. In a Cornish account a brownie was:

> *"a little old man, no more than 3-feet high covered with rags and his long hair hung over his shoulders like a bunch of rushes...having nothing of a chin or neck...but shoulders broad enow for a man twice his height. His naked arms out of all proportion, too squat for his long body, his splayed feet more like a quilkan's (frog's) than a man's."*

The fairies of Wales may be divided into five classes: the Ellyllon, or elves; the Coblynau, or mine fairies; the Bwbachod, or household fairies; the Gwragedd Annwn, or fairies of the lakes and streams; and the Gwyllion, or mountain fairies. The Ellyllon are the tiny elves that haunt the groves and valleys, and correspond with the English elves. The English word "elf" is probably derived from the Welsh *el*, a spirit, and *elf*, an element. Collectively, Wales' invisible race is known as the Tylwyth Teg (the Fair Family). The Cyhyraeth is a ghastly figure seldom seen but can be heard groaning before multiple deaths at

The dreaded Cyhyraeth

times of disaster. Accompanied by a corpse-light, it passes along the sea off the Glamorgan coast before a wreck occurs.

Welsh folklore offers a number of origins for the Tylwyth Teg. One has it that the first fairies were men and women of flesh and blood. Another portrays them as the souls of dead mortals, neither bad enough for hell nor good enough for heaven. They are doomed to dwell in the secret places of the earth until the Day of Judgement when they will be admitted into Paradise, an example of such being the Lady of the Lake who resides in Llyn y Fan Fach in the Brecon Beacons.

While a third story from Anglesey tells of a woman in the Holy Land who felt ashamed of having borne twenty children. So, when Jesus visited her, she decided to hide half of her children away. Those ten hidden children were never seen again for it was supposed that as a punishment from heaven for hiding what God had given her she was deprived of her offspring, which went on to generate the race called fairies, the Tylwyth Teg.

Another name for the Tylwyth Teg is Bendith y Mamau (Mother's Blessing, a term of endearment used to placate the fairies' penchant for stealing away children). Numerous folklore tales highlight the Tylwyth Teg's fatal admiration for handsome children, a compulsion which they must satisfy by stealing infants from their cradles and replacing them with a *plentyn-newid* (changeling).

In 1921, Albert Coe…was told by his 340-year-old (!) alien friend that, as early as 1904, the aliens replaced a hundred terrestrial babies and infiltrated their own. 'In the base of each baby's brain was this little thing that recorded everything that that baby saw or did, from the time they put it there…No one ever knew it was a switch.' Subsequently, as adults, the aliens became active in every major nation on Earth. Their main concern: that we were on the verge of discovering secrets of the atom, which could have disastrous consequences for our planet.[14]

Else Arnhem's photographs of a fairy, taken in Germany, summer 1927
(Mary Evans Picture Library)

The fées of Upper Brittany are young and beautiful while others have teeth as long as human hands, their backs covered with mussels and seaweed indicating their great age. While the Breton lutins are in the same class of fairy as the farfadets in Poitou, the pixies of Cornwall, the English Robin Goodfellow and the brownies of Scotland.

The Irish Celts generally refer to fairies as the Shee, the Gentry or, simply, the folk. The Gentry were described to Evans-Wentz as a folk far superior to us. In Irish mythography they are a unique race between humankind and the spirit world, comprising a military-aristocratic class, noble in appearance. They range in height and build from child-size to

---

[14] Good, T., *Earth: an Alien Enterprise*, Pegasus Books, London, 2013

unusually tall, fully grown men and women. They speak in a sweet, silvery voice and play the most beautiful music (it is not hard to recognize where the Irish inherited their love of the Craic!).

Though they may look human the Gentry have magic aplenty. They can take many forms, make things seem other than they are and time stretch or contract. A witness told Evans-Wentz of a member of the Gentry that once appeared to him. He was stoutly built and appeared to be only four feet tall but told the witness, "I am bigger than I appear to you now. We can make the old young, the big small, the small big." Compare this statement with an exchange between a witness and UFO occupant. The witness said that the occupant told him he would see its form only as he wanted to see it. If I wanted to see the being in the semblance of a duck, said the witness, it would look like a duck. If I wanted it to look like a monster, it would look like a monster.[15]

What may we draw from our study of the Wee Folk? If we have gained one essential perspective it is that the life forms under our lens can neither be described as wholly "wee" nor as wholly "folk." However, one notable aspect in both popular tales and in serious studies is the lack of information regarding detailed physical descriptions of fairy folk. This is hardly surprising, seeing that reported instances of sightings are mostly confined to the "I knew someone who knew someone who thought they glimpsed a fairy" category, while reports of actual encounters are very few and far between.

One is either exceptionally fortunate (or unlucky, depending on what one sees and the actions that follow) to see a fairy; or, by virtue of having through discipline consciously developed certain (positive or negative) faculties of higher perception, one may observe them through an inner eye that in most mortals remains closed throughout materially dominant lives.

From the available data fairies across the spectra of type and classification, with obvious bizarre exceptions, resemble to some degree the human form, ranging in size from inch-high to at least human proportions and exhibit human traits and behaviours.

Pixies the size of a child's hand sport translucent wings, have an oversized head and pointed ears and nose but are still recognisably human in appearance. Viking lore speaks of the light-elves (the Ljossalfs), which inhabit Ljossalfsheim, one of the nine worlds that made up the universe on the upper level of the World Tree above the

[15] Hind, C., *UFOs—African Encounters*, Gemini, Zimbabwe, 1982

human world of Midgard. On the other hand, the unfriendly Swartalfs, the black elves, occupy a region between Midgard and Helheim, an underworld on the lower part of the Tree. Despite differences in appearance, both sets of elves bear humanlike features. Higher up the size scale are the Gwragedd Annwn: beautiful Welsh fair-haired fairy women, the same size as humans, who live in underwater palaces beneath the lakes of the South Wales Black Mountains region.

The same may be said both of the Brownie, a good-natured household fairy with brown skin and brown clothing and its opposite in temperament, the ill-tempered Boggart, characterised by its unkempt dense covering of hair and its ragged attire. The fearsome, elf-like Red Cap, its tam o'shanter dyed with the blood of its wayfarer victims, may have blazing red eyes, grey beard and the claws of an eagle but its humanlike features are unmistakeable. And as for the Coblynau, one has only to turn to Thorin Oakenshield's company of dwarfs in the Tolkien stories to see what the mining folk of Magonia surely resemble.

On first consideration, fairies' similarity to humans may appear to be a counter-intuitive circumstance. It certainly does not follow that beings from the Otherworld should look human-like. In fact, one might expect exactly the opposite, considering the infinite variety of possible evolutionary forms that might abide there.

Increasingly, though, evidence suggests that fairies are energy beings whose home is one or more dimensions that are as much an intrinsic part of the earth plane as humankind and which intersect with our world at an indeterminate number of etheric access points. In other words, they have always been here, whereas humans are the late arrival.

In support of this line of thinking, anthropologist Roger W. Wescott[16] believes that our Earth may exist in a "hyperhistorical" sphere in which beings from our religions and folklore might become intrusions that can be explained rather than passed off as miraculous occurrences. In this case, extraterrestrial anthropology includes not just a study of possible interplanetary phenomena but also that of our own planet with other associated spatial and temporal dimensions added to it. In this model the supporting disciplines would not be astronomy and aeronautics but mythology, folklore and Fortean-style anomalies.

Current scientific thinking supports also the principle of convergent evolution, in which different species will independently evolve similar common features. In this context, it is not unlikely that humans' physical appearance gradually and selectively evolved to incorporate

---

[16] Magoroh, M., & Harkins, A., *Culture Beyond the Earth*, Vintage Books, NY, 1975

features of neighbouring life forms, including those that occupy dimensions that interlace with Earth.

Moreover, in line with the Genesis dictum that "God created man in his own image" there is a common belief in a cosmic archetype of creation that reflects the attributes of the makers of life, the Universal Powers, and with which life forms in all dimensions conform, including humans. The striking human-like being that so impressed George Adamski during their encounters from November 1952 onwards (his illustration reproduced below) told the professor that the human form is a universal archetype, the only differences being in stature, colour and in the shape of details. Interestingly, the visitor told Adamski that he had lived on Earth long ago and since then had evolved through many incarnations.

Remarkably, orthographic projection analysis has confirmed that the very same craft in which Adamski's visitor arrived at California's Desert Center is also the one seen and photographed by ten-year-old Stephen Darbishire over Coniston Lake in the northwest of England in February 1954. Queen Elizabeth's consort, Prince Philip, a UFO buff and a fan of Adamski's book "The Flying Saucers Have Landed," was so impressed with Darbishire's experience that he invited the boy to Buckingham Palace for a full debriefing on the incident.

Humans and the inhabitants of Magonia may indeed share a semblance of likeness but mutual awareness of one another is evidently one-sided. Very few humans can see into the world of the wee folk whereas the Magonians seem to be able to come and go into ours with

relative ease. And when they come their intention is often to tease and torment humans, even to carry them off into fairyland, some never to be seen again: the same practice of torment and seizure observed in so many instances of UFO phenomena.

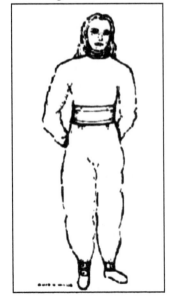

But there I go again, describing the wee folk as fairies as if that is the name by which they have always been known. We have seen that the term fairy is a relative newcomer in language and that its early use related largely to village midwives and healers who, through fear and ignorance, were sent to the stake in huge numbers as "witches" (estimated as up to 600,000 since 1200). No, the residents of Magonia should not objectively be called "fairies" but, for clarity, described simply as non-human entities.

In the next chapter we move from Wee Folk to UFOlk and embark on the Sisyphean task of identifying the one from the other. Like navigating an Escher staircase, we will discover that our journey has neither beginning nor end but rather endless circles, much like Alice found when she tried to find the centre of the Looking Glass garden in her very own Magonia world.

Chapter 3

UFOlk

"Many poets, and all mystics and occult writers, have declared that behind the visible are chains on chains of conscious beings, who are not of heaven but of the earth, who have no inherent form, but change according to their whim, or the mind that sees them. You cannot lift your hand without influencing and being influenced by hordes. The visible world is merely their skin. In dreams we go amongst them, and play with them, and combat with them."

—W.B. Yeats, *Irish Fairy and Folk-Tales*

Francis Crick, co-discoverer of the structure of the DNA molecule, speculated that in the far, far distant past an alien intelligence instigated a panspermia[17] program in which DNA was manipulated to create new life forms on this planet. If Crick was right in his thinking it is inconceivable that these cosmic architects of earth-life would not have wished to keep a watchful eye on their creations. With their incalculable intelligence, the God-men would surely possess the means to monitor us from afar but, like all concerned parents, would also want to observe their offspring close up in their local environment.

It is certainly the case that many victims have spoken of their abductors' claims that they have always been here. It is reported that they come to monitor animal life and vegetation and to test water quality. Contactees report that these practices are concerned with the threat of pollution and a forthcoming large loss of life on Earth. This impending catastrophe results, they say, from man's nuclear waste practices and testing activities that have caused a fundamental change

[17] Greek word meaning "seeds everywhere." The panspermia hypothesis states that the "seeds" of life exist throughout the Universe and can be propagated through space from one location to another.

in chemical composition from which there is no turning back. The visitors claim that their presence here is necessary to try to prevent a chain reaction that would affect more than just humanity. They appear to make their periodic appearances in our skies with avuncular, seemingly loving motives. At least, that is the message they seek to convey.

Isaiah 13:5:"They come from a far country, from the end of heaven, even the Lord, and the weapons of his indignation, to destroy the whole land."

Psalms 68:17:"The Chariots of God are twenty thousand, even thousand of angels; the Lord is among them."

In 1950, 13-year-old Massachusetts citizen, Betty Andreasson Luca, experienced "coming out of myself" and then being taken by little grey men to an underground location. One of these men told her that she "shall enter the Great Door and see the Glory of the One." Betty later told investigators that the Great Door is an entrance into the other world, the world where light is. It is not, she was informed, a world yet available to the mass of humanity. Betty said that she was told this by "the Elders," the masters of the grey men, whose appearance and demeanour are mindful of Crick's God-men. She described the Elders as tall, white skinned, androgynous beings with white-blond hair.

In this startling account we see mention of two distinct life forms that are not of this earth: the "little grey man" of which we read so much in UFO lore and its master, a being that *appears* to belong to the higher spheres of supercosmic consciousness.

In Betty's case the common factor that binds the kindly "God-man" and his loyal servant is that they jointly undertook, as they would on several later occasions, the kidnapping and detention of an earth child, an act identical in nature to the disturbing particulars of countless fairy stories. In the old tales a physical changeling would have replaced the seized child. Today, it returns as a changeling *savante*, enchanted by the "Glamour" of Stockholm syndrome and tells the world of lofty matters.

But let us begin at the beginning. In December 1984 an anonymous but evidently privileged source sent Hollywood film producer Jaime Shandera a package containing a 35mm Kodak film. It arrived in his mailbox postmarked Albuquerque, New Mexico. It bore no sender's address. Wrapped like a Russian Doll, the large envelope contained another sealed with plastic tape and inside that was a third, white envelope imprinted with the emblem of the Marriott Hotel. Inside this last envelope was undeveloped Kodak 35mm film, which Shandera sent to a photo lab for processing.

When it was returned only eight frames had been exposed, each frame consisting of a single page from a classified government document bearing the stamp: "TOP SECRET/MAJIC-EYES ONLY," denoting classification at the highest level consisting of "Sensitive Compartmentalized Information" (SCI). Only those possessing a special access permit designated "MAJIC" had authorization to see it. Its EYES ONLY classification meant the document was for reading only; no notes could be taken nor copies made of its pages. The eight pages contained the preliminary briefing prepared on 18 November 1952 for President-elect Eisenhower by briefing officer Admiral Roscoe H. Hillenkoeter and signed by former U.S. President Harry S. Truman. It stated that the briefing was introductory to a full operations briefing to follow. It revealed that USAF was in possession of an alien spacecraft that had crashed on a ranch near Roswell in 1947, as well as five alien bodies.

The Roswell timeline began on 31 May 1947 when 12 Indian children playing in Gallup, New Mexico, saw a "big ball of fire" shooting over the sky. Some got blisters on their hands when they covered their faces. The ball disappeared in the direction of Socorro.

A few days later a strange girl appeared on the scene. Looking more like a witch from a fairy story than an alien visitor, the girl had greyish skin, grey hair and appeared to be wearing a wig. She was dressed in white clothes and a white veil to hide her face and always stayed close to the river at night. She avoided all contact with grown-ups who tried to catch her but failed.

The girl seemed focused on seeking out the children in Gallup who had seen the ball of fire. During the week that she was around she caused sickness in those she came into contact with; the closer she got the sicker one became. There was something very eerie about her, it was reported. She always appeared from the east and entered the community along the river. After a week she simply vanished.

The wreckage and bodies from the Roswell craft were recovered by 509th Bomb Group, the USA's only atom bomb unit. In charge of the investigations were Major Jesse Marcel of the Intelligence Corps and Sheridan Cavett of the Counter Espionage Unit.[18] The retrieval team found a disc and 4 humanoids lying face down. They were screaming

---

[18] Hesemann, M. and Mantle, P., *Beyond Roswell*, Michael O'Mara Books, London, 1997

loudly and clutching tightly metallic boxes that had indentations to fit their hands.

On 2 June after the discs had sufficiently cooled down the beings were relieved of their boxes with blows from rifle butts, one dying as a result of the force exerted. The other 3 were dragged away and secured with ropes and tape. The document states that a status report was sent to Truman on 19 September 1947, which concluded that the crashed ship was a short-range reconnaissance craft of non-terrestrial origin.

On 30 June a person initially known only as "Jack B." filmed the autopsy performed by Professor Detlev Bronk and Dr. Robert P. Williams. Purported film of the autopsy was subsequently acquired by Ray Santilli, proprietor of a small London-based video production company. Santilli later identified Jack B. as a "Jack Barnett." The infamous autopsy film divides opinion sharply. However, following a review of the film, Dr. Roger K. Leir, a doctor of podiatry medicine at Thousand Oaks, California, said that a flexing of the knee action seen in the film demonstrated that the body was not an elaborate mannequin or dummy. If it were a dummy, Leir maintained, the film director would have had to hire a physiologist and other expert personnel to ensure the necessary external rotation of the thigh during flexing of the knee.

Between 4 and 6 July another disc crashed 40 miles northwest of Roswell, its arrival witnessed by Franciscan nuns at St. Mary's Hospital Roswell. On the 6th, Sheriff Wilcox found 4 beings, one still alive.

Documents shown to Howe by Richard Doty, former USAF special agent, indicated that the survivor NHE from Roswell died 18 June 1952. Another survivor is said to have lived until 1960. Doty told Howe that the normal lifespan for EBEs is 300-400 years and that the 1952 death was a mystery as the being was still relatively young. He was "like a child that had the mind of a thousand men," Doty told Howe.

It appears that the crashing of these two craft was not the end of the NHEs' calamities. A memo dated 22 March 1950 to J. Edgar Hoover states that 3 flying saucers were recovered in New Mexico, each occupied by 3 bodies of human shape but only 3-feet tall, dressed in metallic cloth of very fine texture. Each body was bandaged in a manner similar to the blackout suits used by speed flyers and test pilots. The Government's very high-powered radar set up in the area was believed to interfere with the controlling mechanism of the saucers.

On 24 September Dr. Vannevar Bush and Defense Secretary James V. Forrestal were called to a meeting at the White House in which was agreed the establishment of an oversight group: Majestic-12 (abbreviated to MJ-12, also known as MAJI). Its purpose was to facilitate recovery and investigation of alien spacecraft. The Kodak film document listed MJ-12's members at the time of its formation:

- Admiral Roscoe H. Hillenkoetter (pictured in 1957 opposite top) – designated lead member (MJ-1)

- Dr. Vannevar Bush - tasked with coordinating scientific investigation of alien technology (MJ-2)

- Defense Secretary James V. Forrestal (replaced after his death in 1952 by Walter B. Smith) – responsible for military coordination (MJ-3) – pictured opposite below

- General Nathan F. Twining - responsible for recovery and investigating crashed UFOs (MJ-4)

- General Hoyt S. Vandenberg – responsible for aerospace and for detecting the presence of UFOs (MJ-5)

- Dr. Detlev Bronk – investigation of anatomy, biology, brain function and EBE behaviour patterns (MJ-6)

- Dr. Jerome Hunsaker – responsible for technical evaluation of recovered UFOs (MJ-7)

- Mr. Sidney W. Souers – 1st Director of the CIA on its formation in 1946. Between 1947-1950 was executive secretary for the National Security Council - responsible for coordination of internal security (MJ-8)

- Mr. Gordon Gray – responsible for strategy of "banalizing" UFO reports, witnesses and their accounts (MJ-9)

- Dr. Donald Menzel – astrophysicist – responsible for natural sciences and liaison with scientific community (MJ-10)

- Dr. Lloyd V. Berkner – geophysicist - tasked with developing defense strategies against unknown intruders (MJ-11)

- General Robert M. Montague – responsibility for liaison with AEC (MJ-12)

Brigadier General Arthur E. Exon referred to these members—the "high-ranking team" that had access to the wrecks, bodies and all information about Roswell—as the "unholy thirteen," the thirteenth member of the Majestic coven being the "Old Man," Truman. By the time the film reached Shandera all thirteen had died.

Whistleblowers and investigators have unearthed a good deal of information about Majestic. Majestic and MJ-12 are acronyms: (Manhattan [Engineering District] Joint [Chiefs of Staff] Integrated Command [Z Division, Group) 12. The group is also referred to as MAJI (Majestic Agency of Joint Intelligence), responsible for every aspect of interface with Alien Life Forms (ALFs), including security, intelligence, misinformation and foreign disclosure of the aliens'

presence. MJ-12's OPNAC Team (OPNAC BBS-01) is reported to have absolute autonomy to deal with recovering crafts and ALFs and is not accountable to anyone. These enforcers are known as the "Silver Group."

Defense Secretary Forrestal became seriously paranoid, eventually suffering a series of mental breakdowns. In 1949 he is reported to have run up and down the corridors of the Pentagon shouting, "We are being invaded and are helplessly at their mercy!" During this year he resigned his position and checked into Bethesda Marine Hospital in Washington, D.C. for treatment. At first he was assigned a room on the 2nd floor. Diagnosed as in acute danger of suicide he was then transferred to a room on the 16th floor (my underline) from where he "jumped" to his death from a window on 22 May. Perhaps it is little wonder that Forrestal became so paranoid. As a key insider he was only too aware of the scope and seriousness of the NHE problem that was confronting

humankind. A government insider code-named FALCON, believed by UFO researcher William L. Moore to have been the late high-ranking CIA official Henry Rositzke, told Moore that there were 9 different species of NHEs.

What precisely is known about the various members of the NHE community? We shall begin with the aforementioned grey. MJ-12's SOM1-01 Special Operations Manual provides detailed descriptions of alien forms based on third-party reports and direct U.S Government

44

engagement. I am grateful to Linda Moulton Howe for her kind permission to reproduce the manual's content as conveyed to her by U.S. government insiders.[19] The manual divides the greys into EBE (Extraterrestrial Biological Entity) Type I and EBE Type II. The lengthy term Extraterrestrial Biological Entity is often shortened to "Eben" in official documentation.

EBE Type I creatures are humanoid and might be mistaken for Orientals if seen from a distance. They are bipedal, 5 feet to 5 feet 4 inches tall, weight 80lbs-100lbs, and in build are proportionally similar to humans although the cranium is larger and more rounded. They have pale skin that is chalky yellow-grey in colour and thick and slightly pebbly in appearance. Their eyes are small and wide-set, almond shaped with brownish-black irises and very large pupils. The whites have a pale grey cast. The ears are small and not low on the skull. The nose is thin and long and the mouth is wider than humans and nearly lipless. There is no apparent facial hair. The body hair is very fine and confined to the underarm and groin areas. There is no evident body fat but EBE Type I has well-developed musculature. They have small hands with four fingers with dark nails, no opposable thumb and no webbing between the fingers. The legs are slightly bowed, feet splayed and proportionately large. It is understood that it was the Type 1 Ebens that were found at one July 1947 crash site and at another in 1949, both in the Roswell area.

In 1985 two men claiming to have U.S. government insider knowledge of extraterrestrial matters contacted Linda Moulton Howe. Both, they said, had previously worked for a secret group that was a continuation of MJ-12. They provided further information on the remit of MJ12, adding that it had responsibility to study captured extraterrestrial entities and to back-engineer Eben technology. To protect their identities, Howe referred[20] to the pair as "Sherman."

Sherman spoke of their attendance at a pre-arranged meeting between the Ebens and U.S. officials in 1964 at Red Canyon eighteen miles east of White Sands Missile range, New Mexico. They described the Type I Ebens at the meeting as about four and a half to five feet tall. They had a flat face. Their eyes had a black lid, which covered "cat eyes" underneath. They wore a tight-fitting, greyish-white jumpsuit. (Sherman said that the U.S. had recovered three downed craft.)

---

[19] Howe, L.M. *Glimpses of Other Realities, Volume II: High Strangeness*, p71-72, Paper Chase Press, New Orleans, 1998
[20] ibid p130-131

Insiders told Howe[21] that they believed the Ebens had historical connections to Egypt and to Sumeria. Their language is similar to Bhutan-Tibetan-Sanskrit and they use mathematical phraseology. FALCON said that NHEs are fond of ancient Tibetan-style music. It is claimed that Tibetan monks in the Bhutan region possess Eben scrolls written in early Sanskrit that never wear out. The Ebens know how to capture time and play it back in 3-dimensional images. They claimed at the Red Canyon meeting that they created humankind.

The Majestic-12 Manual goes on to describe EBE Type II greys[22] (described often as grey androids or worker bees). There appears to be considerably more information available on the appearance of Type II greys than for the Type I.

EBE Type II greys are bipedal humanoid entities, height 3 feet 5 inches to 4 feet 2 inches and 25lbs-50lbs in weight. The head is proportionately larger than humans, the cranium being much larger and elongated. The eyes are very large and slanted, black with no whites and nearly wrap around the skull with a noticeable brow ridge. The skull has a slight peak that runs over the crown. The nose is two small slits that sit high over a slit-like mouth. There are no external ears. The skin is pale bluish-grey, being darker on the back of the creature. The face and body are hairless. The creatures do not appear mammalian. The arms are long in proportion to the legs. The hands have three long tapering fingers and a thumb nearly as long as the fingers, the second finger thicker than the others but not as long as the index finger. The feet are small and narrow with four claw-like toes joined by a membrane.

Sherman told Howe that the Type I Ebens manufacture the Type II greys as biological androids to do work for them on our planet. The Manual comments that "it is not definitely known where either type of creature originated, but it seems certain that they did not evolve on Earth…"

Howe's sources told her that EBE Type II alien skin has a pronounced texture and elasticity. Under a microscope it appears to have been woven. Other reports describe it as tough like a reptile hide. (William Steinman wrote[23] that a reptile specialist was consulted during the alien autopsies.) It varies in colour from white to grey-blue to light green. The creature's arms resemble a praying mantis and are very long

---

[21] Ibid p131-132

[22] ibid p71-72

[23] Steinman, W, *UFO Crash at Aztec*, UFO archives, 1987

46

in relationship to the body. Their clawed fingers reach their knees in very thin, short legs. Their skeletons are purportedly hollow like a bird's. Their straight, slit mouth opens to a closed sac or membrane and has no teeth. According to some sources, their digestive and sexual organs have atrophied. The most disturbing aspect of description is that the alien creatures require blood and other biological fluids and substances from animals or humans to survive.

Some reports say the creatures possess two distinct brains separated by a mid-cranial lateral bone partition, which creates an anterior (front) brain and a posterior (back) brain with no apparent connection. The eyes have been described in two ways. In one, there is a pale iris, perhaps pale yellow, which is dominated by a vertical slit pupil like a cat's or crocodile's eye. These eyes slant upwards and reportedly have two or three lids that move sideways from the corners across the eye, the number of lids varying with light intensity.

Further descriptive data relating to the Type II grey were included in Howe's "An Alien Harvest."[24] The information derives from an autopsy report sent by an unnamed doctor to researcher Leonard Stringfield. The doctor explained that he had performed a partial autopsy on an alien creature in the early 1950s. The statement reads:

"SIZE—the specimen observed was four feet, three and three-eighths inches in length. I can't remember the weight. HEAD—was pear-shaped in appearance and oversized by human standards for the body. The eyes were Mongolian in appearance. The ends of the eyes furthest from the nasal cavity slanted upward at about a ten-degree angle. The eyes were recessed in the head. There seemed to be no visible eyelids, only what seemed like a fold. There were no human type lips as such – just a slit that opened into an oral cavity about two inches deep. A membrane along the rear of the cavity separated it from what would be the digestive tract. The tongue seemed to be atrophied into almost a membrane. No teeth were observed. X-rays revealed a maxilla and mandible as well as cranial bone structure. The outer "ear lobes" didn't exist. The auditory orifices present were similar to our middle and inner ear canals. The head contained no hair follicles. The skin seemed grayish in color and seemed mobile when moved. The above observations are from general anatomical observations. I didn't autopsy or study the head portion in any great detail since this was not my area of specialty.

---

[24] Howe, L.M., *An Alien Harvest: Further Evidence Linking Animal Mutilations and Human Abductions to Alien Life Forms,* p159-161, Linda Moulton Howe Productions, Pennsylvania, 1989

"NOTE—the chest area contained what seemed like two atrophied mammary gland nipples. The sexual organs were atrophied. The legs were short and thin. The feet didn't show any toes. The skin covered the foot in such a way that it gave the appearance of wearing a sock. X-rays showed normal bone structure underneath."

American journalist Frank Scully (1892-1964) published two columns in *Variety* in which he passed on information imparted to him by geophysicist Dr. Silas Newton. Newton confided to Scully that he had accompanied a crew sent to retrieve a craft that crashed in Hart Canyon, east of Aztec, New Mexico, 25 March 1948. The object was Saturn-shaped, 99 feet in diameter and 18 feet wide with an oval cabin housed in its middle section.

The team gained access to the interior via a broken hatch. Inside they found 16 deceased small, uniformed humanoids, 35-40 inches tall (Scully likened them to the Singer Midgets who portrayed the Munchkins in *The Wizard of Oz*). Their skin had been burnt chocolate-brown in the crash. These beings appear to have been EBE Type II greys. Scully reported that every dimension of the craft was divisible by 9.

Dr. Newton told Scully that early investigation indicated that the craft seemed to fly along geomagnetic lines of force. The view among the investigating scientists was that the craft had come from Mars or, possibly, Venus. In later pages, we will return to the subject of crafts' purported means of propulsion and likely candidates for their planetary origin. Scully's story was quickly discredited as a hoax but in the late 1970s Leonard Stringfield claimed that not only was the incident real but that the craft involved was one of many captured and stored by the U.S. military.

Former Navy Petty Officer Milton William Cooper released in December 1988 information on Ebens on Compuserve and Paranet computer networks, saying he could no longer live with the secrets. Linda Moulton Howe reproduced Cooper's testimony.[25] In GRUDGE / BLUE BOOK Report No. 13 Cooper saw photos of two different types of grey aliens. One is the EBE Type 1I, seen or reported in abductions; the other is the so-called "big-nose" grey.

In the photos the greys were naked. Cooper saw no mammaries, nipples, belly button or body hair. The Type II's arms reach down to the knees. The hands' four webbed digits appear to end in claw-like manner

---

[25] ibid p198-209

but could possibly be just very tough skin. The head is roughly 1.6 to 1.7 times the proportion of the human head to size of body. The eyes are very large, black and opaque with no pupil. They seem to have a bigger rib cage or bear more ribs than humans. They have no ears, just a hole in the head. There is a very slight raised part where the nose should be and two nostrils flat to the face. Right below where the nostrils are the face drops straight down to a small, slit mouth.

An illustration of the "robotic" grey EBEs as commonly reported by abductees. Sketch by Tim Hogan based on abductee testimonies.

Cooper estimated that if the scale of the head were ten inches high, each egg-shaped eye would have been two and half inches from corner to corner and two inches wide from bottom to top. The eyes have a slight 10-15 degrees slant. They face each other and get larger as they go out. They possess two distinct brains separated by a mid-cranial lateral base partition (anterior and posterior brains) with no apparent connection between the two. There is what appears to be a set of lungs connected together (unlike as in humans) and the conjoined lungs connect with a heart. Additionally, there is another heart in the body.

U.S. government memoranda refer to a small insect-humanoid-like species that takes in liquid chlorophyll-base nourishment. Small amounts of liquid food are absorbed through the mouth membrane and converted to energy through photosynthesis by chlorophyll. Wastes are excreted through the skin. Papers that Cooper referred to as the "Majority" document comment on the chlorophyll base, questioning if the greys had evolved from plant life.

The big-nose grey is a small creature between six inches and one foot taller than the EBE Type II grey. Cooper described it as having a huge nose that "stands out in profile like the Rock of Gibraltar." The bridge is a pronounced bump that descends to a very large hooked nose with large nostrils. It has oriental shaped eyes, one-half to three-quarters of an inch wide and two inches wide from corner to corner. They have a much exaggerated slant about 45 degrees upwards. In the eye there is a lighter portion that encloses a round, circular pupil. The iris is a little over half an inch in diameter. The pupil has a quarter-inch vertical straight slit that has the appearance of almost glowing against the dark rest of the eye (others have described this slit as being light yellow-green coloured). The almond shaped larger part of the eye is toward the centre and gets narrower as it goes out, the reverse of the eye shape in the Type II grey.

Cooper described big-nose's eyes as looking very sinister, almost evil. They have a tendency to rivet the onlooker. Cooper saw no teeth in the photos. They have a large lower jaw. The head is a little bigger than a human's although about the same size as ours in proportion to its body. Cooper described the head as seeming to go back like in Egyptian drawings where the head is exaggerated compared to the neck. The hands have three digits that appear to be thick and clumsy compared to ours. The feet are small in the same ratio as the little alien's feet but they are covered. Its skin is described as being anywhere from a light green (when they have recently fed from the photosynthesis process) to a pasty, doughlike colour with varying shades in between. It wore a one-piece, metallic, light, tight-fitting silver suit that came all the way up and covered the sides of the head.

On the suit were markings: the "tepee triangle" called the Trilateral Insignia, which is a pyramid bisected laterally by three horizontal lines of equal length, the bottom line of which is the pyramid base that extends out a little at each end.

50

Two other symbols that adorned all uniforms and craft were, according to Cooper, the simple tepee with the base line extended on both sides (said to be also used by Ebens to mark landing sights in some way), and the simple tepee without extended base line but with two dots positioned left and right of the apex.

Norton Air Force Base (AFB) official Paul Shartle, Chief of Requirements for the Audio-Visual program in the early 1970s, confirmed[26] seeing 16mm motion picture film of three disk-shaped craft that landed at Holloman AFB in May 1971. He saw three aliens: "human sized, with odd grey complexion and a pronounced nose…they wore tight fitting jumpsuits, thin headdresses that appeared to be comms devices and in their hands they held a 'translator'."

The Majority document said that the big-nosed greys were taking blood and biological substances from humans and animals. It said continuing to do this was a violation of the agreement with the US government forbidding mutilating animals and abducting humans; abductions were supposed to be for medical examination only.

The papers described animal mutilations: organs were removed, the rectum was taken out as a plug and the blood was removed from the body with no vascular collapse. The same process is reportedly undertaken with humans.

Sherman described[27] another distinct creature: the "Blonds" (also called the Talls), human-looking aliens of Nordic appearance standing about 5-6 feet tall that say they are concerned with our spiritual evolution. They have:

"blond or real pale hair. Females have longer hair. Very slender. Nose and eyes similar to humans, but they have invisible, double lids, apparently for filtering light or something. It's confusing, though, because the Ebens have made humanoids that actually look human, a spitting image of a high cheekboned human with Scandinavian features."

The blonds wear tight, brown jumpsuits with matching shoes and belt and a pale yellow stole draped over one shoulder. On their chest is a winged emblem: a circle with "hawk-eagle" in the centre and wings on each side. These have been associated with strange helicopters of different sizes and colours. Reputedly, the Blonds are our early ancestors and need our genetics to reproduce.

[26] ibid p138-139
[27] *Glimpses of Other Realities, Volume II: High Strangeness*, p138

In 1987 "Axle" was flying with ten men over ice and water.[28] The pilot suddenly yelled, "The clock has stopped!" At this point the plane should have been falling from the sky but it kept on flying. They looked out of the window but "there was nothing there." Axle then heard a voice offering to show him something if he wanted to see it. He saw a series of "scenes" or other realities like changing TV stations. He felt himself standing on thin air. He saw he was surrounded by three (EBE Type II) greys. He described them as "glorified bellhops" who took him to where he was supposed to go. Axle said that they didn't appear to be independently functioning intelligences. They smelled like vegetables and spoke with a squeak like the sounds heard in a forest of very fast growing bamboo. They seemed to have been formed out of a mould. Axle was taken to a round room and met a man who resembled the character of Sir Perceval in the Arthurian romances. The man had blond hair, green eyes, stood about five and a half feet tall and wore a white robe.

The blond told Axle that he had to give up something before he could do whatever he is supposed to do. He said that each human could be a Sir Perceval if one aspires with pure heart; everyone has a chance to see what's wrong and right and to choose the proper course of action. He said we are all going to be judged very shortly. Instantly, Axle found himself back in the plane. Two engines were on fire and in emergency mode the crew proceeded to the nearest base.

During the many times that Betty Andreasson Luca was taken to meet the Elders she was told of the yin and yang of dimensional presences.[29] She was given to understand that there are "bad angels" or "watchers" who are jealous of humanity and want to "hurt and devour mankind," while "good watchers" are the eyes and ears of the overseeing Elders. They explained that the grey Watchers are their remote imaging surrogates connected to the Elders with "bio-electric mind projections" and serve as walking or living cameras and do the bidding of the Elders. The Elders, Betty was told, love mankind and watch the spirit in all things. They are the angels, they claimed: the Sons of God in the Bible working in the angelic realms, the caretakers of nature and natural forms. They said that Jesus Christ is the "hypostasis," the divine creator of the cosmos and humanity. (MJ-12 refers to the Elders as "Jesus-Christ types, tall golden-haired, white robed beings.")

<hr>

[28] ibid p113-114
[29] ibid p320-324

On a day in 1910 two men from County Kerry, both aged 23 years, were on horseback near Limerick. Near Listowel they saw a light half a mile ahead moving up and down, to and fro. The light expanded into two yellow luminous flames each about 6 feet tall and 4 feet wide. In the midst of each flame they saw a radiant being in human form. The two beings were a pure dazzling radiant white like that of the sun that appeared as a halo around their heads. They disappeared a short time later.[30]

To confuse matters, Sherman also referred to what he appeared to be suggesting was an additional category of EBE, which he called the Greys.[31] Sherman told Howe that these are the "bad guys," which carry out human abductions and cattle mutilations although Sherman said that MJ-12 had never admitted to this in any official reporting. The "bad" Greys are similar in appearance to EBE Type I except that they wear a different uniform or suit with distinct insignia and colours. Sherman said that Type II EBEs serve as androids for both the Ebens and the Greys.

When asked about abduction reports concerning aliens resembling praying mantis-like insects, Sherman referred to these as very advanced androids, which can oversee projects thousands of years in duration. The pair described[32] the praying mantis that appears in video footage of the Rendlesham Forest event in England as:

"a scary looking creature that looked like an insect raised up on two legs with two more legs held up in front. It (had) big insect-looking eyes and pincher hands...there was a glowing aura around the creature. And in the aura you could see protrusions in the jaw area that reminded (one) of tusks or something."

Linda Porter[33] reported being taken in her mid-teens by a praying mantis type to an undersea base in the waters off Santa Barbara. The year was around 1961. Arising from the seabed was a silver conning tower the size of a two to three storey building, rendered invisible. Porter referred to the aliens' use of inter-dimensional tunnels. The praying mantis was 7 to 8 feet tall, with a very long torso. The arms were very long and articulated back away from the torso. They had three finger-like appendages that moved with much better dexterity than human fingers. Its tiny feet were very thin, narrow and pointed. The

---

[30] Evans-Wentz, W.Y, ibid
[31] *Glimpses of Other Realities, Volume II: High Strangeness,* p138-139
[32] ibid p136-137
[33] ibid p269-271

eyes were reddish-brown with clear bubbles on them that bulged out slightly. Porter said they exuded a feeling of great age, compassion and kindness. These praying mantis creatures deferred to golden-tanned humanoids. Additional descriptive data portrays the mantis type as having green skin and enormous eyes with rust-coloured irises flecked with gold surrounding large, black vertical pupils. They are hideous in appearance but are non-violent.

Howe asked Sherman if there is a pecking order among the alien types.[34] He said that to the authorities' present knowledge no co-operation exists between the different alien groups. Both the Ebens and the Blonds make android creatures to do the grunt work. These androids come in many shapes and sizes including insect, humanoid Men-in-Black (MIBs) and others. All have an advanced brain that can operate independently or under remote command.

Some of these androids are believed to have a greater intelligence than their creators. In terms of hierarchy, the understanding is that below the Type I greys are the big-nosed greys which serve as guards for the Ebens, followed by Eben scientists, MIBs, Reptoids and the Type II small grey worker drones.

MIBs are described as around five feet tall, either with olive or corpse-like skin. They wear human clothes often decades out of style compared to the timeframe of the encounter. They are the genetically engineered counterparts to the praying mantis, both created by the tall, blond species to perform long-term tasks. We will meet shortly the MIBs when they visit remote farmsteads in West Wales during a seriously strange UFO flap in the late 1970s.

Reptilian and lizard types serve as sentries and workers. They possess great body strength but are not as intellectually complex as the greys. The lizard type has been described as six-feet tall with green, scaly skin and large, yellow irises that surround black vertical pupils. Bones protrude under the scaly chest skin and give an impression of body armour.

A contingent of another alien type, reportedly[35] professional medical personnel, landed in three disc-shaped craft in 1971 at Holloman Air Base. Three visitors disembarked. They were 5 feet 2 inches in height with blue-white skin. Their cat-like eyes had vertical pupils and a kind of cover over them. They had a pronounced aquiline nose, a thin, single-line mouth and no chin. They wore around their

---

[34] ibid p139
[35] *An Alien Harvest,* p140-141

heads a rope-like headdress that covered a raised lobe in the back of their heads. Long ear "attachments" hung down, which served as a communication device for English and other languages. They wore silver leotards. In their hands were translator devices.

Also observed from time to time is a red- or copper-haired humanlike visitor known as the "Orange" or the "tall Irish." These are much taller than the greys and appear to maintain a policy of non-interference. A group of "tall Irish" are said to have lived for a time in the village of Pillpinto in Peru around 1981. They were 7-8 feet tall and said that they came from the skies.

What can we learn from all this? The mass of reporting from government insiders, whistleblowers, witnesses, contactees and abductees provides convincing evidence of the existence of UFOlk. Putting aside the "Elders" and the "tall Irish," both of which with little stretch of the imagination could just as easily be associated with the aristocratic Gentry as with extraterrestrial visitors, what can neither be claimed nor determined with any degree of certainty is that any of the UFOlk types, especially the "greys," is a genuine life form as distinct from a manufactured replicant. Maybe there is something in what the much-maligned Lt. Col. Philip Corso said:[36]

> These creatures weren't benevolent aliens who had come to enlighten human beings. They were genetically altered humanoid automatons, cloned biological entities...that were harvesting (for others) biological specimens on Earth for their own experimentations.

Intimating a similar line of thinking but doing so most astutely, John Keel wrote:[37]

> Our studies of the UFO percipients and contactees are teaching us that these encounters are more hallucinatory than real; that some complex hypnotic process is involved, and the real phenomenon is hiding behind a carefully engineered smoke screen of propaganda. Those funny lights and their hypnotic waves of energy are part of something that is related to this planet, and to us. But that something may be far beyond our meager powers of comprehension. There are forces that can distort our reality and warp our fields of space and time. When we are caught in these forces, we struggle to find an acceptable explanation for them, and then the manifestations begin to conform to that explanation and so reinforce it...

---

[36] Corso, P.J.., *The Day After Roswell*, Pocket Books, Simon and Schuster, 1997
[37] Keel, J., *The Endless Procession*, Pursuit Magazine, Third Quarter, 1982

The theme of Keel's intelligent remarks can be summed up as: "things are never what they seem." I agree. Allen Hynek believed that alien visitors are dimensional energy beings; that what we see are the forms they adopt or become once they lower their home frequency to that of Earth.

I believe that Hynek was partially correct. I am convinced that the greater part of UFOlk phenomena is extra-dimensional in nature and origin. However, common factors that characterise Eben personnel such as recovered at Roswell and Hart Canyon betray the absence of natural evolutionary processes and instead strongly suggest mechanical forms of construction, albeit products of unimaginably advanced technology.

Taken together, the Ebens' actions and appearance suggest that they are instruments through which is exercised a deliberate policy of *trompe l'oeil* promulgated by an unknown intelligence.

The effect of the mass delusion is to create a self-perpetuating reinforcement loop that binds our explanations and us in its snare. I submit that this intelligence with its *"funny lights and their hypnotic waves of energy"* is closer at hand than one might care to believe and, crucially, *"are part of something that is related to this planet, and to us."* In later chapters we will return to this vexing narrative.

Having cast doubt upon a genuine evolutionary origin for the Ebens, we will examine in the following chapter, What the Folk, documented instances of contact with an assortment of non-human entities. We must then ask a key question. Is it energy wasted in seeking to compartmentalise NHEs into specific categories? As Michael Hesemann said to Whitley Strieber,[38] "You can't explain one phenomenon you don't understand by another phenomenon you understand even less."

It is evident that the US authorities remain highly exercised in similarly seeking an understanding into the vexing phenomenon of strange things seen in the skies. At time of writing, the *New York Times*[39] has revealed the existence of the secretly funded Advanced Aerospace Threat Identification Program, which ran from 2007 until a reported shut down in 2012. However, its backers have confirmed to the newspaper that officials with the program continue to investigate episodes brought to them by service members while also carrying out their other Defense Department duties.

---

[38] Hesemann, M., *The Fátima Secret*, Dell Publishing, Randon House, Inc., New York, 2000

[39] Cooper, H., Blumenthal, R., & Keandec, L., 'Glowing Auras and "Black Money": The Pentagon's Mysterious U.F.O. Program,' *The New York Times*, accessed 16/12/17

Initially, the programe was largely funded at the request of Harry Reid, Nevada Democrat and the then Senate majority leader, who has long had an interest in space phenomena. Reid was encouraged to establish the programme by former astronaut John Glenn who had his own personal brush with high strangeness. During his 1962 space mission Glenn encountered the mysterious and unexplained "fire-flies," a large luminescent shower of tiny, brilliantly lit star-like particles that swirled around his capsule, 7-8 feet apart travelling at around 3-4 mph.

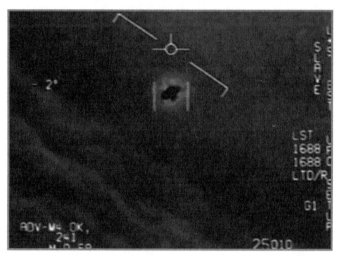

US fighter plane's footage of UFO off the coast of California in 2004. Pilot said, "Look at that thing, dude. There's a whole fleet of them…"

Glenn told Reid that the federal government should be looking seriously into UFOs and talking to military service members, particularly pilots, who had reported seeing aircraft they could not identify or explain.

Most of the money for the programme went to an aerospace research company run by a billionaire entrepreneur and old friend of Mr. Reid's, NASA consultant Robert Bigelow. The program produced documents that describe sightings of "glowing auras" and aircraft that moved at very high velocities with no visible signs of propulsion or hovered with no apparent means of lift. Program officials also studied videos of encounters between unknown objects and American military aircraft including one of a whitish oval object the size of a commercial plane, chased by two Navy F/A-18F fighter jets from the aircraft carrier Nimitz off the coast of San Diego in 2004.

Ultimately, all parties with an interest in the UFO issue—nations, groups and individuals alike—may have to forego attaining a complete, rational solution to the mystery and be content to accept that NHEs exist and that they visit us for reasons in our present stage of our evolution we are hopelessly ill equipped to divine.

My personal feeling is that when we *really* do need to understand just who these beings are that impinge upon our lives in such a bizarre manner all may be revealed in one lightning flash of illumination.

Chapter 4

What the Folk

"Last night I saw upon the stair
A little man who wasn't there.
He wasn't there again today.
Oh, how I wish he'd go away."

—William Hughes Mearns, *Antigonish*

Time and again people have found themselves in the presence of one or more beings for which they are unable to provide a meaningful description. In groping for words that conform to their cultural, experiental and mental parameters, they want desperately to pin a label on what stands before them when, in fact, its unknowable nature defies rational attempts at objective portrayal.

For peace of mind an onlooker will reach for terms embedded in the collective unconscious by centuries of mythological conditioning and, hence, perhaps seize on "fairy" or "alien." There is an element of safety in this psychological process of recall because, frankly, if one truly did know the real nature of what had stepped through that hole in the bedroom wall one's sanity might not be guaranteed to survive the experience. Here are some fascinating examples that underline the dichotomies facing the observer when confronted with instances of "things are never what they seem."

In 1656 Welshman John Lewis of Cardiganshire woke from sleep after midnight. His family remained sleeping. He saw a light enter the room followed by a dozen small men and three small women. They embarked on a wild dance and his room grew lighter and wider than it was physically possible. During their dance the visitors broke off to eat what looked like bread and cheese they had brought with them. They offered Mr Lewis meat. He heard no voices but instead received their thoughts expressed in Welsh. The beings wanted him to remain calm in their presence and bade him hold his peace. After four hours Mr Lewis tried vainly to wake his wife. Eventually the beings departed and Mr Lewis, clearly in another world, pixy-led, was unable to find either the door or his bed in his small room. Distraught he cried out, this time waking his wife and family whereupon he described his amazing encounter.

While travelling to Leipzig during September 1768, Goethe came upon a ravine in which there was a beautifully illuminated amphitheatre. In it were innumerable tiny lights that dazzled the eye. These lights danced and jumped about, here and there. Goethe could not decide if they were will-o'the-wisps or a company of luminous creatures.

A professional gentleman returning home one day in 1905 to his Welsh home in the village of Bryncrug saw a gigantic figure rising over a hedgerow with its right arm extended over the road. A ball of fire appeared from which a long white ray descended. The ray struck the figure, which then vanished

Christmas 1910—a County Kerry man and another young man, both aged 23, were on horseback near Limerick. Near Listowel they saw a light half a mile ahead moving up and down, to and fro. The light expanded into two yellow luminous flames each about six feet tall and four feet wide. In the midst of each flame was a radiant being in human form. The two beings were of a pure, dazzling radiant white like that of the sun, which appeared as a halo around their heads. After a short while they vanished.

Nora, the 18-year old niece of Colonel Henry Jordan of Connacht in Ireland, was visiting her uncle. The year was 1919. Nora was in the bedroom of one of the colonel's young daughters. The younger girl told Nora that a man had appeared from nowhere in the room. He was four-feet tall, wore a green brimless "flowerpot" hat, a close-fitting green cutaway coat, a yellow waistcoat and cravat, buff knee breeches, grey woollen stockings and brogues on his feet. He stood watching the pair for a while and then vanished. He became known as the Thornhill Fairy.

In 1951 two teenage sisters were walking in County Wicklow in Ireland when they saw a little man appear in front of them. He was two to three feet tall and dressed all in black with a black cap. Terrified, they ran into a nearby field. The little man watched them as they ran. They turned and saw he had gone but, curiously, balanced on top of the bar of the gate they had run through was a tin kitchen clock!

In 1954 a Czech living in France met a heavy-set man, medium height, wearing a grey jacket with shoulder insignia, a motorcyclist's helmet and carrying a gun. He spoke an unknown language. The Czech tried Russian and was understood at once. The man asked in a high-pitched voice: "Where am I, in Italy, in Spain?" and then asked how far he was from the German border and what time it was. The Czech said it was 2:30 p.m. The man looked at his watch, which said 4:00 p.m. He then got into a craft that had landed in the road. It was like two saucers glued together, five feet in diameter and three feet high. The craft rose making a sound like a sewing machine.

In the same year a French farmer saw a round object the size of a small truck shaped like a cauldron. It landed and two normal looking men in brown overalls emerged. They asked: "Paris? North?"

Sixty years earlier in 1897 the humanlike occupant of a flying disc was questioned by a Texan witness. He was asked his name and replied that it didn't matter but he could be called "Smith." Asked where he came from, he said, "from anywhere, but we will be in Greece the day after tomorrow." Similar occupants of flying craft have been described over the years, including those resembling GI mechanics and short stocky types with yellow hair cut in a crewcut, yellow eyes, light complexion and wearing Nazi-like uniforms.

While an engineering student was out walking with friends in some trees in July 1961 he became separated from his companions. Shortly afterwards he was lifted into a cabin from within a translucent "elevator." He was taken to a machine, which during the next three hours fed recordings into his brain. At no time did he see any occupants. When he was returned eighteen earth days had passed. All during this time searches were made for him by the police and the military. When he appeared he was still wearing the same fresh flower in his buttonhole, and his suit was still neatly pressed and impeccably clean. He decided the least line of resistance to avoid prolonged questioning about an episode that no one would believe was to admit to a hoax on his part. The case was soon forgotten. Over the next few months he found he needed less and less sleep and that all the things he had been taught during the recordings came back to him during the units of his university course. He discovered he could leave his body at will and also carry out acts of psychokinesis like Uri Geller.

In August 1965 a young woman from Seattle woke at around 2:00 a.m. unable to move or make a sound. A tiny football-sized, dull grey object floated through her window. Its three tripod logs descended to the carpet and a small ramp appeared. Five or six tiny people wearing tight clothing clambered out and engaged in what seemed like repairs of some kind. They finished, climbed the ramp into their craft and sailed out of the window. Only then was she able to move.

Yet another French farmer, Maurice Masse, encountered in 1965 two beings less than four feet tall. They were pilots of a small egg-shaped craft that had landed in his lavender field. They were dressed in one-piece, grey-greenish suits. On the left side of their belts was a small container; a larger one was on the right side. They had human eyes but their heads were three times the size of a human's. They had practically no mouth, only a very small opening without lips. They wore no respiratory device, no headgear and no gloves. They had small, normal hands. When Masse approached them one took a tube from its container and pointed it at him, rendering him immobile. The pilots exchanged communication like the sound of throat gargling. Masse remained paralysed for twenty minutes after they returned to their craft and flew off. The craft disappeared in an instant.

Tiny beings in white suits were seen in Lumut in Malaysia in June 1980. Girl witnesses described them as two inches tall, very hairy and resembling monkeys. One wore a white hat and boots in addition to its white suit. They carried packs and a long weapon.

In Panama City in 1986 three children playing at a stream saw 8-10 little beings. They had claws for hands, very little hair and two small horns. They had no feet and levitated above the water.

November 1978—farmer Angelo D'Ambros of Gallio, northeast Italy, experienced a close encounter while gathering firewood near his home. He was confronted by two beings three feet in height hovering in the air about eighteen inches above the ground. They had bald heads, big pointed ears, sunken white eyes, large noses, fleshy lower lips, two large pointed fangs, very large hands and feet relative to the rest of the body and long fingers and nails. They were dressed in tight, dark garments. Their appearance was terrifying. Angelo asked what they wanted but they replied in unintelligible mumblings. One tried to take Aneglo's woodcutting tool but he managed to hold on to it as they struggled for possession. He felt an electric shock coursing through his hands. He grabbed a branch intending to deal a blow to his assailants and, anticipating his intentions, they fled. They got into a metallic disc 12 feet wide and 6 feet in height standing on four legs and took off.

A 10-year old boy, surname Gowran, was walking up towards Clonmellon Hill in the Irish town of Edenderry accompanied by his 8-year old friend Jack and two 9-year old girls. The year was 1901. The girls suddenly called out. They were looking into a field where was gathered a group of human-sized, dark figures standing in a circle ten yards in diameter. Black capes draped over their heads hung across their shoulders and dropped down to the ground. The figures stood completely motionless. Their cloaks appeared to be made from very fine cloth. Above the black drapes was a casket or coffin similarly covered in the same black material. Lying on the casket was a set of old Irish bagpipes: three drones, each about three feet long. The bag and the mouthpiece hung down over the side of the box. A farmer and his 18-year old son came by and seemingly saw nothing, after which the figures vanished.

At 6:00 a.m. on 4 January 1979, Mrs Jean Hingley of Rowley Regis in England's West Midlands region saw an orange light by the carport at her home. It was coming from an orange sphere hovering over her garden. Three small figures shot past her into the house. They were three and a half feet tall wearing silvery tunics and transparent helmets like goldfish bowls. The figures had large oval wings seemingly fashioned from thin paper decorated with glittering dust. Each figure was surrounded by a halo and thin streamers hung from its shoulders. They had neither hands nor feet and their silvery-green limbs tapered to a point. They pressed buttons on their chests before speaking in unison.

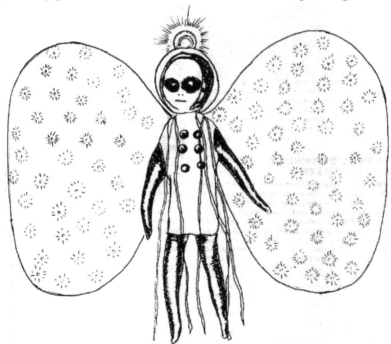

An illustration of one of the winged creatures that visited Jean Hingley, artist unknown

Their answer to Mrs Hingley's question "Where do you come from?" was "from the sky." She felt that the buttons were some kind of translation device. With every word they didn't understand they did 1-2-3 very quickly on their chests with a "bleep-bleep-bleep." She said to them, "You'll learn a lot of things from me with the bleep-bleep," and they said, "Yes, yes." They shone a light at her head repeatedly. She complained, saying it was giving her a headache but they said they hadn't come to harm her. They went around her room touching various things, which lifted up as if being pulled by a magnet. They seemed interested in the drink bottles left over from Christmas. She asked if they wanted some and they answered, "Water, water, water." Mrs Hingley then lit a cigarette to show them how to smoke, an action from which they recoiled, evidently afraid of fire. They then glided out of the house, each taking a mince pie as they went! They returned to their craft and took off leaving Mrs Hingley feeling very poorly. Electrical items in the house were damaged.

A rarely reported event took place one cold night at Hønefoss in Norway on 23 October 1985. Children aged seven to twelve were outside observing a lunar eclipse. An oval light appeared in the sky and moved towards them. One child shone a torch at it. The light's bright glow illuminated where the children were gathered. Inside the light the children saw hundreds of tiny beings less than two feet tall in the road. On their heads were box-like objects of many colours, including white, brown and black. On seeing the children, the tiny beings ran away but over the next three hours were seen time and again. The children thought that they were playing a game of hide and seek. Some ran home to tell parents, none of whom came out to look for themselves. (What is it about us grown ups that we are willing to abandon our innate sense of curiosity and capacity for wonder so submissively?) A passing jogger claimed he saw only a cat. An excited dog defaced the footprints left by the beings.

Isle of Man resident, John L. Hall, was walking with a friend in a wooded valley in Glen Aldyn near Ramsay. It was Sunday 4 September 1994. He felt "odd sensations," "uncanny feelings" and heard "musical sounds and tinkling voices." He wondered if the sounds were being made by the Little People or by a rushing stream. He sensed movement and also felt he was being watched. He looked round but saw nothing. Feeling sick, Hall decided to turn back, taking photographs as he went. On one of them can be seen what Hall described as a "strange-looking green man on a pedestal" up in the leaves.

A boatman named Carr from Sligo took two strange men from the mainland bound for Innishmurry. The two disappeared before his eyes at a place on the water where legend sites an invisible island that reveals itself to mortal sight once every seven years.

Graham Brooke and his son Nigel were out for a run one night in the autumn of 1987 as part of Graham's training for the 1988 London Marathon. Their route took them by the Stocksbridge bypass northwest of Sheffield, which was under construction. As they approached a layby by Wortley village they saw a figure walking towards them with his back towards the oncoming traffic. Graham said later:

"My brain just could not take in what I was seeing. He was dressed in what I would say was eighteenth century costume and wore a dark brown hood with a cape covering his body. He was walking in the ground, not on the level of the road itself and I just could not make out what I was seeing. Then I looked at him directly and saw his face. He was carrying a bag and it was slithering along the surface of the road. It was a dark coloured bag with a chain on it and Nigel said he could hear the chain rattling on the ground. I just gasped and said 'who is this silly person?' and realised my son was seeing him too and at that moment the hairs on the back of both of our heads just stood on end and we could smell something really musty, just like we were standing in an antique shop. I saw him clearly and was looking directly at him, probably no more than fifty yards away from me. His face was towards me and his back was to the traffic. He was so close I could see that every half-inch down the cape there was a button, it was that clear. It was a long cape, dark brown in colour and very worn, with a 'lived in' look about it; it was so real you could have walked up and touched it. He walked straight past as we stood there amazed in the middle of the road. Then a lorry came with its lights on and he just disappeared. I will never forget that musty smell, the cape he wore and the blank face. I looked right into the face and everything was black, just like a miner's face but without any eyes. It was the strangest experience of my whole life."

Ten years later Paul Ford and his wife, Jane, became one of many who subsequently encountered the "Wortley Road Ghost." They were driving to Jane's sister's home in Stocksbridge. To trim their journey time, they were travelling along the new bypass, which runs along the hills high above the Don valley with the town and its steelworks below. It was New Year's Eve, 1997.

Suddenly, Paul spotted a figure. From a distance it looked like someone who was trying to cross the road. As they got closer they could see it was like a man in a long cloak. When they realised it had no face and was hovering above the road, Paul slammed on the brakes and swerved to avoid hitting it. Jane had to grab the wheel to keep the car on the road and avoid an accident.

In Hockley, Birmingham, a grey humanoid creature was seen jumping across the road, kangaroo fashion, although seemingly gaining momentum by swinging its arms. The entity stopped in the road and looked at the witness's car before turning into the grounds of a cemetery.

The town of Nome in Alaska in August 1988 was the scene of five consecutive nights of sightings of little men two to three feet high. They had a greenish luminescence, a trained athlete's broad shoulders and muscular legs. They ran at around 40-50 miles per hour. Men passing by in a car ran right over one but felt no bump or thud. Later the being was seen again, this time turning colour from green to silver before witnesses' eyes.

Every now and again its feet got darker. It chased some kids back to their car. They noticed its red eyes and heard it making a dry whistling, hissing sound. Another night three little green men were seen, one becoming silver, another black and one remaining green. When they changed colour they retained a greenish-blue aura. Another night they were seen dancing across the road.

Between the early 1930s and the mid-1940s an unidentified assailant known variously as the Mad Gasser of Mattoon, the "Anesthetic Prowler," Friz, the "Phantom Anaesthetist," the "Mad Gasser of Roanoke," or, simply, the Mad Gasser launched a number of gas attacks in Botetourt County, Virginia and Mattoon, Illinois. The assailant was described as being a tall, thin man dressed in dark clothing and wearing a tight-fitting cap. Another report described the gasser as being a female dressed as a man. Some saw it carrying a flit gun, an agricultural tool for spraying pesticide, purportedly used to discharge the gas.

Investigators of Fortean phenomena have categorised the Mad Gasser of Mattoon as belonging to that strain of entities known as "phantom attackers." These appear to be human but often display superhuman abilities, their seeming paranormal nature making them unapprehendable by the authorities.

Victims commonly experience the "attack" in their bedrooms, homes or in other seemingly secure environments. In one case a 6-year Irish girl woke in the middle of the night to see a little man, unclothed and grey all over. In its hand was a big ball of wool, which unravelled as the little man backed out of her room. He then vanished upon the stair. The girl was fortunate. Often victims report being pinned or paralysed or describe a prolonged state of siege during which they try desperately to fend off one or more menacing intruders.

The Mad Gasser has been likened to Victorian cryptid, Spring-Heeled Jack. Press reports in Britain of a "peculiar leaping man" appeared as early as 1817 but his activities resumed twenty years later. On 18 February 1838 18-year old Lucy Scales was attacked while walking through East London's Limehouse district. A black figure leapt out from the dark shadows, spat a blast of blue flame in the girl's face, leaped onto a nearby rooftop and vanished.

"Spring-Heeled Jack" went on to terrorise more victims. 18-year old Jane Alsop, an East End resident of Bow, described her attacker as wearing a tight-fitting black cape or cloak that felt like oilskin. On his head he wore a helmet. His hands were icy cold with sharp claws and he had staring, orange eyes that protruded from his head. A week after her attack a similar one was attempted on a servant boy who noticed a gold filigree "W" embroidered on the front of "Jack's" costume.

In 1843 Spring-Heeled Jack appeared in Northamptonshire, Hampshire and East Anglia where he frightened the drivers of mail coaches. In November 1845 a fire-breathing "Jack" confronted a 13-year old prostitute named Maria Davies in Bermondsey. He breathed fire into her face then threw her into a ditch where she drowned.

Throughout the 1850s and 1860s this strange creature was seen all over England. People stayed off the streets at night. Concerned Londoners formed vigilante committees to patrol the streets in an effort to track down the assailant. Police put out extra patrols in search of the villain but no one even came close to catching "Jack." In 1877 he appeared at Aldershot Barracks. He was seen in Liverpool in September 1904 when the newspapers reported a figure seen "jumping over a building in William Henry Street."

"Jack" made dozens of appearances between 1938 and 1945 in the U.S., belching flames and making gigantic leaps, then "melting" into the darkness. In the 1970s he returned to England while also still being seen in the U.S., but by this time he had grown his hair long. In 1976 at least a dozen residents of Dallas saw a creature that leaped across a football field in a few strides. He was 10-feet tall, thin and had long ears.

Other like characters regularly pop up throughout European folklore: from Uomo Nero (the Black Man) in Italy, to Wee Willie Winkie in Scotland and Der Kinderfresser in Germany. They punish naughty children by nipping their toes, stealing their presents or, in classic fairy fashion, removing them entirely. Spring-Heeled Jack played a particularly vindictive trick. He would leap up to a bedroom window and stare at a terrified child in its bed.

19th century investigators sought for clues to Spring-Heeled Jack's identity. Naturally, their first thought was that the malevolent prankster was to be found from within the ranks of British menfolk. One theory popular among the educated and literate upper classes was that "Jack" was dissolute nobleman, Lord Henry de la Poer Beresford, the 3rd Marquis of Waterford. Waterford and a small group of aristocratic friends were notorious for playing unpleasant and vicious pranks that were widely chronicled in the newspapers of the day. These included perpetrating practical jokes that occasionally resulted in savage beatings of random pedestrians. Waterford was killed in a riding accident in 1859. Although there is conjecture that places Waterford in London during the winter of 1837-38, there is no evidence that he was responsible for the assaults in that period.

Having fruitlessly searched for a human assailant, investigators of the Spring-Heeled Jack phenomenon have increasingly turned to the paranormal option. His non-human appearance: retro-reflective red eyes, phosphoric breath and his superhuman jumping ability deriving, it is suggested, from life on a high-gravity world are mindful of an extraterrestrial origin. Others interpret these abilities and his bizarre, malevolent behaviour either as those of a demon summoned into this world by occult forces, or that "Jack" simply manifested by his own volition to foment fear and turmoil.

In 2012 it appears as if Spring-Heeeled Jack made a dramatic re-appearance as a road ghost in the English county of Surrey. Scott Martin and his family told the *Surrey Comet* that while on a taxi ride late on Tuesday 14 February they were confronted by a "dark figure with no features" that vaulted over a dual carriageway and a 15-foot embankment. The experience left Scott, his wife and four-year-old son Sonny shocked whilst the taxi-driver "admitted he didn't want to drive back alone" along the Ewell bypass near Epsom afterwards. Mr Martin described the figure as:

> *"dark...with no real features, but fast in movement with an ease of hurdling obstacles I've never seen. My last image was of him going through the bushes at the top of the bank. I'm not usually one to be freaked...but the cab driver was petrified."*

It was the Martin family themselves that likened the figure to nineteenth century Spring-Heeled Jack, although investigation of media reports at the time of the Ewell bypass sighting indicated that the last previous sighting of "Jack" was in Birmingham in 1986! Jack appears to come and go as he pleases.

How about this for the height of high strangeness, a story of the "Little Blue Man of Studham" kind but with extra bells, whistles and a trumpet voluntary. Make what you will of the extraordinary tale of the "Gnomes of Wollaton" (children's illustrations below and opposite). To readers who are familiar with the British television puppet characters, Noddy and Big Ears, the account will evoke memories of that bygone time. The event took place in September 1979 at Nottingham's Wollaton Park in England. The park surrounds stately Wollaton Hall, home of the Hollywood blockbuster, *The Dark Knight Rises*.

Six children aged eight to ten—Angie and her siblings Glen and Julie, brother and sister Andrew and Rosie, and Patrick—were enjoying late-summer playtime in the park grounds at around 8:30 p.m. Light was beginning to fade. The children's attention was attracted by a bell-like sound coming from a nearby fenced-off boggy area. To their astonishment, they saw a group of around sixty little men about two feet tall. They had wrinkled faces with a greenish tinge and they laughed joyfully but in a quirky manner. They sported long white beards with red tips although one boy said the beards were black. They wore what the children described as old-fashioned nightcaps, just as puppet Noddy wore, with a bobble on the end. They also wore blue tops and yellow or green tights. Some tights that were torn were sewn with

yellow patches. One child said they didn't talk; another said they shouted at each other but not in a language he understood. Despite the looming darkness, the children were able to see them all plainly. One child said he could see them clearly because there was a light hanging in the trees. Patrick later explained to their Headmaster, "I could see them in the dark. They all showed up."

For most of the fifteen minutes that they were under observation the little men rode around in little bubble vehicles, once again appearing to behave just like Noddy and Big Ears. The cars were of mixed colour: some were green and blue, others red, or red and white. They had no steering wheels but were equipped with a round thing with a turning handle. There was no sound of engines but the cars travelled quickly and could jump over obstructions like logs. The gnomes chased the children in a playful manner.

One child mentioned that they had seen the gnomes on a previous occasion during the long summer holidays but then the little men had just ran off. Another child said that on that earlier occasion while being chased by the men he ran out of the wooded area through a gate whereupon the gnomes immediately stopped their pursuit. Interestingly, the child said they did this because "they don't come out in the light and might have died."

At no time did the children touch the little men or were touched by them. The children's parents roundly disbelieved their account but, just like the pupils at Broad Haven Primary School two years earlier (see chapter 5), they insisted on the truth of it. Their Headmaster interviewed them separately soon afterwards and, despite a few minor discrepancies in their accounts and differences in emphasis, the children's reporting was consistent.

The Wollaton case is echoed by an event that occurred in 1929 in the English town of Hertford. A five-year old girl and her eight-year old brother were playing in the garden. Alerted to the sound of an aeroplane, the children looked up to see a biplane with a wingspan of twelve to fifteen inches swoop down over the garden fence. In the cockpit was a tiny pilot wearing a leather-flying helmet. The plane

narrowly missed overturning a trashcan before landing briefly. Waving cheerily to the children, the pilot took off and flew away.

Wollaton swamp area where the gnomes were at play

There are other recorded episodes during which percipients, like Mr Lewis of Cardiganshire, become pixy-led. In Ireland the phenomenon is described as the stray sod (*Foidin Seachrain*). It is said to occur when a person steps on turf on which a fairy spell has been laid. Consequently, the hapless person who finds themself in the wrong place at the wrong time cannot find their way out of a familiar place they have walked hundreds of times before. Wearing one's coat inside out is supposed to be one way in which to counter the stray sod experience. In Scandinavia the way to turn the tables on the mischievous Lygtenand or Lyktgubhe is to turn one's cap inside out.

> *"William found a mean for our deliverance*
> *Turn your cloakes*
> *Quoth he, for Puck is busy in the oakes.*
> *If ever wee at Bosworth will be found*
> *Then turn your cloake, for this is fair grounde."*[40]

[40] Keightley, T., *Fairy Mythology, vol. 2*, VAMzzz Publishing, Amsterdam, 2015

In 1935 an Irish girl lost herself on Lis Aird, a fairy fort in Co. Mayo. When she tried to leave the hill an invisible force kept her from passing through the gap in the outer bank. The force physically turned her around so that she was always walking towards the fort. She felt an atmosphere of strong hostility build around her. Darkness fell. She could see the lantern lights from the search party. She heard the men call her name. She shouted but no one heard her and the searchers went away. All at once, she felt the barrier disappear and she was able to return home.

An early nineteenth century event in Wales powerfully illustrates the baffling conundrums of perception and psychology facing those that seek to compartmentalise events of high strangeness. One night David Williams, a servant living at Penrhyndeudraeth in the county of Gwynedd in north Wales, was walking some distance behind his mistress, carrying home a flitch of bacon. He arrived back three hours later insisting he had been gone for only three minutes. He told of how he had seen a meteor overhead and a hoop of fire. In the hoop were standing a handsomely dressed man and woman of small size. With one arm they embraced each other and with the other they held on to the hoop, their feet resting on its concave surface. When the hoop reached the earth the pair jumped out and immediately inscribed a circle on the ground. Out of the circle emerged a large number of men and women who straightaway danced around to the sound of sweet music. A subdued light lit up the ground. After a while the meteor and hoop returned. The pair boarded and went off and the fairies vanished from the circle.

Mr Williams had never heard the term UFO or flying saucer and so his "hoop of fire" simile makes perfect sense in describing the unusual couple's extraordinary mode of arrival. But then what happens? No sooner do the man and woman, the only reported passengers in the hoop, alight from their fiery orb than the circle they inscribe on the ground, clearly an act of invitation, becomes filled with Little People that emerge out of the earth.

All at once, what we have is a unique and remarkable account of Wee Folk meeting UFOlk, an episode that connects them in common purpose and, for all we know, origin. As Janet Bord noted,[41] it is the apparent incongruity of such events that provokes the deepest questions. What was the reason for the Wee Folk and the UFOlk to meet in this fashion? Did they really come from different places at all?

---

[41] Bord, J., *Real Encounters with Little People*, Michael O'Mara Books, London, 1997

What was the purpose of the dance and why the abrupt departure? Did David Williams temporarily step into another world like so many have been reported doing in centuries of fairytale telling?

Few can resist a great vampire story but how many are told that are claimed to be true? Here is the remarkable story of the Vampire of Croglin Grange. Its authenticity has never been satisfactorily resolved but its points of interest make it a worthwhile fireside tale. Was the entity that reputedly scared Amelia Cranswell half to death a malevolent fairy, a bad alien or an energy form that belonged to an entirely order of existence?

Croglin Grange in Cumberland in the northwest of England was a one-story stone dwelling on a hill near a remote church. Around 1875 it was home to the siblings Edward, Michael and Amelia Cranswell. One hot summer's night Amelia, unable to sleep, saw from her window two flickering lights in a belt of trees that separated the lawn from the nearby churchyard. Gradually, she saw emerging from the trees a "ghastly" something. Little by little the "something" got nearer, increasing in size and substance. Amelia was horror-stricken. She wanted to shout but her voice was paralysed. She heard "scratch, scratch, scratch" at her window and saw a hideous brown, shrivelled face staring in at her. The scratching stopped and was replaced by the noise of the monstrosity pecking at her window. It was unpicking the lead! It wanted to get in!! A diamond pane fell into the room and a long bony finger turned the handle of the window. The thing entered the

room. It came to her bed and twisted its fingers into her hair and dragged her head over the side of the bed, biting her violently in the throat. Awakened by her screams, Amelia's brother chased the thing across the churchyard.

After recuperating from her ordeal in Switzerland on doctor's advice, Amelia returned home only to endure the same terrifying encounter the following March. As before, the thing looked in on her through her bedroom window but this time it was pursued by Amelia's brothers into a vault in the churchyard. During the chase it

was shot in the leg. The next day the vault was examined. It was full of coffins. They were broken open and their grisly contents were strewn over the stone floor. Only one coffin was undisturbed. When it was opened there lay the same creature that had terrified Amelia. Its leg bore evidence of a fresh bullet wound. The family then burned the evil "Vampire of Croglin Grange."

I referred earlier to the Rendlesham Forest event. I am including it in this chapter because the NHEs that communicated to witnesses during this incident claimed that they were time travellers from our far future. The event took place in the vicinity of two military bases (both now decommissioned): RAF Bentwaters, north of the forest, and RAF Woodbridge, which extended into the forest from the west and was bounded by its northern and eastern edges. At the time, the United States Air Force was using both under wing commander Colonel Gordon E. Williams. The base commander was Colonel Ted Conrad, and his deputy was Lieutenant Colonel Charles I. Halt.

The encounter occurred in the early hours of 26 December 1980. The craft fired a pencil-thin mean of light into the nuclear weapon storage bunkers, penetrating beneath the surface. On that night three small humanoid beings glided down from the craft in a beam of light and landed in front of General Williams. They looked like children: 3-4 feet tall with large heads and catlike eyes. They were dressed in silvery overalls.

Staff Sergeant James Penniston and Airman 1st Class John Smith (alias) encountered the alien ship a few hours after Penniston had had Christmas dinner with his family. Under hypnosis in September 1994 Penniston described the appearance of blue and red lights at the Bentwaters East Gate at 2.00 a.m. He saw a white light and a large disc-shaped craft with raised symbols on its surface. He reached out and touched them and received binary code information. The occupants told him they needed people to interpret the lights. He was told that there were many interpreters. Human interpreters such as Penniston, he was told, may come from a bloodline that carries memory files locked inside genes that are necessary for communications between mankind and our future selves. The decoded message was "Explain. Mission. Purpose": the mission being "Contact," the purpose "Research."

The future Earth "time travellers" said they needed something connected with chromosomes from the interpreters, which they take from abductees. They can only travel back into the past; future travel is impossible. They need sufficient speed to make the time travel possible. They can go back a maximum of 40,000-50,000 years; any further they might not be able to return. They have been coming to Earth for 30,000-40,000 years. They took nothing from Penniston because they were interrupted. Penniston was not supposed to understand the program but by touching the symbols he activated them. He did this unseen while they were making repairs. They have a physical problem trying to sustain their children. To address this, they use us not like breeding stock but like band-aids. They take foetuses when necessary. One of the photos from the Bentwaters landing showed the insectoid type of greys (EBE Type II). Eyewitnesses described them as 1.5 metres tall wearing what appeared to be nylon-coated pressure suits with no helmets. They had claw like hands with 3 digits and an opposable thumb. One struggles to reconcile these all too familiar "greys" descriptions with what one might expect time travellers from Earth's future to look like!

We conclude this chapter by restoring the much-maligned reputation of the "little green man." So often the term is derided. Although the Majestic-

12 manual does refer to some greys as having a green or greenish tinge, for example, Ufologists often treat the term "Little Green Men" disparagingly. In fact, it should be accorded with a good deal more respect when one looks at the weight of evidence in favour of green visitors. Here are five such cases.

Case number 1—in 1947 Italian artist, Professor Rapuzzi Luizi Johannis, was on a geology trek. Johannis was making his way up a short valley called the Chiarsò near Villa Santina, Carnia, in northeast Italy when he saw a large disc of a vivid red colour. It was seemingly of varnished metal, lens-shaped with a low central cupola with no apertures. From its tip protruded a shining metallic telescopic antenna. It appeared to be embedded in the valley rock.

Johannis decided to take a closer look and saw what he first perceived as two "boys" slowly coming towards him. As they got nearer Johannis saw that they were not boys but dwarf-like figures that were approaching with tiny strides, hands at their sides and heads motionless. They halted a few paces from his position, at which point Johannis felt all his strength drain away. Unable to move, he was now able to see them perfectly.

They were no more than 90 centimeters in height and were wearing dark blue-coloured overalls made of some material that I would not know how to describe. 'Translucent' is the only term for it. They had collars and rather deep belts, all of a vivid red colour. Even the cuffs and the shins of the legs ended in 'collars' of the same type. Their heads were bigger than the head of a normal man, and gave them a caricaturish aspect...They had no signs of hair but in place of it they were wearing a sort of dark brown, tight-fitting cap like an Alpinist's bonnet. The 'skin' of their faces was an earthly green. The only colour that comes close to it is the plasticine commonly used by sculptors, or of clay dipped in water. The 'nose' was straight, geometrically cut and very long. Beneath it was a mere slit, shaped like a circumflex accent, opening and closing again at intervals, very much like the mouth of a fish. The 'eyes' were enormous, protruding and round. Their appearance and colour were like two well-ripened yellow-green plums. In the centre of the eyes I noticed a kind of vertical 'pupil.' I saw no traces of eyebrows or eyelashes, and what I would have called the eyelids consisted of a ring, midway between green and yellow, which surrounded the base of those hemispherical eyes, just like the frame of a pair of spectacles.[42]

[42] Creighton G., *The Villa Santini Case*, Flying Saucer Review, 1969

Unwisely, Johannis waved his pick-carrying arm toward them and asked if they needed any help. Interpreting the gesture as threatening, one dwarf touched his belt and Johannis was struck by a puff of vapour that felt like an electrical discharge. He fell to the ground. The dwarfs came to where he lay and reached for his pick allowing Johannis a good look at their claw-like hands, which were green with eight jointless fingers, four of them opposable to the others. He saw that their chests were quivering. Like a dog's when it pants after a long run, was how Johannis described it. Johannis managed to get into a sitting position and saw the dwarfs return to the disc, which shot straight out from its "embedded" position in the rock and rose into the air.

Case number 2—on the evening of 15 November 1957 John Trasco had just returned from work at the paper mill to his home in Everittstown, New Jersey. He was feeding his half-blind, ill-tempered dog, King, when his wife, standing at the kitchen window, saw a light in front of the barn about sixty feet distant. She thought that "it was a pond or a puddle" reflecting the day's last gleams of sunlight and then realised that it was coming from a luminous egg-shaped object 10-12 feet in length, which was hovering while moving up and down a few feet above the ground. She saw no occupants.

Meanwhile, her husband, having gone outside to see what was causing King to bark so furiously, came face to face with a little man 2.5 to 3.5 inches tall with a putty-coloured face and frog-like eyes. It was dressed in a green suit with shiny buttons, a green tam-o'-shanter cap and gloves with a shiny object at the tip of each finger.

It said to Mr Trasco, "We're peaceful people, we only want your dog." Trasco grabbed the little man's arm and told him angrily to "get the hell out of here" whereupon the visitor got back into the ship without apparently opening any door or porthole. The object then rose quickly in the sky "like a scrap of flame which escapes from a campfire and goes up" as Mrs. Trasco imaginatively described it. Keen eyed readers will, of course, realise that what Mr Trasco actually met in his yard that autumn night is a close match for that classic Wee Folk favourite—a leprechaun.

Case number 3—retired policeman, Philip Spencer, was taking an early morning walk to his father-in-law's house across Ilkley Moor in Yorkshire. The date was 1 December. A keen amateur photographer, Spencer was carrying his camera, hoping to take photos of reported strange lights on the moor. Ilkley occupies the highest part of the moorlands between Ilkley and Keighley in West Yorkshire. It is a place of mystery and legend. UFO reports abound. There are strange lights that come and go eerily in Ilkley Moor's dense fogs. Not many miles distant lies Menwith Hill Station, which fronts as a Royal Air Force facility to provide "rapid radio relay and conduct communications research." NSA Whistleblower Edward Snowden claimed that Menwith Hill Station, in collaboration with U.S. partners, eavesdrops on satellite and other wireless communications around the world.

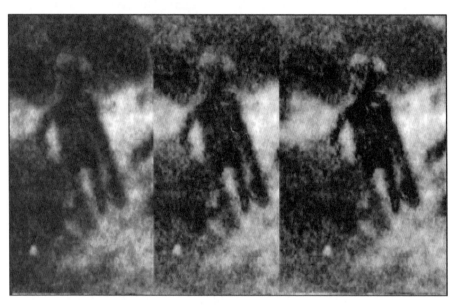

Philip Spencer's original photo, with level adjusted, and with his suggested colorisation

Spencer was equipped with a compass to ensure he kept to the right direction before sun-up. His camera was a Prinz Mastermatic loaded with 400 ASA Kodak film. He was keen to take some decent shots of the town in the valley below. At around 7:45 a.m. while heading for the village of East Morton Spencer heard a humming noise and then saw through the fog a small being on the slopes of the moor. It had a dark green appearance and a large head. Spencer took aim and snapped a shot. He felt that the being was trying to wave him away. The bizarre creature then ran off behind a rocky outcrop.

Spencer was very curious to know more about the being and ran after it. As he did so Spencer was stunned to see a flying craft "like two silver saucers stuck together with a square box with holes sticking out of the top." It rose up from the ground and quickly disappeared into the sky. He was not quick enough to photograph it. Giving up his plans, Spencer returned home expecting it to be about 8:15 a.m. but, bewilderingly, the church clock was showing 10.00 a.m. Spencer boarded a bus to Keighley and had his film developed at a 1-hour photo shop. The shot of the strange green entity came out. Kodak laboratories subsequently confirmed that this photo had not been produced by trickery. After taking comparative photos on Ilkley Moor, Spencer calculated that the being was around four and half feet tall.

Spencer decided to consult a clinical psychologist and in two sessions Jim Singleton hypnotically regressed his subject. Afterwards Singleton was convinced that Spencer was describing events that he truly believed had taken place. In the sessions more pieces of the timeline fell into place, Spencer recalling that he had been taken aboard the UFO by a number of the green entities. Inside the craft he encountered a strong magnetic field, which attracted both his compass and camera. He also recalled being subjected to medical examinations.

Subsequent study of local folklore records unearthed accounts of a similar green entity being seen in and around the White Wells area of Ilkley Moor. The event was was written up by investigators as an example of an encounter with a grey alien of UFO fame. It is evident from the photo that the little green figure could just as easily be described as one of the fairy folk.

These three encounters raise important questions around perception and psychology. When something appears on a Yorkshire moor, in a farmyard barn and in a rocky valley: events that are so far removed from percipients' frames of reference as to preclude any possibility of recognition, identification or categorisation how does one even begin to explain it in absolute terms? If a neighbour's dog or cow wanders on to our property we see in a nanosecond what it is, understand the situation immediately and take steps to redress the matter. Substitute a frightful green dwarfish character that steps from a flying disc and its human observer can only search his mind for an answer relative to present day conditioning.

In the circumstances described, had the three parties experienced their encounters in the nineteenth, even in the early decades of the twentieth century they would have had nothing to help identification and description other than stories from folk tradition. The first and obvious thought at the time the scenes unfolded would have been, "I'm witnessing the fairy folk," no other explanation being at hand which their conditioned consciousness could bring forward. Such descriptions would certainly have been of the type to provide rich source material to Evans-Wentz and inspire his groundbreaking early twentieth century folklore studies.

Not many more years would have to pass, however, before the emergence of a startling, new cultural and psychological phenomenon. 1947 became the nascent year of UFO reporting beginning in May with sightings in Alaska, Canada, Hungary, Guam and Japan. On 24 June private pilot Kenneth Arnold's observation of 9 discs over Mount Rainier in Washington, D.C. became worldwide news.

From this date forward UFO sightings proliferated, including the infamous Roswell event of 2 July. By the end of July the U.S. national press had made approximately 850 announcements on UFO events,[43] and local papers more than 2,000. News was now travelling very fast around the globe about this extraordinary new phenomenon.

Nevertheless, Johannis disregarded any preconceived impressions and spoke not of seeing a UFO and aliens but of a disc and two dwarfs. It was as if his instincts were telling him that, fundamentally, he was observing a "Magonia" event but was not inclined at the dawn of the the atomic age to speak of fairies.

By 1957, and certainly by 1987, the prevailing cultural memes, influenced by growing numbers of sightings of "alien" spacecraft and little green and grey men, added even more weight to the expectation that witnesses of high strangeness were more likely to say, "Ah, I'm a

---

[43] Bloecher, T., *The Report on the UFO Wave of 1947*, Washington, D.C., 1947

witness to a UFO event." However, the Trascos and Spencer, just like Johannis, did not speak about experiencing a UFO encounter (Spencer only doing so later under hypnosis) but instead spoke respectively of seeing a little green man and his ship and a little green entity and its curious looking craft. It would appear that all three parties spoke from the shared perspective of a deep and powerful subconscious archetype over which the increasing weight of mass media reporting had little influence.

Cases 4 and 5 are presented neither as encounters with Wee Folk nor with UFOlk but with remarkable people by all appearances human except for their greenness.

Case 4 relates the famous twelfth century English legend of the green children of Woolpit who claimed after their spontaneous appearance that their true home was a subterranean world. One day at harvest time during the reign of King Stephen (1135–1154), the villagers of Woolpit in the English county of Suffolk discovered by one of the wolf pits that gave the village its name two green-skinned children. They were brother and sister. Apart from their unusual skin colour the siblings were of unremarkable appearance although their clothing was unfamiliar and they spoke in an unknown language. Villager Richard de Calne took the children into his home where for the first few days they refused all food until they came across some raw broad beans, which they consumed eagerly.

Traditionally, green is the Celtic colour symbolizing death and beans are traditionally the food of the dead. Eventually, the children learned to eat other food and lost their green pallor. After a while the boy, the younger of the two, turned sickly and died. His sister was baptised shortly afterwards, given the name Agnes. After she learned to speak English the girl explained that she and her brother had come from a land where the sun never shone and the light was like twilight. She named it Saint Martin's Land, a subterranean world where everything was green, including its inhabitants.

She was unable to account for how they had left their mysterious homeland and arrived in Woolpit. All she could remember was that they had been herding their father's cattle and became lost when they followed the cattle into a cave. After being guided out from the cave by a loud noise (the Abbey bells of Bury St Edmunds, a town six miles from Woolpit), they suddenly found themselves by the wolf pit where they were found. Agnes was employed for many years as a servant in de Calne's household where she was considered to be "very wanton and impudent." She eventually married a royal official named Richard Barre from King's Lynn.

Finally, Case 5 is an account of what was described in 1910 as a fairy encounter. The story was passed on to Alasdair Alpin McGregor by Reverend Alexander Frazer, Minister of the Small Isles, as told to him by the family concerned. McGregor recounted it in his book, *The Peat-Fire Flame*. The encounter took place on the island of Muck off the west coast of Scotland. Local man Sandy McDonald's two sons, aged 10 and 7, were playing on the seashore when they found an unopened tin. While trying to open the tin they saw a little boy dressed in green standing beside them. He invited the lads to look at his boat. They saw a tiny boat on the water a few feet from shore. A little girl three feet high and a dog the size of a rat were aboard. The girl offered the lads biscuits, which they ate. After the lads had been invited to make an inspection of the boat, the green children said that it was time for them to leave. They said they would not be coming back but that *others of their race would be coming* (my italics).

The foregoing examples demonstrate that it is impossible to seek to compartmentalise NHEs into specific categories. Let us imagine we are members of an audience watching a circus show: "Marvello's Magnificent Men and Monsters of Magonia."

Marvello, the gun toting, grey-jacketed motorcylist ufonaut, is acting as ringmaster. The ring is full of performers. Among them we see the Little Blue Man doing somersaults, the grey-skinned, white-veiled Roswell girl of Gallup performing acrobatics, Axle's Blonds and bellhops doing clown antics and stilt walking, the Ilkley Moor green man breathing fire, the human flame forms of Limerick juggling hot coals, the Hopkinsville goblins tormenting hapless volunteers from the audience, Portunes cavorting round on a white mare doing bareback stunts, and David Williams' petite man and woman, high over the arena, swinging inside their magical hoop of fire. Scores more figures of bewildering varieties of shape, size and character are scampering around in madcap manner, kicking up sawdust and making whoopee.

Observing the whacky scene we do

not, cannot discriminate. We don't point and say to our partner, "Look, there's a fairy figure," or, "Hey, over there, isn't that one of those UFO types?"

To our eyes, they are a homogenous collection of performers, each weird and wonderful in its own way, merging together as a single troupe of colourful characters as if viewed through an old fashioned SeeBackroScope.

Our process of perception does not permit objective judgements on form or type because the home base for Marvello and his players exists outside our physical plane of reality.

In essence, Marvello's marvels are neither Wee Folk nor UFOlk. They are indecipherable emanations of dark matter whose energy spectrum is of a Bohmian "implicate" quality, which cannot conceivably be interpreted objectively by life forms native to our "explicate" (physical) order of existence.

Chapter 5

Grimm Tales

"When, lo! as they reached the mountainside,
A wondrous portal opened wide,
As if a cavern was suddenly hollowed;
And the Piper advanced and the children followed,
And when all were in to the very last,
The door in the mountainside shut fast."

—Robert Browning, *The Pied Piper of Hamelin*

Among reported encounters with NHEs are those that may not be remotely described as airy-fairy, pleasant experiences. Indeed, they are terrifying and, occasionally, deadly.

Time and again, folklore highlights the illusory nature of humans' contact with fairies and elementals and the way the mind is manipulated on such occasions. For example, there is an old belief in the Welsh county of Cardigan. It describes how when local people encounter elementals the ellyllon put a cap of oblivion on their heads to prevent them from describing clearly their adventures in the Otherworld and, in the worst cases, from leaving it. This is the practice of "pixilation," a policy of obfuscation and confusion so often associated with modern day UFO encounters.

An Irish mystic told folklorist Evans-Wentz that there are many Otherworlds. He explained that Tír Na nÓg of the ancient Irish, the home of the Sidhe, could be described as a radiant archetype of this world, although this definition does not at all express its psychic nature. In Tír Na nÓg, he said, one sees nothing except harmony and beautiful forms. Then came the punchline. The mystic added that there are other worlds in which, if one has the sight, can be seen "horrible shapes." Evidently, all is not sweetness and light in Magonia. It appears to be full of beings that delight in taking humans for sport or experimentation and feel no compunction about keeping them captive permanently.

Legends say that fairies have to kidnap a child for sacrifice every seven years so that can pay a tribute (a *Teind*) to Hell. Fairies prefer to kill a mortal child rather than one of their own. A motive assigned to fairies for seizing children is that of preserving and improving their race. Another reason given is that fairies are devoid of souls for which reason they steal children so they can acquire a mortal soul for their descendants. In Greek mythology, for example, the shape-shifting female *nereids* cast spells on animals and maladies on humans, kidnap children and leave behind changelings. According to Breton legend there are little figures no more than 2-feet high with bodies as aerial and translucent as wasps, given to abducting human children. Breton folk lived in terror of them.

Kirk described fairies that seize women to nurse fairy children, a lingering voracious image of theirs being left in their place. To perpetuate the deception, the fairy-image "woman" left behind makes pretence of eating meat but secretly spirits it away.

In fairyland the child with food and other necessities are set before the captive nurse as soon as she enters but she never perceives any passage out nor sees what the fairies do in other rooms of their lodging. When the child is weaned the nurse may if she is fortunate be conveyed back to our world but oftentimes stays in fairyland until she dies. In olden days, to prevent the fairies from stealing away womenfolk householders would put cold iron in their beds. Folklore holds that spirits are terrified of iron because it reminds them of the Hell in which they are doomed to be cast in the hereafter.

The Gentry take the whole body and soul of young and intellectual people who have interesting and engaging personalities. Once they take someone and the unfortunate captive tastes the Gentry's beguiling food they can never come back. They are changed to one of them and must live with them forever. In Irish folklore, Knock Ma in the west of the Emerald Isle is threaded with excavated passages and palaces where people seized by the fairies are taken.

In 1856 Ronald Rhys was walking home from his work as a farm labourer in the Vale of Neath when he saw a strange light in a nearby field. It was making a whooshing noise and, being of good Welsh stock, Rhys went to investigate. The next thing he knew he was floating in the air. After that his memories were patchy. Tiny people with swords collected his blood and one bald-headed green being cut into his stomach and took out his organs. When Ronald woke up he was lying in the field. He returned to work (presumably with his organs back in the right places!) and discovered he had lost a full week. In common with many modern encounters, Rhys afterwards exhibited symptoms similar to radiation exposure. His skin was pink and scarred and his hair was falling out.

Donald McKinnon, at 94 the oldest man on the Isle of Barra in Scotland's Outer Hebrides at the time of interview, told Evans-Wentz that fairies appear to us as men and women, often dressed in green. He told stories of fairies seizing cattle. He also spoke of the fearsome "hosts": witches and the spirits of mortals who have died, which fly about in great clouds up and down the face of the world like murmurations of starlings. The hosts abducted men, rolling them up in cattle hides. If they were very unfortunate the captured men would then be lifted and transported to neighbouring areas and islands to do the hosts' bidding, including killing other men. McKinnon explained that hosts could only take a human with the help of another human. Occasionally, an assassin would elect to kill an animal to ensure that the hosts' demand for a slaughter was fulfilled.

Fairytales tell of people seized by the Wee Folk and, bereft of their senses, being held captive in flying chariots (folklore code for a UFO-type) for up to a month before being dropped none too ceremoniously into a meadow or upon a mountainside.

Welsh folklore speaks of country folks' apprehension of meeting fairies in a mist for fear of being the object of their sport in carrying men in mid-air from place to place and leaving them to return home as best they can. Edward Jones ("Ned the Jockey") of Llanidloes in mid-Wales was one such victim. He was coming home one misty evening and came across a troop of fairies. They were annoyed by the intrusion and politely asked him how he would like to be carried off: high wind, middle wind or low wind. He chose high wind and was immediately whisked up into the air and, seemingly moments later, dropped into a garden near Ty Gough several miles from the spot where he started his unusual journey.

In 1816 the celebrated German folklorists, Jacob and Wilhelm Grimm, published their new collection of folk tales: "Deutsche Sagen." Included in the compendium was an account of the mysterious Pied Piper of Hamelin. The story has a chilling, supernatural character. One day in 1284 a stranger appeared in the Lower Saxony town of Hamelin close to the river Weser. Rats were plaguing Hamelin and its citizenry was desperate to see the vermin exterminated. The arrival of the quirky visitor, clad in a coat of multi-coloured bright cloth that earned him his soubriquet, appeared to be a godsend because he declared that he was a rat catcher.

For a certain sum he promised to rid Hamelin of its vermin. The citizens were an unscrupulous lot and struck a cash bargain they never intended to keep. Unaware of their planned deceit, the exterminator took a small fife from his pocket and began to play. Immediately, a horde of mice and rats streamed from every nook and cranny in the town and followed the piper towards the Weser. On reaching its shore, the piper hitched up his clothing and waded into the water followed by the mesmerised animals, which drowned one and all. Naturally, the piper requested payment for services rendered. The townsfolk refused.

On 26 June while the Hamelin citizens were in church celebrating the feast day of Saints John and Paul the piper, dressed now in the forest green of a hunter, took his awful revenge. Once more he played his fife but on this occasion the magical pipe attracted not rats and mice but one hundred and thirty boys and girls of Hamelin. The piper lured them into a cave and the children were never seen again. Two children were left behind. One was blind and the other was lame so neither could follow the others.

Make believe? Within the records of Worms Cathedral is a facsimile of a page from an early fourteenth century chorus book, together with a cleric's note of explanation. The page bears a description in verse of the event as told by an eyewitness, the grandmother of Ludwig, Deacon of Hamelin. Her account confirms its principle details, including corroboration of events surrounding the kidnapping of the town's children by a travelling player and their subsequent disappearance. Here is a first hand contemporary record of a monstrous incident that struck while Hamelin townsfolk were celebrating the midsummer Saints' Day.

The cathedral archive also offers supporting evidence in the pages of a manuscript compiled soon after the event in Hamelin's neighbouring town of Lüneburg. The document narrates the classic components of the story but adds the chilling footnote that the children were: "brought to the place of execution, Golgotha, the place of the skull, where they lost their heads."

130 children led into a cave by a peculiar man vanished off the face of the earth. Where might they have gone? It's unlikely that it was anywhere in this world, otherwise the children, dead or alive, would have surely been found. One is left to surmise that with his magical reed the piper played "open sesame" before a door that should forever remain sealed and led the youngsters into a frightful dimension of existence from which they would never return.

The practice of taking children by Otherworldly beings continued down the centuries. The scene is the Vale of Neath in South Wales, an area renowned as a famous centre of fairyland. In order to avoid the severity of his preceptor, 12-year old Elidurus ran away from school and hid under the hollow bank of a river. After he had fasted in that situation for two days two little men appeared to him and said, "If you will go with us, we will lead you into a country full of delights and sports." Happy to go with them, Elidurus followed his guides through a dark, subterraneous path, which opened into a most beautiful country that was not illuminated with the full light of the sun. The days in that country were cloudy and the nights extremely dark.

Elidurus was brought before the king who delivered him to his son as a companion. The men of this country, though of small stature, were very well proportioned, fair complexioned and wore long hair. They had horses and greyhounds adapted to their size. They neither ate flesh nor fish but lived on milk-based dishes made up into messes with saffron. They abhorred humans' materialistic ambitions, infidelities and inconstancies. Elidurus frequently returned to our world in company and alone: sometimes by the way he had gone, sometimes by others. He made himself known only to his mother and described to her what he had seen.

Elidurus wanted to give his mother a precious gift of gold, with which the secret country was blessed in abundance. Without asking permission, Elidurus stole a golden ball and brought it in haste to his mother. The little men were soon hot on his heels and when Elidurus stumbled at the threshold and dropped the ball they seized it angrily. For his misdemeanour Elidurus was scolded severely but at least he was allowed to return home. In 1909 Welsh lad Oliver Thomas was not so fortunate.

The Christmas Eve party at the Thomas' remote hillside house situated above the Elan Valley reservoirs in the Cambrian Mountains of Breconshire was in full swing. Grandfather Thomas was playing Yuletide carols on his harmonica while other family members were poking chestnuts into the embers of the fire. Others present comprised a Minister and his wife, the local veterinary surgeon and an auctioneer from a nearby town. All gave evidence at the subsequent inquest into the shocking and inexplicable disappearance of Owen Thomas' son, Oliver.

A few minutes before 11:00 p.m. Owen noticed that the water bucket by the sink needed a re-fill. He asked eleven-year old Oliver to go out in the yard and make a visit to the well. With five inches of snow on the ground the boy put on his boots and coat to perform the errand, a chore he had carried out scores of times before. The wind had abated and the night was black and starless.

About ten seconds after Oliver went out into the yard the people in the kitchen heard him screaming for help. Chairs were overturned as they made a frantic dash outside to investigate the commotion. The minister snatched up a paraffin lantern, which sent its weak rays flickering around the dark snowy yard. The yard was empty but the air above was full of noise. Scream after scream chilled the gathering. "They've got me, they've got me, help me, help me," Oliver screamed. The screams became fainter and fainter until soon they could be heard no more.

By the light of the lantern they traced Oliver's footsteps and saw that he had walked 75 feet across the yard before they ended abruptly. The bucket lay on its side about 15 feet away from the tracks as if Oliver had abruptly hurled it aside. There were no other marks of any kind in the snow. The following morning police from Rhyader police station made a thorough search although their whole demeanour was one of doubt and scepticism. Ultimately, though, they were forced to accept that Oliver had vanished—upwards.

In the daylight it was clear that the boy had not reached the well, nor had he paused or turned to either side of his path. The one single logical explanation was that Oliver had been plucked bodily from the ground. Official records showed no balloons were flying anywhere in the country that winter night. The boy weighed 75 pounds, far too heavy to have been carried off by any bird.

British journalist and UFO investigator Nick Pope has considered the correlations between fairy folklore, UFO events and abductions.[44] He notes that in folk tales child changelings often have only a vague memory of what they experience and also suffer time distortions. He writes:

These cross-cultural folkloric beliefs about the taking of babies, and about changelings, are mirrored in accounts of alien abductions where the creation of hybrid human/alien babies is a central theme, Variations on this theme include the accounts of marriages between

---

[44] Pope, N., *The Uninvited: An Exposé of the Alien Abduction Phenomenon*, Thistle Publishing, London, 2015

fairy folk and humans and intriguing stories of midwives being
abducted to assist with fairy births. Again, there is an inescapable
parallel with the whole concept of the genetic breeding program that
many ufologists insist lies behind the modem abduction phenomenon.
Have humans been participants, sometimes willing, sometimes not, in
an age-old but still continuing program to unite two intelligent races?

MJ-12's investigations indicate that NHEs need blood and other
biological fluids in order to survive, their sustenance converted to
energy by chlorophyll via photosynthesis. They abduct humans and
animals to procure these vital fluids. Reportedly, the NHEs periodically
provide a list of abductees to MJ-12.

It is reported that as a result of the use of binary language between
the U.S. and NHEs a meeting was arranged at Holloman AFB in 1964.
It is claimed that this was the occasion of an exchange of hostages: a
human abductee for an NHE captive named Krll. After this a second
meeting took place where a formal agreement treaty was signed. This
specified that NHEs could abduct humans for medical research and
return them unharmed with no memory of their experience, in return for
which the USA would not reveal the alien presence on Earth and would
receive technological know-how.

In 1991 Hopkins, Jacobs and Westrum commissioned a Roper Poll
in order to determine how many Americans might have experienced the
abduction phenomenon. Of nearly 6,000 polled, 119 answered in a way
that Hopkins *et al.* interpreted as supporting their extraterrestrial
interpretation of the abduction phenomenon. Based on this figure,
Hopkins estimated statistically that nearly four million Americans
might have been abducted by extraterrestrials or had experienced
abduction related phenomena.

By any measure this is a staggering statistic. Professor John E.
Mack, psychiatrist at Harvard Medical School, observes that the
abduction phenomenon, "an invisible epidemic," has the potential to
revolutionise our worldview, concluding that:

"...it has important philosophical, spiritual and social
implications...we participate in a universe of universes that are
filled with intelligences from which we have cut ourselves off,
having lost the sense by which we might know them."

Putting aside these abstract implications, the experience of being
forceably kidnapped just the once by NHEs must be absolutely
terrifying but some abductees speak of multiple instances of involuntary
captivity.

In 2002 Steven Spielberg's 10-part mini-series, *Taken*, was aired to general critical acclaim. The production image design team was tasked with creating a striking fairytale environment, a brief that they pulled off magnificently. The hero of the series is a part alien, part human little girl named Allie, the latest progeny of the Keys dynasty. She is not just special but endowed with full-on superpowers. She can control time with ease, making it slow down or speed up. In one episode she makes an entire company of U.S. soldiers and scientists enter a UFO that she has modelled from her own thoughts. To them it is as apparently solid as the ground beneath their feet. Allie is as comfortable living in David Bohm's "Implicate" reality (see chapter 7) as she is in our "real" world. Other members of the Keys family fare far less well than Allie in their dealings with UFOlk that have a penchant for kidnapping and torture.

Jesse Keys, son of Russell, captain of a bomber from which he was abducted in flight during WWII, goes to bed one night in 1953. He sees a character from a children's story (a giant squirrel) peeking into the window. Jesse follows the squirrel, jumps from the roof of the house and walks to a tree with a door. The tree lights up, morphs into a flying saucer and takes off. Nine years later Jesse is riding his bike down an alley and sees a truck that is part of a traveling circus. The truck chases him. It turns into lights and the lights take Jesse away, leaving his bike abandoned in the alley. By 1980 Jesse is an ambulance driver. One day he is getting a badly injured girl out of a rolled sports car and trying to calm the new paramedic guy, saying, "You can always make it better." At that moment Jesse hallucinates the driver of a passing citrus truck as the dreaded circus carnie. He has a panic attack and finds himself alone at the accident site. The new guy comes back for him and explains that he's been missing for two and a half to three hours. During every instance of abduction, and there are very many, Jesse endures the agony of extremely painful procedures.

In real life, many victims experience similarly unpleasant encounters. When Linda Porter was 16 an oval-shaped hole appeared in mid-air in her bedroom. Its sparkling edges were ragged and gold. From it emerged two featureless three-dimensional entities (shadow beings), which took her away, the scene witnessed by a grey standing in her bedroom. Porter described then seeing a very thin figure about 7-feet tall wearing a long purple robe with a high collar. It had whitish-grey skin, eyes like a cat's, no hair, a round top to the head, a big prominent nose and a lipless mouth. Its hands were very long, white and thin.

On the evening of August 21, 1955, five adults and seven children arrived at the Hopkinsville police station in Christian County,

Kentucky, claiming that small alien creatures from a spaceship were attacking their farmhouse. They said that they had been holding them off with gunfire for nearly four hours. Two of the adults, Elmer Sutton and Billy Ray Taylor, claimed they had been shooting at 12-15 short, dark figures (subsequently becoming infamous in UFOlogy as the "Hopkinsville Goblins") that repeatedly appeared at the doorway or stared into the windows. They had oversized heads, almost perfectly round, with large pointed ears and eyes that glowed yellow. Their very long arms terminated in huge clawlike hands armed with talons. Like the Pembroke visitors we shall meet in the next chapter, they wore a glowing aluminium style suit. At times they floated through the trees or walked upright on spindly legs. When fired upon they ran on all fours with extreme rapidity, their arms providing most of the propulsion. The sound of bullets striking them "resembled bullets striking a metal bucket." There was an odd luminous patch along a fence where one of the beings had been shot. In the woods beyond there was a green light of indeterminate source.

In 1957 in Tennessee a party of NHEs tried to seize a family horse. A boy who witnessed the event said that the ufonauts conversed between themselves like German soldiers he had seen in movies. Later they walked directly through the fabric of their closed oblong craft.

Steve Bismarck was clearing a trail behind his house in Snohomish, Washington just before Easter 1977.[45] After a while he took a break and set off home. En route he came to a pool of water. Not wanting to wade through it, Bismarck turned round and was astonished to see a little old man. He was about 4-feet tall, very slender but well muscled. His pale brown skin, "like a light-complexioned Filipino" Bismarck described it, had an appearance as if scarred by fire. He was wearing a sparkly metallic blue uniform and carried under his right arm a helmet of clear plastic with a white coloured section at the back. The man saw him too and was clearly spooked. His face contorted and his body vibrated so fast (like he was doing the "jitterbug") that he appeared to Bismarck as a blur.

Bismarck then saw a transparent egg-shaped object on the ground. Sticking out from the top was a rod attached to a small curved blade. The little man stepped inside the egg at the same time as a second humanoid came down through the trees and landed his own oval machine with a sound like a beehive. It appeared to Bismarck as if these "eggs" were in a kind of wind tunnel.

---

[45] *Glimpses of Other Realities, Volume II: High Strangeness,* p145-146

Both beings then got out of their eggs and walked off about sixty feet. The eggs ascended skyward and a 60-foot diameter UFO appeared overhead with a roaring noise, stopping above the trees. The two little men stood staring at Bismarck. Underneath the UFO was a 50-foot diameter, bell-shaped object. A bearing on the underside was going clickety-clack like a train. Streams of wind were being expelled from its bottom. Bizarrely, specks in the air coalesced into the form of a wolf with horns and a long lion-like tail. The frightening form reached Bismarck who felt a shock and heard cackling laughter. It came at him and delivered its shock several times.

Later, under hypnosis, Bismarck recalled that he was taken aboard by four other small men who also wore metallic blue uniforms and helmets that sparkled. Their heads and necks were covered with light brown fuzz. Horrifyingly, he recalled having a needle stabbed into his eye, his eye coming out of its socket and then feeling numb. The next thing he remembered was being back on the ground. To conclude this utterly bizarre and terrifying episode, a Sasquatch was lowered on a cable in front of him. The creature was 8-feet tall with a cone-shaped head. Its body was covered in 4-foot long hair. Bismarck recalled seeing a total of 9 little men on the ground, each equipped with small tanks on their backs.

Late one night in October 1972, Arizona resident, Ed Foley, was travelling on Highway 10 near Casa Grande, Arizona.[46] Foley stopped to relieve himself, turning off the engine but leaving on the radio. He walked over to a ditch and heard a high-pitched squeal coming from the radio. Looking up, he saw a bright star that was growing larger. Soon he saw that it was a yellowish-gold luminous disc. When the disc descended Foley saw inside it many humanoid creatures busily working at various consoles and control apparatus. The bronze coloured creatures were about thirty inches tall and shaped like little human-formed doughmen with very flexible appendages, simple domed heads and round black eyes. Their arms and feet ended in stumps with hard looking knobs that projected from the ends that could extend outward like flexible tentacles. On some the right arm seemed longer than the left. He received information that the beings needed blood, vital fluids, brain juices and secretions from glands of various animals in order to help replenish their diminishing supply of life essence. They told Foley that they carefully avoid humans as much as possible in their harvesting of fluid substances.

---

[46] *ibid*, p163

Robert Taylor parked his pickup truck and began a walk with his dog along a forest path up the side of a local hill, Dechmont Law, near the town of Livingstone in Scotland's county of West Lothian, not far from Edinburgh. The date was 9 November 1979. Minutes later Taylor saw a "flying dome" approximately 7 yards in diameter hovering above the forest floor in a clearing about 500 yards away from his truck. He later described it as a dark metallic material with a rough texture like "sandpaper" featuring an outer rim set with small propellers. Taylor smelled an acrid odour "like burning brakes." Two smaller spheres, "similar to sea mines," descended to the earth from the dome with a plopping sound and attached themselves to Taylor's trouser legs. They pulled him to the ground and dragged him in the direction of the dome. At this point he lost consciousness. When he awoke the objects had gone. Disoriented, Taylor backed his truck into a mud patch and so he walked home.

Taylor's wife reported that on his return her husband was dishevelled and muddy with torn clothing and ripped trousers. She called the police and a doctor who treated him for grazes to his chin and thighs. Police accompanied Taylor to the site where he claimed he received his injuries. They found "ladder-shaped marks" in the ground where Taylor saw the dome and other marks made by the smaller spheres. Police recorded the matter as a criminal assault.

In 2009 a film was released which relates the horrifying account of a purported series of abduction events in Nome, Alaska, in October 2000. *The Fourth Kind* was directed by Olatunde Osunsanm and starred Milla Jovovich as psychologist Dr. Abigail Tyler, Elias Koteas as her colleague Dr. Abel Campos and Will Patton as Sheriff August. The plot relates how in August 2000 Tyler's husband, Will, was mysteriously murdered one night in his sleep, leaving her to raise their two children, Ashley and Ronnie. The story then widens to describe the experiences of Nome citizens, who under hypnosis sessions conducted by Tyler see every night a white owl staring at them through their bedroom windows. One resident refuses to admit what he sees and returns home. That night, before killing his family and then himself he says he remembers everything and asks the meaning of the phrase, "Zimabu Eter."

Tyler comes to believe that the affected citizens have been victims of kidnapping by NHEs. Evidence in the form of a tape that confirms that something broke into Tyler's home and attacked her indicates that she, too, may have been similarly kidnapped. Dr. Campos is suspicious of Tyler's claims, as is Sheriff August. Philologist Dr. Awolowa

Odusami identifies the mysterious language on the tape as Sumerian.

A patient then calls Tyler in a panic urging her to come to his house to hypnotize him in order to get something horrific out of his head. While hypnotised he suddenly jerks and lifts upright, hovering above his bed. In a distorted electronic voice the patient then tells Tyler: "Abbey Tyler…respond…no need pray…I…here…end (your) study." The man's seizure is so violent that three upper vertebrae are completely severed, leaving him paralysed.

Sheriff August tries to arrest Tyler but Campos comes to her defense and so she is instead confined to her house. Meanwhile, the footage of a dashcam recording made by August's deputy while later keeping a watch from outside, shows a large black object flying over the Tyler house. The video playback then distorts but the deputy is heard describing people being pulled out of the house and calls for backup. Deputies rush into the house, finding Ronnie and Tyler who is screaming that Ashley was taken into the sky. Sheriff August accuses her of her daughter's disappearance and removes Ronnie from her custody. Ronnie goes willingly, not believing his mother's alien abduction theory.

Under hypnosis Tyler describes both seeing Ashley's abduction and details of her own, including scenes depicting parts of the abductors' ship and of the aliens' extracting human egg cells from her. The camera scrambles and Tyler begs the aliens to return her daughter. The creature replies by saying that Ashley will never be returned.

When the encounter ends, Campos and Odusami rush over to the now unconscious Abbey and notice something out of camera's view. The camera scrambles again and a volatile voice yells, "Zimabu Eter!" When the camera view clears it shows that the three of them are gone. The film cuts to an interview with Tyler in which she explains that all three were abducted during that hypnosis session and that no one has any memory of what happened.

After her hypnosis session Tyler wakes up in a hospital after breaking her neck in the abduction. Sheriff August tells her that Will had actually committed suicide, indicating that she has deluded herself about everything. Eventually, Tyler is cleared of all charges and moves to the East Coast where she becomes bed-bound requiring constant care. Ronnie remains estranged from Abbey and still blames her for his sister's disappearance.

The film divided opinion. Some panned it while others held that with repeated viewings one increasingly feels that there is something to its remarkable narrative. What cannot be denied is that Nome is a mysterious area. It lies on one of Alaska's remotest boundaries, beyond which is the icy Bering Sea. It is said that from 1960 onwards up to 40 men, women and children have gone missing. No bodies have ever been found. In 2005 a group of homicide detectives investigated these unexplained disappearances. If they came to any conclusions their findings were not placed into the public domain. However, the Anchorage Daily News stated that a majority of the victims were "Native American men who had travelled to Nome from surrounding villages." Police seized on this to assert without a shred of proof that the victims were killed by "excessive alcohol consumption and a harsh winter climate." In other words, the disappearances were nothing to do with little green men.

Others looking for answers have looked to the skies. According to local UFO watchers, there are regular UFO sightings in the Nome region, which, for whatever reason, are believed to signify a sort of command centre for alien life on Earth. A sizeable element among the Nome community sincerely believes that there is a baleful non-human presence in the area.

Investigators have estimated that 5 out of every 1,000 people go missing in Alaska each year, more than double the USA average. Most of the Alaska vanishings take place in Nome. Erin Marie Gilbert was last seen on 1 July 1995 in Girdwood. She was driving to an event with a date when suddenly the car broke down. The date went off to get help and on his return Erin was not to be seen, nor was she again.

It is striking just how many Nome citizens appear to hold repressed memories of being abducted by NHEs. Intriguingly, many share the common experience of waking in the night, often observing a white owl and then seeing by the clock showing the precise time of 3.33 a.m.

The film's owl motif is reflected in Sumerian and Babylonian mythology, for example with the Sumerian deity Moloch and the goddess Inanna. The owl theme also features in *Twin Peaks*, including the recent third season, as a creature whose presence denotes evil or supernatural occurrences (the ominous "the owls are not what they seem" being a recurring line).

There are two Sumerian messages in the movie. Sumerian scholar Aleksi Sahala of the University of Helsinki made exhaustive efforts in 2010 to translate them. He had to conclude that the shorter message is untranslatable. However, he had more success with the longer, concluding with a degree of speculation and imagination that the message is: "en-e-ne me-na-am-me-en-dè-en; ki-úlutim igi-kár; a el sá i-e kax-e sug-zag gu," which translates as:

"We are the masters, divine beings of the heavens; examining the place of creation; fetching the offspring to compare (it); taking (it) away to KA; destroying (it) completely."

Sahala suggested that "Zimabu Eter" might possibly be a phrase in Akkadian / Old Babylonian that translates as: "save the father's / ancestor's face / appearance." The Nome phenomenon's connections with an ancient civilisation are a recurrent theme shared by many UFO events. In fact, the "Sumerian" link to UFOlogical phenomena is so prevalent that it will be addressed in chapter 8.

The mutilation of animals by NHEs is a sobering and serious subject, which has formed the substance of numerous books by distinguished investigators. I touch on it here in passing. Typical mutilations may include removal of one or more among: sex organs, limbs, eye, ears, nose, mouth, tongue, udders, lung, throat, head, jaw, entrails, penis and mammary glands. The mutilations are characterised by complete exsanguination leaving pink-white muscle tissue. Incisions resemble cookie-cutter shapes. Somehow the mutilators are able to separate cells instead of cutting the tissue. The dissections appear to be performed with laser instruments, leaving no blood signs. In one event, "Lady's" mediasternum was emptied and the mare's cavity was dry. No tracks led up to the carcass.

Associated with mutilations are appearances of silent black helicopters without rotary blades, or low, small fix-winged "planes."

These craft seem to be able to anticipate mutilation events. Human-like figures and hairy beasts have been seen gliding over terrain and nearby fences. There have been instances of mutilated animals being found inside perfect circles of bare earth. Liquid will not soak into these bare areas.

Investigative journalist Linda Moulton Howe presented a paper at the July 1991 MUFON International Symposium in Chicago titled *Further Evidence Linking Animal Mutilations and Human Abductions to Alien Life forms*. In her remarks Howe referred to the experiences of a woman from Missouri who had been subjected to repeated episodes of alien abduction since childhood. In a series of exchanges she asked her captors why they engaged in the mutilation of animals. These are extracts from their reported replies (key phrases in bold type):

"Increase in tissue sample collection of bovine species. Similarities in genetic makeup of human tissue. Samples extracted for varied uses. Pollutants registered in areas selected for study...Tissue from selected bioplasms are collected, stored and processed for many uses. Bovine tissue most easily processed for replication...Pollution levels in mucous membranes registered and analyzed for signs of genetic deviation caused by increased radiation bombardment. Continued sampling will increase as the need increases...Polymorphic indoctrination will continue. Speciation is necessary to guarantee continuation in the event of catastrophic annihilation. Necessity supersedes diplomacy...Genetic splicing of individual chromosomes within DNA matrix can be used to eliminate unfavourable traits and physical flaws, which make a stronger race. The improved product can pass on advanced biological systems to future generations, which effectively evolves the species."

Here we have an instance in which UFOlk reportedly seek to rationalise and defend their mutilation of animals in order to help preserve the human race in the face of impending cataclysmic annihilation. Is one prepared to believe that their actions are carried out for such altruistic motives? Or is their apparent regard for our survival just a smokescreen to conceal distasteful actions carried out for much more sinister purposes?

The British UFO Investigation and Research Unit have undertaken numerous investigations into paranormal activity in Wales. Its 12-strong team has also been investigating animal mutilation through its Animal Pathology Field Unit. In April 2010 *The Sun* newspaper reported on the team's activities. In the preceding 12 years there had been many reports of bizarre animal deaths in Wales, particularly along a corridor from the Berwyn Mountains down the Shropshire-Powys borders to the Brecon Beacons, a mountain range and moorland area in South Wales notorious for UFO activity, which opens the narrative of the next chapter.

The Animal Pathology Field Unit was established to conduct research into the phenomenon and its connections to increasing appearances of red and orange spheres in the vicinity of animal deaths and disappearances. In 2010 the team established a surveillance point on a hill farm that overlooked some of the most active sighting areas around Wales' Radnorshire Forest. From their vantage point the team observed the mysterious spheres as they came and went, occasionally morphing into different shapes that fired beams to the ground and discharged small spheres that darted backwards and forwards across the valley floor as though they were looking for something. In interviews all but one local farmer reported having suffered some unusual disappearances of animals or deaths with strange injuries. Many reported seeing flashing lights and red or white spheres over the area.

We turn now to a particularly "Grimm Tale" of an extremely unsavoury element of NHE activity in Wales. Other investigators who contributed to the Animal Pathology Field Unit's studies included Richard D. Hall whose "Richplanet" website is crammed full of topics of the kind loved by fans of conspiracy theories. After Hall had broadcast a documentary, *Silent Killers*, on animal mutilations he received a call from a UFO buff who asked him why he was not also investigating human mutilations. Hall had no idea what he was talking about; the subject had not previously arisen in connection with Wales.

Hall discussed the matter with fellow investigator Derek Gough. Gough had a source that was a soldier in the UK military. He had formerly been a member of a secret British operation reputedly named "5-8," which worked in liaison with the NSA and NATO based at the Brecon Beacons. This group was reportedly founded by former Prime Minister Margaret Thatcher to monitor UFO events. The source reportedly told Gough that his job was to cover up cases of human mutilations in the U.K. and in Europe, as well as in Australia where, allegedly, there had been a case of 30 mutilations occurring in one day. He said that his unit would actually arrive 5 minutes *before* a UFO incident involving mutilations. His job was to keep people away. He said that on two occasions he was able to actually touch a UFO. He said that the aliens looked exactly like demons; they were exceedingly strong and could move 60 feet in one second.

The source had photos of the mutilated bodies of a 20-year old man and a 16-year old girl who had gone missing from their car, which was found with its headlights on and the engine running. Additionally, the late former policeman and top UFO investigator, Tony Dodd, told fellow researcher David Cayton of three other cases of human mutilation in the UK, including one in the Brecon Beacons where a family of four was found laid out beside their vehicle. Gough was provided with photographs. Subsequently, he received death threats and had his house burned down. Gough turned the photos over to the police but despite their initial confidence that those responsible would be identified there was reportedly no follow up.

It is claimed that factions of the military shoot down reptilian craft regularly over the Brecon Beacons, the hypothesis being that the NHEs arrive through a form of "stargate." It is further allegedly reported by contacts within Group 5-8 that members of Delta Force "arrive out of nowhere when the craft come down and communicate to each other telepathically when involved in the sealing off and clear up."

Reportedly linked with the NHE activity in South Wales is the spate of suicides of young people in the Bridgend area, a highly alarming series of events that attracted UK-wide media attention in 2007. Richard Hall said that while TV reporters were interviewing local people about the deaths, members of MI-6 and Group 5-8 Special Forces were working in the background on telephone poles and in telephone boxes. These operatives were searching for an "item," which had recently gone missing from a purported underground genetics facility below the Brecon Beacons known as "Trapdoor." The story goes that this so-called item was an alien human-like chimera that had escaped the facility. The chimera was described as a "feeder" because it telepathically feeds on the taste of fear; anyone standing within its field of influence experiences intense suicidal tendencies and depression. It is claimed that the chimera came to the town of Bridgend and engaged some young people in conversation, telepathically hypnotizing them with various subliminal suggestions to encourage an act of suicide.

Afterwards the chimera went back to the place it was staying (possibly a local guest house) and performed remote viewing to the location where the individual was in the process of committing suicide and "fed" off the energies being released before and during the act.

The intelligence operatives in the news background were apparently seeking to convey a silent message to the community saying, "We're attempting to get the situation under control and track this thing down."

These are shocking stories purporting to tell of monstrous events that have taken place just 50 miles from my home in my adopted Celtic nation of Wales. It is scary stuff. One can only hope that it is with no more than a pinch of salt with which these gruesome stories should be digested.

In the next chapter we stay in Wales but go back in time to a 70-year period beginning in 1904. In particular, we will explore a series of remarkable events that took place in the 1970s. The nature of the flaps and sightings inside the "Welsh Triangle" echo much of the content of "The Landing Lights of Magonia" thus far, and will lead us into a fascinating review of the cutting edge scientific thinking behind the new concept of the Implicate Order—the home of Non-Human Entities that come and go into our world with such alacrity.

"When I came home last night at three,
The man was waiting there for me
But when I looked around the hall,
I couldn't see him there at all!
Go away, go away, don't you come back any more!
Go away, go away, and please don't slam the door."

William Hughes Mearns, *Antigonish*

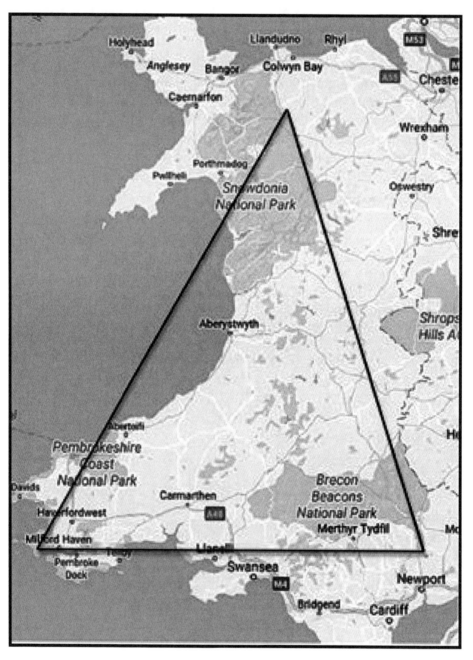

The Welsh Triangle

Chapter 6

The Welsh Triangle

The causal source of the UFO and UFO abduction phenomena is not extraterrestrial...Explore Jacque Vallée's Passport to Magonia *again for more close parallels between the 'faerie' manifestation of the NHEs and current events. Dr. Vallée was so close to the truth of the situation, with the exception that the ultimate manipulators are not human.*[47]

—U.S. Dept. of Defense agents, 1994

I was born and raised in England but in the early 1990s work brought my family to Wales and we never left. It is a tiny nation but vast in the richness of its cultural and mythological history. As I approach my eighth decade I am becoming increasingly aware of its unique mystical qualities. I now cannot imagine living anywhere else.

Wales, one thirty-fourth the size of Texas and with a population of three million, is a Celtic land filled with beauty, magic and mystery. Its legendary fare is epic. In the White Book of Rhydderch, the Red Book of Hergest and the Hanes Taliesin, the three volumes that make up the "Mabinogion," the earliest prose stories of Britain, we read marvellous tales of enchantment.

Spellbound, we are gripped by Arthur's fantastical exploits in which the Once and Future King quells mountaintop monsters and troublesome dragons. In the pages of "Llud and Llefelys" we read of fairies, the bad ones of the bunch that want to seize and do harm to humans. Wales' ancient power exists today in its haunting hills and valleys. Stories persist about the presence of dimensional gateways in the Black Mountains area of the Brecon Beacons in the southeast and in Pembrokeshire's Preseli hills in the southwest, the origin of the Stonehenge bluestones. Sensationally, the Preseli gateway is said by

---

[47] *Glimpses of Other Realities - Vol II: High Strangeness*, p126

some to be a time portal.

There is a tradition that Shakespeare visited Brecon for background material for *A Midsummer Night's Dream*. The story goes that Shakespeare's friend, Robert Price, showed the playwright Cwm Pwca, the haunt of the ellyllon in the Clydach Gorge and the purported glen setting on which the work is based. The fairies are reputed to inhabit a cave in the wooded gorge. The three pointed slots that radiate above it give the cave a magical appearance. Today, the gorge and cave are popularly known as the Valley of the Goblins and Shakespeare's Cave.

The western regions of Wales are favourite haunts of the Tylwyth Teg. Legends speak of them living on Pembrokeshire's enchanted islands, in underground dwellings in Cardiganshire and under lakes in Carmarthenshire close to the hillside cave where Merlin sleeps with his fairy consort, Vivian.

The Berwyn Mountains incident – the Welsh "Roswell"

We begin our investigation of Otherworldly tricksters in 1974 in the northeast of this tiny, folklore-rich nation. Wales is noted for its own Otherworldly "triangle," an area rich in UFO phenomena dating back to 1904.

The Berwyn range of peaks sits at the apex of the isosceles triangle. Pembrokeshire, the site of the Dyfed Wave of 1977 shortly to come under scrutiny, occupies the triangle's bottom left corner, while its bottom right point is situated in the Brecon Beacons. Of the three points the Brecons has a decidedly more sinister history of NHE phenomena.

It can be said that the Berwyn Mountain event of 1974 cast its shadow 70 years earlier. The town of Barmouth, 35 miles west of the Berwyn event epicentre, is the location of a fascinating event known as the "Egryn Lights" phenomenon, which occurred between December 1905 and March 1906. This account has all the usual features of a UFO flap, including unworldly lights and the presence of Men in Black.

In December 1905 residents of the villages of Egryn, Bryncrug and Towyn described seeing in the surrounding hills an enormous luminous star with intensely brilliant white light, its circumference emitting dazzling sparks. It poised in midair, a mass of fire of every conceivable colour spreading on all sides and descending into a rainbow shower to the surface of the mountain. Even more spectacular events were seen at nearby ancient megalithic remains. Several multicoloured columns of light emerged out of the ground and leapt upwards. One appeared to flutter before producing spheres of light, which slowly rose up its length before exploding at the top.

The Berwyn Mountain range

The lights took the forms of starlike bodies, spheres, ovals, glowing arches, bars, and luminous forms "suspended" upon incandescent "arms." On one occasion a bloodred light no more than a foot from the ground appeared before startled onlookers in the centre of the village street. On another a group of villagers walking near Barmouth suddenly saw a soft shimmering radiance  that was flooding the road at their feet. Some described it as a brilliant snowy whiteness, others as brilliant blue. Immediately, it spread around them; every stick and stone within twenty yards visible as if under the influence of the soft light. Villagers said later that it was as if some large body between earth and sky had suddenly opened and emitted a flood of light from within itself. The effect was like that of a bursting firework bomb, yet wonderfully different. They looked up and saw an oval grey mass, half open, disclosing an interior kernel of white light.

Investigators later mapped the precise locations of the many sightings in the four-month period and discovered that they were strung out like beads on a thread centred round the deep seated Mochras Fault, which runs north-south between the coastal towns of Harlech and Barmouth and passes almost directly under the village of Egryn. The nearby northeast–southwest Bala geological fault also passes by Egryn. It was learned that the area had been subject to tremors immediately around and after the occurrence of the lights, which culminated in a minor earthquake under the Swansea area in southwest Wales in 1906. Ground-lights were also seen in nearby Llangollen to the east in April 1905. Three local vicars who had gathered to see what all the fuss was about saw them "burst luridly" and fly off.

In the 17th century balls of flame were seen crossing the sea near the west coast of Wales. Harlech residents claimed that in 1672 these strange lights were setting fire to crops and barns and infecting grass, although they did no harm to people who were in the fields at the time. In 1877 blue lights were seen over Pwllheli and the Dysynni Estuary.

Local investigators advanced the notion that the phenomenon went back much further. They suggested that people who lived in this northwestern area of Wales 3,000 years ago might have witnessed similar lighting phenomena and marked the appearances by building stone edifices to mark the sites. This interpretation supports the increasing belief that there is a connection between the flight paths of UFOs, earth energies and ancient civilisations.

Lay-preacher Mary Jones and her Welsh Revivalist congregation immediately adopted the Egryn Lights as proof that God was trying to communicate with them. It is little wonder that Jones arrogated to herself ownership of the lights because she had a history of invoking similar strange lights that would appear at places where she was about to preach. They lights appeared for the first time on the night that Mrs Jones commenced her public mission at Egryn. A star of light was heralded by a luminous arch that witnesses likened to the Aurora Borealis, one end resting on the sea, the other bathing the little hilltop chapel in a soft luminescent glow. The star then appeared, its light flooding the chapel. From that night the star and the lights always accompanied Mrs Jones' preachings. Each night the star would appear above a particular house, its occupant afterwards coming to the Egryn chapel as a new convert. Some witnesses saw the lights around Jones making jumping motions, rushing or coming together (sometimes with a loud peel of thunder), or balls of fire rising from the ground and bursting.

Returning home one night well after midnight from one of her mission meetings Mrs Jones dismissed her driver, telling him that her brother would walk her the rest of the way home. She pointed to the figure of a man she believed to be her brother approaching up the lane. The car drove off and Mrs Jones walked on to meet her chaperone. The man then turned and walked before her down the lane. Puzzled, Mrs Jones called out to her brother by name. The figure looked back over his shoulder and she realised it was not her brother. Afraid, she began singing softly one of the Revival hymns. The man stopped abruptly and, according to Mrs Jones, transformed into an enormous black dog which ran from bank to bank across the road in front of her as though to prevent her advancing any further. There and then she believed that the figure before her was the Devil who was angry about her Christian evangelist work. She prayed aloud for strength whereupon the black dog rushed growling into a nearby hillside.

Mrs Jones' story would sound absurd and fantastical were it not for the testimony of another Egryn villager. A highly intelligent and well respected young woman of the parish reported that on three nights in succession at midnight she was visited in her bedroom by a man dressed in black whose appearance corresponded with the person seen by Mrs Jones in the lane. The young woman said that the visitor gave to her a message and forbade her to reveal its contents. The theme of "secret messages" conveyed to a parishioner in a deeply devout Christian community has its parallels with celebrated events such as at Lourdes, Garabandal and Fátima.

High strangeness returned to North Wales in 1974 in the Berwyn Mountains, an area approximately bound by Bala in the southwest, Corwen in the northwest, Llangollen in the northeast and in the southeast by Oswestry in the English county of Shropshire. The range largely consists of sparsely populated moorland, thick with heather, interspersed with grassland and bracken. Its main summits are Cadair Berwyn (832 metres above sea level), Moel Sych at 827 metres and Cadair Bronwen at 784 metres.

Welsh folklore speaks of unusual aerial phenomena in the Berwyn hills. Terrifyingly, the westerly part of the range that abuts the mountains of Snowdonia, in particular Cader Idris ("the Chair of Idris the Giant,") is the home of the Cŵn Annwn, the Hounds of Hell. These are the fabled hounds of Annwn, the Celtic Otherworld. In the Mabinogion the Cŵn Annwn run with the Wild Hunt led by Arawn, King of Annwn, and at other times by Gwyn ap Nudd, King of the Fairyfolk. If one is unfortunate enough to hear the howling of the hounds, the die is cast—one's death is nigh. Legend has it that anyone who stays the night on Cader Idris will find death, go mad or become a genius. On the first night of each New Year mysterious lights can be seen around its peak. Note that the events in the nearby Berwyn Range took place in the month of January.

In addition to the Cŵn Annwn, villagers living in the shadows of the Berwyn hills tell tales of being plagued by flying dragons, a synonym in medieval times for UFOs. If this were not enough, the region suffers phantom bombers, lake monsters and, in common with many other places in Britain, "ABCs" (Alien, or Anomalous, Big Cats). One might say that the Berwyn hills' impressive mythological pedigree makes what occurred in 1974 at least as suggestive of a modern day fairytale as a UFO story.

From a study of all the reported facts, notably those unearthed by investigators such as Andy Roberts, Scott Felton and Tony Dodds who deserve grateful acknowledgement, a fascinating account emerges. During the twelve months prior to the Berwyn incident the north of England bore witness to a phenomenon dubbed the "phantom helicopter." More than one hundred credible sightings were reported, including over the Cheshire skies a few miles to the east of the Berwyn range. It appeared at night at low altitude, often over difficult terrain, dangerously close to power lines and in very poor weather. Witnesses felt that the phantom crafts were engaged in looking for something. The phenomenon ended on or around the date of the Berwyn incident.

On the night of 23 January 1974 villagers in Landrillo and Llandderfel near Bala witnessed over a period of several hours strange lights streaking across the sky. The authorities officially attributed the lights to a bolide meteor shower. A bolide is categorised as an extremely bright meteor, especially one that explodes in the atmosphere. Astronomers refer to bolides as fireballs about equal to the brightness of the full moon. That night bolide meteors were recorded at 7:25 p.m., 8:15 p.m., 8:30 p.m. and 9:55 p.m., the latter appearance being the most dramatic. These times coincide with witness observations of the Berwyn incident.

At around 8:30 p.m. the villagers heard a colossal explosion, closely followed by a deep rumbling. One witness recalled it as being "like a lorry running into a house." Its shockwaves reverberated through homes, overturning furniture, knocking objects off shelves, rippling walls and upsetting pets and livestock. Scientific instruments registered the tremors between 4 and 5 on the Richter scale. Frightened, the villagers congregated outdoors. The tremors were felt in Wrexham, Cheshire, Wirral, Liverpool, and even as far as the Isle of Man

Locals at first thought that something, perhaps an aircraft, had crashed into Cader Berwyn Mountain. Others believed they had seen something else. One farmer described seeing an object the size of a bus, white in the middle, travelling along the mountain. It then dipped and the farmer thought it was going to crash.

Other witnesses spoke of red and amber pulsing lights and an egg-shaped craft flying past them. Witness Elfed Roberts reported seeing from his car a green light in the sky ahead of him. He described it as an arcing light. Many telephoned the local police to report these strange events. The Gwynedd Police Constabulary Major Incident Log for that night includes these calls:

> ➤ Explosion. PC receiving 999 calls of UFO. A witness who saw an object on the hillside reported: "Saw bright red light, like coal fire red. Large perfect circle. Like a big bonfire. Could see lights above and to the right and white lights moving to bottom. Light changed colour to yellowish white and back again."

> ➤ "There's been a large explosion in the area and there is a large fire in the mountainside. I am speaking from ... and can see the fire where I am."

> "Saw bright green lights, object with tail - travelling west. Saw about Bangor direction - dropped down."

> "Saw a circular light in the sky at an estimated height of 1,500 feet. This object exploded and pieces fell to the ground. Mr X estimates the pieces would have fallen into the (Irish) sea between Rhyl and Liverpool."

Fearing an aircraft crash, a team from RAF Valley on Anglesey conducted a search and reportedly found nothing. Evidently, they didn't look that hard.

Llandrillo district nurse Pat Evans contacted Colwyn Bay Police HQ to report the explosion. Pat was told that it was probably caused by a plane crash. Her first thought was to put her training to good use and assist the injured until the arrival of emergency services. Accompanied by her two teenage daughters who were St John Ambulance trained in first-aid, Pat set off. After climbing above the tree line Pat rounded a bend on the B4391. Abruptly, she slammed on the brakes as she and her daughters saw a large red-orange pulsing ball of light on Cader Berwyn a few miles to their left.

Unable to identify the object in detail, Pat drove on for a few minutes before returning to the same spot. The light was still there so she parked and observed it for a while with her daughters. A light drizzle was falling but the night was otherwise clear and Pat was able to describe the ball as "large" and forming a "perfect circle," but it did not appear to be three-dimensional. Pat's first thought was that the glow was from the flames of an aircraft but was straightaway unconvinced because the glow wasn't moving in the manner of flickering flames. Perfectly spherical and still, the glow pulsated between red and orange. In an interview she recalled, "There were no flames shooting or anything like that. It was very uniform, round in shape...it was a flat and round."

As Pat and her daughters watched in puzzlement, the light changed colour several times from red to yellow to white. The three women also observed smaller white lights lower down the mountain. These were flashing like "Christmas tree fairy lights" and making a zigzag movement towards the glowing object. The astonished witnesses firstly assumed that they were seeing the lights of handheld lanterns. However, Pat quickly realised that a rescue team could not possibly have been organised in such a short time so as to arrive at the mountain before her.

Pat Evans continued driving to the mountain, still intent on helping any survivors but even as she was making the initial climb she realised that the crash had probably occurred on an inaccessible part of the peak. She said she then turned around and returned home.

Moel Sych Mountain in vicinity of crash site

In 2010 Pat stated that the object "couldn't have gotten there any other way apart from being flown there...It had to be a UFO of some sort!" Stories later circulated that Pat had seen alien bodies but was ordered to keep quiet by the Ministry of Defence. Pat firmly denied that she had seen anything of the kind

Paul Devereux[48] describes the Berwyn incident and attributes the "earthlights" seen on Cader Berwyn to geophysical stresses. Devereux adds that colleague, Keith Critchlow, got into discussions with scientists who were investigating the mountain in the days after the incident. Their Geiger counter gave off extraordinarily high readings at the Bronze Age archaeological stone circle known as Moel ty Uchaf on the slopes of Cader Berwyn. Devereux went on to map approximately 85 UFO sightings in Wales against tectonic and geomagnetic factors. Interestingly, together with geologist colleague Paul McCartney,

---

[48] Devereux, P., *Places of Power*, Blandford Press, London, 1990

Devereux found that sightings corresponded more with earth (epicentre) movements rather than with the positions of static fault lines.

Devereux and Critchlow's investigations should be considered in tandem with John Michell's remarkable insights[49] on the true nature of megalithic constructions. Michell saw Stonehenge both as a model for a UFO and as a gateway to the higher dimensions. He pointed out that seen from above Stonehenge's resemblance to a UFO is remarkable. He pointed out the significant features that characterise the resemblance: the well-defined outer rim consisting of low bank and ditch, and within this the Aubrey holes and small circular pits around the perimeter like portholes seen in UFO craft. In the centre is the perfect stone circle of the UFO's raised cabin enclosing the horseshoe-shaped trilithon construction that appears above the surrounding rim like a domed cockpit. The smaller Prescelli bluestones stand inside the circle, visible through its openings just as witnesses observe occupants inside UFOs, as in 1959 when teachers and pupils in New Guinea saw a UFO hovering in full view over their school.

In 1994 British researcher Jenny Randles lectured on the Berwyn case at the Fortean Times UnConvention. During her presentation she mentioned the anomalous radiation count at the Moel ty Uchaf circle. Following her lecture a member of the audience, a science correspondent from *The Sunday Express*, told Randles of rumours of a leukaemia cluster among children in the Bala area, which had arisen in the years following the Berwyn incident. The correspondent told Randles that at the time he connected the rumour with possible leaks from the Trawsfynedd nuclear power station (25 miles east of the Berwyn crash site) but he could not prove this. He told Randles that in the light of later claims of UFO crashes or secret military hardware, however, it could be implied that whatever had crashed in the Berwyn Mountains had possibly been radioactive in nature and of sufficient strength to subsequently generate the leukaemia cluster around the Bala district.

Police participated in the search for a downed aircraft; in some cases commandeering vehicles to assist but their public position was that nothing was found. Locals spoke of a substantial military presence after the incident and of the arrival of official-looking "Men-in-Black" strangers who went around questioning the villagers about what they had seen that night. Military jets and helicopters criss-crossed the area. Roads were barricaded and people shepherded away from sensitive

---

[49] Michell, J., *The Flying Saucer Vision*, Abacus, London, 1974

locations. A few even claimed they had seen strange boxes being carried away in lorries. Farmers reported that they were forbidden from tending their cattle. The feeling among locals was that something was obviously being sought.

Documents leaked in 2008 showed that many of the reports made to police that evening were from residents convinced they had seen a UFO before the "earthquake" struck. One resident reported seeing "a bright red light, like coal fire red" on the mountainside, as well as "light above and to the right...and white lights moving to the bottom." The documents also reveal a police officer's testimony. He said "large explosion in the area and...a large fire in the mountainside. I can see the fire (from) where I am." A local hotel manager told investigators that the conversation in the bar was increasingly about the military "sealing off the area." Just as we will find in the account of the Pembrokeshire UFO flap of 1977, there were also rumours about an American military presence.

A few days after the incident a family driving along a quiet road twenty miles from the Berwyn range heard a humming sound filling the air. Seemingly out of nowhere a saucer-shaped object passed in front of them above the treetops and then vanished. In the same period, two truckers driving home to Lincolnshire noticed a cigar-shaped object hovering over Bala Lake. Three weeks after the event Geraint Edwards saw a UFO by Cader Berwyn. It was a Friday evening. He was in a car with others on the way to play a pub darts match. At 6:45 p.m. they saw something to the southeast. It looked like a rugby ball but its ends were more "pointy." It hovered for at least ten minutes. Five other reports of UFOs seen over the UK at about 10:00 p.m. on 23 January 1974 were unearthed during the Ministry of Defence investigation. Three sightings were in the Home Counties, one in Lincolnshire and another in Sussex.

Replying to a letter in May 1974 from local Member of Parliament, Dafydd Elis Thomas, Brynmor John, then a junior RAF minister, explained that:

"The phenomena could well have been caused by a meteor descending through the atmosphere burning up and finally disintegrating before it reached the ground. Such a hypothesis would also explain the absence of any signs of impact. It has also been suggested that at 8:32 p.m. that evening there was an earth tremor in the Berwyn Mountains which produced a landslide with noises like detonation."

It was reported that the tremor's epicentre was in the Bala area at a depth of eight kilometres. However, officials maintained that a reading and depth of those proportions ruled out a cause that could be attributed to something crashing into Cadair Berwyn. Such an object, they stated, would have to be several hundred tons in weight and leave a massive crater.

A few months after the event a curious organisation emerged from the shadows. UFO investigators in the north of England received "official" documents from a group that called itself the Aerial Phenomena Enquiry Network (APEN). At this time APEN was not an unknown body and had been linked with the Men in Black phenomenon. On previous occasions it had contacted UFO researchers via letter and cassette tape offering pieces of information but never contact details. The format of the letters received was heavy with bureaucratic terminology references: "Code=7 Case number 174L 74-71/349 ST Classification = Jasmine Clearance date=02 DE 74," in one case.

Jenny Randles was one such recipient. On the one-hour audiocassette tape she received was an introduction from a male American claiming to be someone called "J.T. Anderson, Supreme Commander of APEN." It contained television and radio broadcasts of UFO reports, occasionally interrupted by other voices, evidently terrified and in panic, claiming that UFOs were hostile and that the listener should be wary of their nature and intentions.

It has been speculated that APEN may have been part of a government disinformation unit whose remit was to cover up the true facts and divert attention from secret weapons testing. APEN issued similar communications in connection with other notable UFO events, including the Rendlesham Forest case.

During interviews in 2006 British ufologist Nick Redfern claimed that APEN had a far right wing agenda and was under investigation by Special Branch. It is the case that some of the cassette tapes sent to UFO researchers included the sound of Nazi marching and Nazi marching music. Redfern also said that APEN manipulated and spread misinformation amongst various British UFO groups in the form of smear campaigns and false allegations in efforts to undermine the groups and, ultimately, to bring them together under the umbrella of APEN.

The APEN documents sent to the Berywn event investigators claimed that an extraterrestrial craft had come down on the Berwyn Mountains and was retrieved by an APEN crash retrieval team, which had been on the scene within hours. More significantly, APEN claimed that they were recommending for hypnotic regression an unnamed key witness to the event. In 1974 hypnotic regression was virtually unknown in the British UFO community.

In the 1990s witnesses began coming forward to say that they had been part of a UFO recovery operation in the Berwyn area. Sensationally, they claimed that NHE bodies were taken from the wreckage and transported to Porton Down in Wiltshire for analysis. Porton Down is the site of the U.K.'s top-secret Chemical and Biological Defence Establishment. It was also said that the crashed UFO had been accompanied by other alien craft that subsequently submerged in the Irish Sea and were eventually flushed out by the Royal Navy and Royal Air Force.

Seasoned investigators took up the cudgels and discovered startling new facts and lines of enquiry. Scott Felton claimed that a relative of Pat Evans told him that, on her return home, Pat was stopped by a military patrol, which ordered her away from the mountain to allow them to close the road. Pat denied that this happened. However, Felton also received testimony from a number of people who said that police or soldiers had stopped them. A hotel chef was stopped whilst returning from Corwen, a reporter from Bala had his camera confiscated and two students noted a very heavy police presence in Llandrillo just after 9:30 p.m.

Felton also poured cold water on the oft-quoted suggestion that the lights seen on Cader Berwyn were from poachers' lamps. It is a fact that police were looking for poachers that night. However, this activity was going on several miles away on Cader Bronwen and had finished by 9:00 p.m. His investigations confirmed also that the plane accident that residents spoke of did not take place around the time of the event but became conflated with the circumstances surrounding one in 1982 when a light training aircraft crashed with very little disturbance to the locals.

Scott Felton's research ultimately led him to conclude that a UFO had landed in the Berwyn hills on many occasions prior to the January event. He understood that the military was very much aware of this activity and that on the night of the 23rd they were to conduct an operation, using the meteor story as a cover if needed. Felton reviewed his evidence and concluded that the object that had been visiting Berwyn in recent days returned. Observed by the waiting military personnel it came down, stayed for about an hour and a half and departed unhindered. Felton believed that it came and went in this fashion for another three weeks afterwards.

Tony Dodd (formerly a contributor to "UFO Magazine") claimed in 1996 that he was contacted by a serviceman whistleblower who said he was present at the Berwyn event. The soldier said that he had been attached to a barracks in southern England at the time. A few days before the incident they received orders to head for Birmingham, then west to Chester and, finally, to the Welsh town of Llangollen where they set up base. Believing they were to be part of a live drill of some kind, the unit awaited further orders. As soon as the "earthquake" occurred they were ordered to move to Llandderfel and not to stop under any circumstances until reaching their destination. On arrival, still expecting to participate in a drill the 5-man team found themselves being ordered to place two oblong boxes onto their military truck. They received strict orders to leave the boxes shut and not to stop until they reached Porton Down. Unwisely, the team stopped for refreshments, whereupon their tail, a plain-clothed man carrying high-level military police ID, appeared and ordered them to get back into their truck and not stop until they reached the Wiltshire facility.

At Porton Down the soldier and his buddies watched from behind transparent screens as scientists opened the boxes to reveal two frail "grey alien" creatures. Each had been placed in a decontamination chamber, presumably done at the Berwyn site. As they were being removed, the soldiers saw the creatures' obvious "not of this world" appearance. In the following days there were rumours that some of the creatures collected were alive.

Nick Redfern[50] provided further details of the soldier's testimony, assigning him with the pseudonym "Prescott." Redfern claimed that Prescott was one among scores of troops despatched to recover the wreckage from Cader Berwyn. He describes the delivery of the oblong boxes to Porton Down and adds Prescott's description of the greys as about five to six feet tall, humanoid in shape but thin to the point of being skeletal with covered skin. In an earlier work[51] Redfern suggested that the "phantom helicopters" seen in the preceding months were crewed by UFO crash retrieval teams on permanent standby. Redfern gave serious consideration to the idea that there existed a jointly funded CIA-Ministry of Defence rapid response project.

Researcher Russ Kellet did great work in 2000 to uncover a Marine and Coastguard document, which refers to an exercise carried out by RAF Jurby Head during the late afternoon and early evening of 23

[50] Redfern, N., *Cosmic Crashes*, Simon & Schuster UK, London, 2000
[51] Redfern, N., *A Covert Agenda*, Simon & Schuster UK, London, 1998

January 1974. RAF Jurby Head was a Royal Air Force air weapons range that operated on the northwest coast of the Isle of Man between 1939 and 1993. Bombing practices were carried out at sea with the use of dummy bombs, including inert nuclear weapons. Tellingly, the main user of the range was the United States Air Force.

The document names the exercise as "Photoflash." It relates that coastguards were advised to expect at least 10 aircraft taking part and around 80 flashes in the Liverpool Bay area and along the North Wales coastline. The document did not elaborate on the nature and purpose of these "photoflashes" but Kellet believed that their role was to light up the sea to reveal the position of submerged craft. Kellet concluded that three separate craft were flushed out of the sea that night and, crucially, that military craft were involved and that there was an engagement. A fisherman saw one craft come out near Puffin Island, an uninhabited island off the eastern tip of Anglesey. His colleagues told him to say nothing about it.

Kellet was also in correspondence with witnesses who claimed they were moved on by military personnel on the roadside at Llandrillo where one of the craft came down. The men told Kellet that they saw aliens getting out of the craft and helping two of their own that were injured. The aliens were then loaded onto the back of a flatbed truck and taken away. Kellet understood that there were actually two craft that came down, one crashing near Bala at a position that corresponded with the epicentre of the supposed "earthquake." The other ship smashed into one of the Berwyn hills. Kellet also claimed to have in his possession fragments from one of the craft.

Taken together, these reports provide the foundation for an intriguing opinion among investigators that the features of the Berwyn incident compare with those of the well-known US Kecksburg event.

On 9 December 1965 a large, brilliant fireball, generally assumed to be a meteor, was seen by thousands in at least six U.S. states and in Ontario, Canada. However, eyewitnesses in the village of Kecksburg, 30 miles southeast of Pittsburgh, claimed that something crashed in the woods. A boy said he saw the object land. His mother saw blue smoke arising from the woods and alerted the authorities. Others reported finding an object in the shape of an acorn and the size of a Volkswagen Beetle.

In both the Berwyn and Kecksburg events the military rapidly sealed off the area and resolutely denied what local witnesses had seen with their own eyes. Much has been written about the Kecksburg case, including its alleged connection to "Die Glocke," the infamous "Nazi Bell" reportedly built by Hitler's scientists in the latter part of WWII.

All kinds of sensational claims have been made about the purpose of Die Glocke, including its alleged ability to generate images from the past and to open dimensional gateways. In my book on German philologist and Grail explorer Otto Wilhelm Rahn,[52] I referred to this seemingly farfetched agenda in my description of the reported work of the Prometheus Foundation. According to the American research sources that made public this account, the Foundation's aim

A model of Kecksburg object

was to repair damage caused by Hitler's scientists in their efforts to conduct time-travel experiments and open gateways to hostile dimensional visitors. I return to this topic in later pages.

In his book *The Hunt for Zero Point* Nick Cook expressed his belief that the Nazi Bell was transported to the United States under an agreement made between SS General Hans Kammler and American officials. The mooted existence in Wales of a joint British-American taskforce on permanent standby to deal with UFO events indicates that the powers-that-be remain extremely concerned by the NHE phenomenon and its threat to the safety and stability of our planet.

There are numerous stories in Welsh folklore that point to prior appearances of strange objects seen on the land and in the skies of the Berwyn region. One such is the ceffyl dŵr (water horse), which will allow a traveller to ride it but often throws them off and kills them. An especially frightful and malicious creature is the Llamhigyn Y Dwr, the Water Leaper. It is a giant, limbless frog or toad with a bat's membranous wings (sometimes even a bird's feathery wings) and a long, reptilian tail with a large stinger at the tip. It leaps across the water using its wings, hence its name. Its favourite prey is sheep that wander too close to the water's edge…and fishermen. It is said that its appearance alone will strike one dead. To me, the Llamhigyn Y Dwr

---

[52] Graddon, N., *Otto Rahn and the Quest for the Holy Grail*, Adventures Unlimited Press, Illinois, 2008

sounds very much like a Welsh Mothman! The Water Leaper's neighbours in nearby Llyn Dulyn (black lake) by Craig Dulyn are shoals of disfigured fish, which have bulbous eyes and deformed bodies.

The region also accommodates the dreadful afanc, a cross between an alligator and a dwarf that lives in Llyn yr Afanc on the River Conwy. Long ago it caused floods in the Conwy Valley, which drowned cattle and ruined crops. Villagers made a plan to get rid of the monster, using a maiden as bait. The maid sat on the side of the lake and sang. Enchanted by her presence, the afanc approached slowly and rested its head on her lap, with its claws upon her breast. Local man Hu Gardan and his helpers threw chains over the monster, which angrily leapt back into the water, ripping the maiden with its claws as it left. However, the chains held firm and the afanc was dragged back out of the lake by oxen. Instead of killing the monster, Hu Gardan took the afanc to Glaslyn on the eastern flank of Snowdon where it lives to this day. In fact, the journey with the afanc was so difficult that one of the oxen's eyes burst from its socket, causing it to cry many tears. So that now there is a field called Gwaun llygad yr ych (meadow of the ox's eye), containing the Pwll llygad yr ych (pool of the ox's eye), which never dries out.

There is a fascinating precursor to the Berwyn event. In 1972 Manchester citizen, Peter Taylor, was driving home from work one night. As on the two previous nights, Taylor reached at 7:30 p.m. the tiny Cheshire village of Daresbury, the birthplace and childhood residence of Alice's creator Charles Dodgson ("Lewis Carroll"). The village is a relatively short distance from the eastern limit of the Berwyn range. It has long been my suspicion that young Dodgson saw or experienced something extraordinary at Daresbury that he later wove into his Wonderland and Looking Glass stories.

On this third night the lights of Taylor's brand new Ford car faltered at precisely the same spot as before. However, events then unfolded in a very dramatic fashion. To his utter dismay, Taylor found that he was on an unfamiliar road and completely lost. Astonishingly, he discovered that he was forty miles north of Daresbury near the town of Preston in Lancashire. He phoned his wife Sandra from a roadside call box and learned that he had gained two hours in as many seconds.

Daresbury, centred round the Ring o' Bells inn, is at the epicentre of a zone of high strangeness where witnesses have repeatedly claimed all manner of bizarre goings-on. These days the area around Daresbury and the neighbouring villages of Moore, Helsby Hill and Runcorn is known by researchers as "Wonderland." Over recent years there have been repeated reports of car engines cutting out, the appearance of bright lights, a golden ball hovering above Sankey Way and a huge cigar-shaped object the size of an aeroplane that travelled beside a car near Preston Brook. The Berwyn mountains flap (or "Roswelsh" as some call it) was a "Wonderland" event that was seemingly fated to happen.

The Pembrokeshire Wave 1976-1977

Move forward three years to the beautiful Welsh county of Pembrokeshire. Pembrokeshire has played host to the greater part (25 events, termed the Dyfed wave) of the Welsh Triangle's approximately 85 NHE occurrences, counting forward from the Barmouth wave of 20 events in 1904-05. All sections of the Dyfed community witnessed aspects of the phenomena, especially over St. Brides Bay and Stack Rocks. UFOs were seen at Brawdy, Clarbeston Road, east of Nolton, Haverfordwest, Llangwm, Lawrenny, Benton Castle, Pembroke Dock, Milford Haven, Herbrandston, Ripperston Farm, Roch, Camrose, Johnston, Broadhaven, Little Haven and near Martletwy.

In his classic work[53] on Welsh fairies Wirt Sikes, U.S. Consul in Cardiff from 1876 until his death in 1883, described Pembrokeshire as:

> *that isolated cape...looked upon as a land of mystery by the rest of Wales...A secret veil cover(ed) this sea-girt promontory...and out of its misty darkness came fables of wondrous sort and accounts of miracles marvellous beyond belief.*

The shadows cast by coming events in this "isolated cape" were observed forty years earlier. In 1935 young Warren Davies was living with his grandmother in Freystrop, five miles east of the 1977 wave's epicentre at the coastal village of Broad Haven. One late afternoon as he and his sister were walking through a wood to return home from school they saw a bright yellow object. It was floating in the trees. The children thought at first it was a balloon. In the same way as identical objects would behave in 1977, it swung back and forth in short 6-foot arcs like a pendulum. It was roughly the size of a bicycle wheel. Frightened, the children ran home.

Seventeen years passed before the next event. It happened in 1952 in Castlemartin, a coastal village blessed with a spectacular coastline of limestone cliffs, large sea caves, natural arches and tall rock stacks. At

---

[53] Wirt, S., *British Goblins; Welsh Folk-Lore, Fairy Mythology, Legends, and Traditions*, London, 1880

the time of the sighting, most of the limestone downland had been cleared for use as an artillery range. During one lunchtime, date unknown, a Mr Thomas was walking along the sand dunes when he found a partially concealed metallic object. As he approached he saw two men standing by it. One whom Thomas judged to be the leader warned him not to get any closer or powerful rays would hurt him as he was not wearing protective clothing. The men also told Thomas that they had been visiting the Earth for hundreds of years and were concerned that it was on a path to self-destruction. Thomas said that they told him the name of their planet but he had forgotten it.

Twenty-five years passed and then, once again, Pembrokeshire bore witness to high strangeness. What became a series of events that occurred during the winter of 1976-1977 and continued until early summer began 9 December. On that evening school meals supervisor Dorothy Cale, her 10-year old son Daniel and two friends, Yvonne Andrews and Anne Berry, were in a car travelling a long and lonely road between the village of Broad Haven and Milford Haven, one of the largest oil ports in Europe. Mrs Cale described how they saw a very bright, vaguely dome-shaped, flashing light above the nearside high hedge. In the centre of the flashing dome they discerned a zigzag arrangement like that in an electric bulb filament. It emitted a yellowish-white light so bright that it illuminated the whole of the surrounding area and the sky above it. The driver stopped the car, thinking they were about to collide with something. The light flashed four times then disappeared. During the few seconds that the light was visible Mrs Cale got the impression they were seeing the top of something whose lower part was hidden by the hedge. They guessed the size of the flashing object as 5-6 feet across and 3 feet high, the distance above ground level being 15-20 feet.

Eight weeks later the weird stuff ramped up big time. On Friday 4 February 1977 at 4:50 p.m. a humming UFO was seen in a boggy field 400 yards from Broad Haven Primary School by 14 boys and 1 girl aged between 9-11 years. Broad Haven village sits in the southern corner of St Brides Bay. It forms part of the Pembrokeshire Coast National Park, an area of outstanding natural beauty.

The craft's appearance was witnessed at first by relays of pupils as they emerged after lunch into the school grounds and adjacent fields from the school canteen and then later by two lads after school had finished for the day. One young witness, Michael Pugh, said that he assumed that what he saw was a UFO because a few days earlier he had noted the national reports of a spaceship sighting in Yorkshire whose description matched that of the Broad Haven craft.

Pugh likened the UFO's shape to two small saucers put one against the other to make a sort of dome, on top of which was another, smaller dome which resembled an ashtray. He thought that he saw windows, three or four of them round the edge of the dome and a flashing light on top. When asked if the machine resembled any kind of farm implement, Pugh said the nearest he could think of was a muck-spreader but that they were never that flat in appearance.

Two children were reported as seeing a moving figure. David George, 9, said he saw a "silver man with spiked ears." The children's overall description was that the UFO was a silvery yellow-green cigar-shaped object with a dome and a red-orange light on top.

The witnesses went to tell "Sir"—headmaster Ralph Llewellyn—about the sighting but his first response was to dismiss the claims as "poppycock" and made no attempt to see for himself. This was unfortunate because some of the children were very scared and wanted grown-up reassurance that there was a rational explanation for the bizarre sighting.

The children continued observing the ship until 2:00 p.m. when they had to return to class. When school finished at 3:30 p.m. David Davies said that he set out to look for the vehicle because "we'd heard about it before, in the classroom, so I decided to go look for myself." Accompanied by classmates, Davies went to the boggy field but didn't see anything. However, while his friend Philip Reece was trying to find a way to navigate a stream to get a better look Davies saw a silvery cigar-shaped object pop up from behind a hedge, time of sighting 3:35 p.m. Davies later described it as being a bit longer than a coach. He saw no visible windows or portholes but being an intelligent lad he made the astute remark to Randall Pugh that the winter sun that day could have been shining on them to match the colour of the ship.

Intriguingly, Davies said the object seemed to be tugging at a silver object. Several boys felt that the ship was stuck and was labouring to free itself, a task in which it appeared to succeed partially. Witness Tudor Jones wrote: "ship seemed to be stuck—tried to take off and then disappeared behind a bush."

Upset that their claims were being ignored, Davies and his classmates handed in a petition to the police station. Now under pressure to act, headmaster Llewellyn separated the children and asked them to draw what they had seen under exam conditions. He was amazed to find their drawings were almost identical to each other, albeit with small variations. Andrew Evans and David Ward, for example, thought they had seen landing legs beneath the craft.

Witness Michael Webb's father, Tim, was at the time a serving Squadron Leader at RAF Brawdy's Tactical Weapons Unit. He said he believed his son's account absolutely. Very curiously, he said that he felt the encounter was something "supernatural or paranormal." Would a serviceman have used this kind of subjective terminology in the seventies? It sounds like the RAF was aware of unusual activity in the area and suspected a paranormal basis for it. Also curiously, Webb said that the UFO's matt silver finish was a logical choice to enable an unobserved departure. Why might he say that? It seems obvious that he was trying to say within the bounds of what was deemed permissible that he / the RAF knew much more about these affairs than they could disclose officially.

Two months later a "spare military fuel tank," 25 feet tall, was delivered to the school playground one morning. No one knew where it came from or who had had it delivered. The school converted it into a fun "space rocket" and exhibited it at the Queen's Jubilee celebrations.

Thirteen days later the UFO reappeared, witnessed on this occasion by adults: teacher Mrs Morgan who saw a large, shining metal, oval-

126

shaped, ridged object and, a short time later, two school canteen ladies who saw an object on the ground and a figure climb into it. The two women then saw the vehicle move up a slope and disappear behind trees. As it was raining, they interpreted what they saw as a local council tanker used for carting sewage. They went to the headmaster to report the matter and what they believed they had seen. Having the previous sighting and its evident authenticity in mind, Lllewellyn was not prepared on this occasion to accept the women's mundane explanation, pointing out that because the ground was so boggy no vehicle could cross it.

Another young neighbour who did not want to be named also said that around this time he saw a huge silver-suited figure one night after leaving the local pub. It was without helmet and had large, slightly protruding eyes. It was terrifying. He believed he had come face to face with the devil.

Steve Tyler, a 17-year old lad who lived with his parents in the village of Llethr in St Brides Bay, was walking home at 9:00 p.m. Sunday 13 March 1977 from his girlfriend's house. He looked up and saw a glowing orange disc at a location called Hendre Bridge. He called into some friends to tell them of his sighting but they merely laughed at him. At 9:30 p.m. while walking along a remote lane with high hedges Tyler looked into a field to see why the customarily bright lights from the nearby Brawdy NATO base were not visible. He saw that a very large dome-shaped object about the size of a house was sitting in the field and blocking the light. There was a faint light glowing around the edge of the object.

Tyler was suddenly alert to movement to his extreme right. He turned to see a tall, skinny man approaching. He was about six feet in height, hairless, had high cheekbones (like an old man's, was how Tyler described him) and large fish-like, glazed eyes twice the size of a man's. The figure was wearing a one-piece, zipped transparent suit and had a box-like device where its mouth would be and a thick, dark tube that led from this over its shoulder. It came right up to Tyler. Alarmed, Tyler took a swing at it but he said his fist hit nothing. Tyler took to his heels and didn't stop running until he reached home three miles away. When Tyler got home the family Pomeranian cross terrier that usually greeted him with a tail wag growled and barked as if he were a stranger.

Folklore indicates that long before Brawdy became home to mechanical craft it gave shelter to an unusual flying creature. Tales tell of a winged serpent that lived in Grinston Well in Brawdy Parish. Winged serpents and worms are common synonyms for UFO activity that occurred in times when terrified witnesses, confronted by mysterious lights, flying objects and silver suited visitors could only describe them as fiery dragons. Does Brawdy's winged serpent live there still?

High strangeness in the Welsh Triangle reached its peak in April 1977 at Ripperston Farm, four miles from Broad Haven. It is one of the most westerly farms in Wales, lying along the cliffs running out to Wooltack Point. Since 1974 it had been the home of Pauline Coombs and dairyman husband Billie, sons Clinton and Kieran, daughter Tina and twin daughters Joann and Layann. Here the family (pictured opposite) reared cattle-herds of between 120-150 animals.

Before getting into the remarkable detail we should understand that Roman Catholic Pauline Coombs was by all accounts a gifted psychic, an incipient medium, as one researcher described her. In her early years of married life she and Billie lived in a farm trailerpark in Pembroke Dock. It was in the caravan that Pauline experienced a distinctly religious phenomenon. Pauline did not state the actual year it took place but in her interview with researchers Pugh and Holiday she mentioned that it was during the time of the British Teddy Boy movement, which had its heyday in the pre-rock and roll skiffle era of the 1950s.

The image Pauline saw took shape upon the caravan's windowpane, just as the silver suited giant would do many years later at Ripperston farmhouse. Pauline described seeing a life-size figure holding an infant materialise inside the caravan window glass. It appeared to be

128

"floating" in mid-air. Because of her Catholic belief Pauline interpreted the figure's likeness to be a representation of the Virgin Mary. The figure was robed in a white dress that came down to its toes and wore a veil like a nun's with a cowl. The infant was swaddled in white. Around the figure's waist was a rosary. While Pauline and Billie looked on the materialisation transformed into the figure of Christ with outstretched hands. There was no sign of a cross in the vision. The Christ-figure had long hair and was dressed in pure

Pauline Coombs og hendes familie.

white. It wore what Pauline described as a robe like a woman's long dress with a low neckline, long flowing sleeves and sashed around the waist. The image persisted for about thirty minutes. Thereafter, the "Christ" appearance recurred every night around 10:30. Word of it quickly got round with the result that hundreds of people from the local church community flocked to the caravan to see the phenomenon for themselves. Pembroke's Roman Catholic vicar was one of the percipients. He came with the entire Sunday School group and proclaimed the vision as beautiful. Pauline claimed that the event garnered significant attention and coverage, including local press stories and an interview with BBC Radio Wales.

In answer to interviewers' questions about any accompanying psychic phenomena in the caravan, Pauline said the only effect was that the wardrobe latch would lift and the doors would swing open. Surprisingly, although the Vicar had earlier expressed delight at the "beautiful" image of Jesus in the caravan window he told Pauline that he wanted to conduct an exorcism. Pauline refused, saying she had no wish to be exorcised. Afterwards, Pauline went into hospital to have a baby. While she was there the farmer burned the caravan and provided the Coombs with a new one. He said he was fed up with people coming and gawking at it.

Fast forward twenty years or so to Ripperston Farm when in early 1977 Pauline saw a bright ball of light hovering in the sky. The object floated back and forth and then sped off. She thought it might be a flare, so woke Billie who went to look for it. He found nothing.

One evening a short time after this episode Pauline and her children experienced a terrifying event. Pauline was driving home from St Ishmaels, three miles from Ripperston Farm. Joann and Layann were beside her in the passenger seat and Kieron was in the back. Suddenly, Keiron shouted out, "Look at that light in the sky, it's coming towards us." Pauline looked out and saw a luminous rugby-ball shape, yellowish in colour with a hazy greyish light underneath like a torch shining downward. Pauline had reached the point in the journey where she now had to turn off the main Dale road into a narrow side lane. Keiron called out that the UFO had performed a U-turn and was following them. The girls began crying and Pauline, very jittery, drove faster and faster. As she tried to put distance between the car and the object Pauline was dismayed to see it that it was keeping pace. Although throughout the journey the car's headlamps had been switched to main beam, Keiron told his mother to turn them on. In fact, they had suddenly dimmed.

All at once, just as they were approaching the farmhouse the engine died and the car had to coast the last stretch. Pauline dashed in to tell Billie. Billie and sixteen-year old Clinton ran outside, the lad in time to see the UFO heading out to sea. Billie turned the key in the car, which started straightaway.

A few nights later Pauline saw the UFO from her kitchen window. On this occasion the circular object was much bigger than a rugby ball and had a reddish-orange tail that glowed. Soon it disappeared into some nearby clifftop fields known as Mount Vanor. "It seemed to come straight in and go into a hole waiting for it," Pauline told investigators.

Drama for the Coombs would reach Shakespearean proportions in late April but not before neighbouring townsfolk and villagers witnessed their share of weirdness. Lower Broadmoor, a stone's throw from Ripperston Farm, was home to Roland and Josephine Hewison and their children. Neither husband nor wife would have been expected to make up fantastical tales, being professional farm managers (managing both Ripperston and Broadmoor farms at this time) and each holding agricultural degrees. On Saturday morning, 26 March, Mrs Hewison, enjoying a brief lie-in, saw through her bedroom window a three-tiered round object sitting on the grass in a field in front of their large greenhouse. It was fully daylight. Mrs Hewison stared at the object for a couple of minutes before it dawned on her that what she was looking at was not an item of farm machinery but something extraordinary. She said that it resembled a squashed Rowntree's jelly-mould. It was a smooth, aluminium coloured, bulbous round shape, approximately 15 feet high by 35-40 feet wide. It made no sound and she observed no activity around it. Mrs Hewison could not be sure but she felt that it was a lightweight object because of its aluminium-like appearance. She thought that she should find somebody else to verify what she was seeing and so went to wake her three boys. When she returned less than a minute later, this time with the intention of getting a better look at the object from around her bed, it had gone.

On inspection the area in front of the greenhouse bore no signs of an object having been parked there. The one unusual event that appeared to have been associated with the phenomenon was that the family pony was not to be seen standing at its usual feeding place by the field-gate but instead was later found 400 yards away.

Interestingly, Mrs Hewison told investigators that to her knowledge none of the eight families that had lived at Broadmoor Farm within living memory stayed as tenants longer than 5-6 years, a puzzling fact because the land around the farm was of very fertile Grade 2 agricultural standard. The Hewisons had joked about this among themselves, saying that the farm must have a resident ghost.

Milford Haven citizen, 64-year old retired house decorator Cyril John, was all set to drive a group of Senior Citizens to London on 7 April. He woke at 4:45 a.m., an hour earlier than he had planned. He saw that what had woken him was an orange light pulsing off his bedroom walls. It was coming from outside. He peered out of the window and saw two silvery-coloured objects in the night sky's bright orange light. One was shaped like a giant Easter egg about four feet in diameter. It was swinging pendulum-like in an arc of roughly fifty to sixty feet in length above neighbouring chimneys. John then saw that the second object was a very large figure in a silvery boiler suit that was hanging motionless about forty feet above the window between the house and the "egg." Its arms and legs were outstretched parachutist-style. He saw no facial features but the size and shape of the head seemed normal. The figure and "egg' remained in place for about twenty-five minutes. The "egg" then moved up and away over the roofs of the houses, as did the silvery-suited figure.

On Easter Monday, 11 April, 12-year old Mark Marsden, son of Pauline Coombs' brother, Terry, said that while looking for birds eggs with four friends at dusk in the fields near his home in Herbrandston village (near Milford Haven and four miles from Ripperston Farm), he was chased by "a man from outer space." It happened on rubbish-strewn rough ground known locally as "the beach," which contains an enclosed sewage plant. Mark's friends had gone to a nearby haystack to search for eggs while he checked a nest that he knew was on the beach.

He told investigators that while making his way down the slope to the beach he had seen a red glow on one of the grassy banks that surrounded the nearby fields.

Mark heard a rustling sound behind him and then something jumped out of the bushes. He heard very deep heavy breathing and saw a huge figure in a silvery, aluminium-like suit that seemed to be a little inflated. Terrified, Mark began walking backwards as fast as he could and then went off at a run. The figure ran after him with a stiff-legged gait. It halted its advance under a streetlight, allowing Mark a good look at his pursuer. It was a massively proportioned figure with broad shoulders and a stocky appearance. It wore "funny black boots" with no heels that came halfway up its legs, gloves and a helmet that encased its head, which was square-shaped and featureless, totally black. It had what appeared to be an aerial 6-8 inches high sticking up from one shoulder. The 12-inch long bootprints it left behind had no tread.

While it stood still, feet slightly apart under the lamp, the figure kept its face fixed on the boy and wriggled its fingers in gesturing movements. It kept this up for a short while before turning away and running in its awkward gait around a corner and back into the sewers.

The very light indentations in the cow slurry over which the figure moved indicated that it was extremely light or that its weight had either been mechanically supported or had some kind of anti-gravity support. Mark also saw a red glow in the field behind the figure and the vague shape of an "upside-down saucer."

Also on that day Marsden's neighbour's 13-year old daughter, Debbie Swan, said she saw a UFO the size of a football hovering near a hedgerow. She also saw a silver-coloured red glow in the vicinity

Four days later, the 19th, Mrs Rose Granville, the Spanish owner of the Haven Fort Hotel in Broad Haven's neighbouring village of Little Haven, witnessed a strange light in the sky. Formerly a seventeenth century fortification, the Haven Fort Hotel sits on a high knoll overlooking the sea. On this night there was very little moonlight.

Mrs Granville retired at 2:00 a.m. The previous night was a New Moon and so there was very little light in the sky. As was her custom, Mrs Granville read a book while listening to Spanish music on the radio. Suddenly, the mains power to the radio failed and she heard a humming noise. At first, Mrs Granville thought it might be the central heating system she had forgotten to switch off. Eventually, she decided to get out of bed and check the boiler. During her passage to the boilerhouse Mrs Granville thought that the sound was actually more like a ship passing by in the bay.

She looked out of the bathroom window over the adjacent field and saw that the night sky now appeared to be brightly lit with moonlight. Circling the field was a shapeless, "bluey" flash of light she later described as like that from a painter's blowlamp. At first she thought it might be a helicopter. It circled round and round for a while then vanished. She said it pulsated like a lighthouse. Mrs Granville feared that someone was trying to break into the outbuildings, which comprised a small cottage and some chicken coops.

Fetching her binoculars, Mrs Granville was then able to get a good look at the scene in the field about 120 yards distant. She saw that the object emitting the light was an oval shape about two yards in diameter. It was resting on the ground in a corner of the field. Between the object and the field-gate stood two figures that appeared to be men, six and a half to seven feet tall. They were dressed head to toe in whitish, plastic clothing like a boilersuit. She noted that their arms seemed to be overly long for their bodies: gibbon-like, she described them. They were stooping down and measuring something, then one of them climbed up the grassy bank that borders the field on all sides. She described the head of the latter figure as coming to a point like the cowl of a monk's habit. At one point they turned round and she saw that their faces were totally blank and featureless. At the same time, she knew the figures were corporeal forms and that she was not seeing ghosts.

Mrs Granville tried yelling for her husband but found she was speechless. By now extremely frightened, she feared for the security of the house and went round it to switch on all the lights. When she returned to resume her vigil the object and visitors had gone. The night was once again pitch dark. Later that morning Mrs Granville went into the field and saw crescent-shaped indentations in the grass.

In an adjacent field was a locked concrete nuclear shelter used by the Royal Observer Corps. It has been speculated that the silvery-suited figures were intent on examining this facility.

Mrs Granville contacted her local Member of Parliament, Nicholas Edwards, about her experience and he, in turn, contacted nearby RAF Brawdy. Squadron-Leader Cowan came out to see Mrs Granville and told her there was nothing going on at Brawdy that night that could account for the strange craft. He suggested she might have seen workers from one of the local oil refineries, wearing protective suits. However, he asked her not to tell anyone about the event as it could cause alarm amongst the public. Although Cowan did not appear to have taken Mrs Granville's account very seriously, behind the scenes an investigation was underway.

On 24 April events at Ripperston Farm ramped up several notches on the weirdness scale. While watching TV with Billie, Pauline Coombs investigated a noise at the window and saw staring in at them a 7-foot tall figure in a silver suit. Pauline reported that, "it didn't have no eyes, nose or nothing." From the lower central point of its helmet was a thick, dark coloured pipe that went back over its left shoulder. The figure was surrounded by a luminous glow. It stood there for the longest time, seemingly fascinated by the images zigzagging across the Coombs' television set. All the while the figure was present, the window was banging repeatedly as if rattled by a strong wind but there was no wind that night and the window, in any case, was securely fastened. Later on hearing this statement, Josephine Hewison said that exactly the same thing had happened with her window.

Pauline grabbed the phone and made calls, firstly to the Hewisons at Broadmoor then to investigator, Randall Jones Pugh. She told Pugh that the thing was still standing outside the window. He advised her to ring the police, which she did straightaway.

Billie waited for these calls to finish and then called his cross-Labrador dog, Blackie, to join him outside while he checked the yard. Blackie, frantic, didn't want to leave the house and stayed inside running round and round in circles. Billie ushered Blackie outside and together they searched the yard. The figure had gone. Pauline Coombs was convinced that the figure had simply dissolved in place just as farm manager Mr Hewison and the police were arriving ten minutes after the calls were made. They, too, saw nothing on investigation.

On another occasion, one of the Coombs girls who was one night sleeping in the mother's bed because of her fear of the NHE visitors claims she saw a hand come through the window and float towards Pauline, which then touched her on the arm. The next morning Pauline's arm had swollen and she could barely move it. Her eyes were also swollen and irritated much like an allergic reaction.

Keiran and Layanne also described seeing three UFOs near the cliffs. One was just 50 feet above them. It lowered a metal ladder from which descended a silver-clad figure. The UFO dropped a bright red fluorescent box into the long grass, which afterwards the children searched for but couldn't find.

An interesting manifestation attributed to the accumulated visitations at Ripperston Farm was the effect on the family's garden rosebush. Two of them grew side by side close to the window where the silver figure had stood and peered in. One bush remained untouched but the other fared differently. Although its buds were seemingly healthy they hadn't opened like its neighbour's and the rest of the bush had assumed an unhealthy, desiccated appearance. Billie remarked that it looked as if "someone had gone over the rose-tree with a blowlamp."

Astonishingly, the Coombs' claimed that on at least half a dozen occasions their cattle were "teleported" from the farm's bolted stockyard to a field at Lower Broadmoor, a half-mile distant. The number of cattle kept on the farm varied between 120 and 150. The yard was ringed with steel piping and its gates were secured with industrial bolts designed to cope with day-to-day, heavy agricultural use. Billie Coombs had adopted the practice of nightly strapping the bolts in the locked position in case a cow managed to move the bolt with its nose. He did this by winding several layers of strong twine around the handle of the bolt. Despite these precautions the Coombs's herd would inexplicably vanish *en masse.*

On one truly bizarre occasion, 15 April, Billie and son Clinton were standing just 10 paces away in the milking parlour when 16 in-calf heifers vanished from the yard. This had taken place during a period of four minutes while father and son were in the parlour switching on six milking machines. On coming out to check that the milk was coming through, not a single cow was in sight. The pair insisted that during those four minutes they heard and saw nothing.

After each episode of disappearance Billie checked the stockyard and, sure enough, the bolts were still in place and the winding twine intact. Billie would spend at least an hour fetching the cows back to his farm, while enduring comments from his managers, the Hewisons, that he was being careless with his work and inattentive to his animals' welfare and security.

On each occasion the cows were very restless and milk yields very poor. Significantly, each time the cows performed their vanishing act Blackie seemingly heard nothing: very much a telltale case of the dog not barking in the night. What mystified the family was that if the cows had somehow travelled, invisibly, on foot on their nocturnal journey (there being no evidence of any kind as to how they did actually make the trip) they chose not to make the straightforward walk down the lane outside the farm to the main road but took a left turn and headed specifically for Broadmoor Farm. The Coombs family never got to the bottom of the mystery of the "Silver Giant," as the alien figure came to be called, nor of the vanishing cattle.

Consider the baffling affair of the Coombs' cattle alongside this story from Welsh fairlore. Llyn Barfog, the "Bearded Lake" near the seaside town of Aberdovey in West Wales, is the scene of the famous descent to earth of a cow that belonged to Gwragedd Annwn—the elfin wives of the lower world. It was their habit to make their appearance at dusk clad all in green, accompanied by their milk-white hounds. Besides their love of hounds the green ladies of Llyn Barfog were exceedingly proud of their herds of beautiful milk-white kine, the "Gwartheg y Llyn." One day an old farmer caught an Otherworldly cow named "Fuwch Gyfeiliorn," which had fallen in love with the cattle of his herd. From that day the farmer's fortune was made. Such calves and their milk, butter and cheese produce had never before been seen in Wales. Some years later the unthinking farmer took it into his head that the green ladies' cow was getting old and that he should therefore fatten her for the market.

Came the day of slaughter Fuwch Gyfeiliorn was tethered, regardless of her mournful lowing and her pleading eyes. The butcher raised his arm and brought down his bludgeon hard. At that moment shrieks filled the air and the butcher's cudgel passed clean through the fairy cow's head as if it were composed of mist and knocked over nine men standing hard by. All those present then lifted their astonished gaze to behold the appearance of a green lady of the Gwragedd Annwn on a crag above the lake.

She called out her spell: "Come yellow Anvil, stray horns, speckled one of the lake. And of the hornless Dodlin, arise, come home." Whereupon, not only did the elfin cow rise above the gathered assembly but she was joined in her ascent by all her progeny up to the fourth generation. Together, the great herd rose high in the air and disappeared over the hilltops, never to return. Only one cow among the farmer's herds remained and she had turned from milky white to raven black. Distraught, the farmer drowned himself in the lake of the Gwragedd Annwn and the black cow became the progenitor of today's prized race of Welsh black cattle.

The Pembrokeshire wave of 1977 still had plenty of surprises in store. Three notable events occurred in mid-May. On Sunday, the 15th, Layann and Joann Coombs were walking with the dogs to the clifftop fields to play a game of roly-poly. During the game Layann saw what she described as a silver human being with a square head and no face about fifty yards away walking up to a hedge. Its silver suit had no buttons, zip or fastenings. It walked in a slow, ponderous fashion with its long straight arms at its side. Hairs prickling, the dogs barked and growled. The figure then walked through the hawthorn hedge and passed through a waist-high barbed wire fence without breaking it.

At around the same date, a 17-year old Milford Town resident who wished to remain anonymous woke at 3:00 a.m. to see a small humanoid standing on her bedroom windowsill. It remained motionless, staring in at the frightened teenager. Hovering just above it was a space ship emitting a green beam. The long haired-figure was about three-feet tall and wearing a silvery, high-necked, collared suit and mitten-like gloves. It had normal eyes, slanted eyebrows and, like a good old-fashioned fairytale, had a nose like Mr Punch. After a few moments the teenager got up, closed the curtains and went back to bed.

This is the kind of incongruous action that one would expect of someone who is experiencing a vivid or waking dream. However, the girl told investigators that a few days later at 5:00 a.m. she saw another, smaller green-beamed UFO from her window. It had a round bottom and what appeared to be a glass compartment over it with portholes. It had positioned itself by her father's car and then moved upwards to hover at roof level near her sister's bedroom. A by now familiar figure emerged from the craft and performed its midair walking trick. It had an oval face, long wavy brownish hair, slanted eyebrows, normal eyes and the same Mr Punch nose. It walked forward and backward several times then returned to the ship, which disappeared.

Compare this teenager's experiences with Breton legend. Breton folk believed that "corrigans" (fairies) can assume any animal form and are able to travel from one end of the world to another in the blink of an eye. They are tiny, no more than 2 feet high with bodies as aerial and translucent as wasps, given to abducting human children. Bretons lived in terror of them.

Considering that UFO percipients often experience more than one sighting, it is not surprising that Warren Davies' sister (later becoming Mrs Miller) had a second close encounter that May, forty-two years after she and her brother saw the bright yellow "balloon" while walking from school in Freystrup in 1935. Mrs Miller was woken at 3:30 a.m. at her home in Houghton village by an extremely loud whistling-sucking noise like that of a giant vacuum that was reverberating all round the house. The following morning she saw that the gravel in the road outside her house had been formed into a cone as if by design. All at once, Mrs Miller's two dogs began acting up hysterically. While she was trying to calm them Mrs Miller saw over the house a silver upside down saucer with an orange light. An instant later it vanished. She had the impression that the object had come from a nearby mountain and had deliberately stopped over her house in order to suck it up inside. These thoughts scared Mrs Miller out of her wits.

A few weeks later, 26 June, between 1:30 a.m. and 2:00 a.m., locals in the St Brides Bay area saw an object out at sea. It was a sharply defined large orange ball moving left to right slowly in the sky. Two dark lines bisected it horizontally. It emerged from behind Stack Rockss and drifted left towards the land. It was oscillating, moving within itself. As it moved it got smaller and smaller and then disappeared.

At around the same time as this sighting two "men in black" visited Pauline Coombs' neighbour, Caroline Klass. Dressed in grey-blue, two-piece suits and highly polished shoes, the pair arrived in a large futuristic looking sports car. Each was exceptionally tall. Class first saw them when they were about a hundred yards away from her property but, impossibly, a moment later one was standing by her front door while his companion remained in the car outside. The MIB at the door had a highly domed forehead and his hair was swept back over his head. The pair resembled identical twins.

The one at the door spoke in accented English, asking Class where was Pauline Coombs. She told him Mrs Coombs was away from home. He produced a detailed map of the area and asked Class where he was. He also asked her about any UFO sightings in the area. Class told him of the Broad Haven School event. He expressed an urgency to visit Croesgoch, a small village directly across St. Brides Bay opposite Stacks Rock. He then went back to the car, which moved off up the lane.

Moments later Pauline Coombs returned home, expecting to be greeted by her eldest son, Clinton. In fact, he was hiding upstairs because he had been frightened by the appearance of two strange men at the door. Gradually, Pauline coaxed Clinton downstairs and he told her what had taken place. He was certain that his mother must have seen the two men because they had driven off only moments earlier. There was only one road leading from the farm and, moreover, it had no passing places along its half-mile length. But Pauline had seen no one. The MIB's car had simply vanished. The car re-appeared a short time later at the Haven Fort Hotel and the occupants asked if Mrs Granville was in. Her daughter said she'd be back later but they went off saying they would return.

The Coombs family was fortunate that the visit from the MIB ended without serious mishap. In *Our Haunted Planet*[54] UFO researcher John Keel set out his findings about the sinister visitors of Oriental appearance. Often arriving in threes, they drive around in black automobiles, usually Cadillacs in the U.S., some with purplish interior

---

[54] Keel, J., *Our Haunted Planet*, New Saucerian Books, West Virginia, 2014

glows. They engage in mischievous behaviour and scare tactics, bullying UFO witnesses and investigators into silence about what they have seen or discovered.

Remarkably, Keel stated his opinion that the MIB are parahumans, able to make egress into this world via Gateways in the Earth's etheric field and can vanish at will. Some witnesses have spoken of being seized and bundled aboard the black autos, afterwards describing strange psychedelic lights on the dashboards that induce in them a trance state. Some report seeing insignia printed on the car doors: a triangle with a bolt of lightning passing through it; while others describe an eye within a triangle, a common symbol found in many ancient cultures from Egypt to Micronesia. Indeed, MIBs have actually identified themselves as "agents for the Nation of the Third Eye."

Albert K. Bender wrote[55] of three dark-skinned gentlemen with glowing eyes who materialised in his apartment. Dressed in black clothes and Homburg style hats like clergymen, the trio floated a foot above the ground while conversing with the astonished Bender. Coming, they said, from a secret UFO base in Antarctica, their purpose was to collect a rare element from Earth's oceans. After the completion of the project in the early 1960s they and the UFOs would disappear from Earth and he would be allowed to write about the story. Before dematerialising they left Bender with a shining disc with which to contact them. He claimed that the MIB subsequently took him to an underground base where, he was told, aliens were extracting chemicals from seawater for use on their own planet. His disc subsequently disappeared and he told his story to the world in his book. Perhaps not coincidentally to his bizarre story, Bender was a student of black magic. He suffered from sulphurous odours in his apartment, strange poltergeist happenings and was plagued by chronic headaches and memory lapses, all common symptoms of the contactee syndrome.

MIBs often turn up as doppelgangers of the men they are imitating. After the JFK assassination, the circumstances of which bear close comparison with many features of UFO incidents, there were sightings of doppelgangers of Lee Harvey Oswald. One of these made a visit to a public rifle range prior to the assassination, made a big nuisance of himself and surprised people by using a strange gun that spat out balls of fire. The real Oswald couldn't drive and it is known that he was nowhere near the rifle range on that particular day.

[55] Bender, A.K., *Flying Saucers and the Three Men*, Saucerian Books, West, 1963

Unsurprisingly, in June the head of S4 (Air), the Ministry of Defense branch that dealt with UFOs, asked the Provost and Security Service of the Royal Air Force Police to make discreet enquiries into events in Wales. Early in 1977 the P&SS moved to RAF Rudloe Manor in Wiltshire. UFO authors Tim Good and Nick Redfern have claimed that Rudloe is the home of the British Government's UFO investigation authorities.

On 27 August truck driver Francis Lloyd and sixteen-year old John Dwyer were heading for Crosshands in Carmarthenshire on the A48. They were loaded up for a long haul to Continental Europe. As the truck began to ascend Nantycaws Hill, a location 40 miles east of Broad Haven, the vehicle's eight forward headlights illuminated two huge figures about 7-feet high standing on the right-hand grassy verge. They were reddish-orange in colour and seemed to be wearing single-piece celluloid suits. Their heads were elongated as if they were wearing tall helmets. The pair were standing, slightly turned to each other. They appeared to be holding between them an instrument of some kind. They stood motionless as the truck trundled slowly up the steep incline of Nantycaws Hill.

As they passed by the bizarre figures, Francis Lloyd felt a cold tingling over his body and experienced a distinctly weird feeling. He described the figures as having arms but neither he nor Dwyer saw any legs. They had faces but to the witnesses it seemed as if they looked straight through them. Lloyd saw a kind of flap on the shoulders.

The "monsters," as the witnesses described them, had their arms raised, holding what might have been radios and another object that couldn't be identified. The beings also had a sort of aerial coming out of the left side of their chests that reached up to head height. These glittered in the headlights, casting a chrome-silvery colour. Dwyer also glimpsed a smaller aerial coming from the side of one figure's head. The witnesses held the pair in sight for five to six seconds while the truck negotiated its climb up Nantycaws Hill.

Three months later Nantycaws Hill was the scene of a grim postscript to this remarkable sighting. In the afternoon of 23 November a gas tanker *en route* from Carmarthen to Swansea reached the bottom of the hill and jack-knifed across the three-lane highway. This action caused the tanker to overturn. A BMW carrying four men to a Welsh Counties rugby cup-match smashed into the tanker at speed and was literally torn in two. The four rugby supporters and the tanker driver died instantly, their bodies later described as almost unrecognisable.

Had tanker driver Roger Goodreid seen a reappearance of the 7-foot monsters and, scared out of his mind, lost control of his vehicle? Might the August visitors have left something behind on Nantycaws Hill that caused the devastating accident? Certainly, other UFO investigators have linked the two episodes but the truth will probably never be known.

In October the Coombs once again found themselves occupying centre stage with UFO goings-on. On the 30th Pauline Coombs, accompanied by her mother and children Tina, Layann and Joann, was returning from the local shop. She stopped the car at Broadmoor to enjoy the sea view. As they went on to Ripperston they saw a small silvery disc flash across the sky. It headed for Stack Rocks, a tiny reef in St Brides Bay that rises about 90 feet above the sea. Pauline stopped the car to get a better look.

To their amazement, a rock appeared to open. At great speed the UFO dove inside and vanished from sight. The rock face "door' abruptly closed. The onlookers couldn't believe that the UFO hadn't collided with the rocks and broken apart. Pauline then saw what by now were two familiar 7-foot figures walking on the rocks. Not wanting to stick around, Pauline and the girls drove back to Ripperston to tell Billie what had happened. They had barely walked into the front door when Rose Granville phoned to ask if the Coombs had a line of sight on Stack Rocks because two humanoids were walking around the reef.

Stack Rocks

With the twin girls and sons Clinton and Keiron, Pauline went into the Cliffside fields and stopped at a west-facing slope to see what was happening on Stack Rocks. The two humanoids were still walking around. They were wearing whitish-silver outfits that reminded the Coombs of frogmen's wetsuits. Pauline described them on this occasion as having orange heads. The heads (or helmets) were extremely large and rectangular in shape and rounded at the corners with no observable features.

One of the humanoids, described by Keiron as being the colour of fire, looked like it was climbing up steps *out of the rock* while the other was bending by the water as if looking for something. A "door" then appeared on the right hand face of the rocks, sliding alternately open and shut like that of a dumbwaiter. One of the figures entered this doorway and appeared to descend a stairway. It disappeared into the darkened interior and then reappeared. The stairway was not visible to the viewers. On this final vanishing act, the door closed and disappeared from view. To the left side of the rocks, the second figure appeared to "walk" out over the water's surface. Suddenly, the rock at the water's edge seemed to lift up and the figure stepped forward and disappeared.

The display had lasted for fifteen minutes. Meanwhile, the Granvilles were seeing precisely the same train of events. Billie Coombs later told investigators that, on reflection, he believed that the silver-suited humanoids had the ability to blend their craft with natural features such as Stack Rocks.

A few days later while watching the scene alone Clinton saw windows in Stack Rocks. He described the windows as square, roughly the size of television screens. The windows were to the right of the door in the rock. Clinton's description reminds one of a fairy house depiction with fairy silvery-suited inhabitants. The entire coastline of St. Brides Bay is riddled with deeply penetrating sea caves, some hundreds of yards long. Along the coast are Celtic raths, forts, earthworks, mottes, burial chambers and standing stones dating from the era of the Windmill Hill and Beaker peoples of prehistoric Britain.

It is noteworthy that Stack Rocks is adjacent to a ley-line that connects a burial chamber on Kilpaison Burrows, Broadmoor Farm, St Nonn's Well at St David's Cathedral, and terminates at a burial chamber at St David's Head. Note that St Nonn was traditionally known as the "King of the Fairies." Incidentally, a ley-line runs adjacent to Broad Haven Primary School. The Haven Fort Hotel is also bisected by a ley-line, and yet another runs through Ripperstone Farm.

Pauline Coombs reported that one time she saw the sea shake, the vibrations radiating out from a point in St Brides Bay, similar to what might be caused by an underwater explosion or by seismic activity.

Consider this with "the riddle of the bumps," a series of regular and violent rumblings, vibrations and sounds of explosions that shook the West Country, especially around the Bristol Channel during the latter part of 1976 and throughout 1977. Windows rattled and cracks appeared in plaster. On several occasions an orange glow was afterwards seen in the sky, one time in the form of a fireball that sped at high speed across the sky.

Naturally, the Stack Rocks event has its parallels in Welsh folklore. Sailors once spoke of green meadows of enchantment that lie in the sea off the Pembrokeshire coast. For the most part they are invisible to human sight but occasionally they appear for a brief period, then suddenly vanish. Some even claimed to have ventured ashore on these magical isles, not knowing them to be such until they returned to their boat and were astonished to see the isle vanish in an instant. The folk of Milford Haven claimed to be able to see the isles distinctly, lying out a short distance. They knew them to be filled with fairy folk that travelled to the shore through a subterranean gallery under the bottom of the sea.

The old tales also tell of a magical lake in which the Gwragedd Annwn lived in a sunken city. Every year on the morning of New Year's Eve an open door was to be seen in a rock by the lake. Those who had the courage to enter this door were led by a secret passage to a small island in the middle of the lake. Here they found the enchanting garden of the Gwragedd Annwn. Noted for their courtesy and kindness, the elfin wives gathered fruit and flowers for each of their guests, entertained them with the most exquisite music, disclosed secrets of the future and invited them to stay for as long as they desired.

Hugh Turnbull, journalist for local weekly, the "Western Telegraph," evidently didn't go along with local fairytales and held that "something military" lay behind the Stack Rocks sightings. Other parties favoured a more sensationalist theory, namely that aliens had established an underground base beneath Stack Rocks in St Brides Bay where UFOs had been seen to hover and disappear. Such speculation was founded on the fact that within a 20-mile radius of Broad Haven there was a welter of military establishments. To the north at Aberporth was the top secret rocket testing station, while the NATO base at RAF Brawdy near St David's served as a pilots training centre on advanced aircraft and weaponry and as a base for both a Tactical Weapons Unit and a US Navy underwater research station that tracked Soviet submarines. Former Navy pilots have remarked that it was very strange to have a training facility at Brawdy because of the area's atrocious weather. After the very low profile arrival of a large U.S. contingent, locals spoke of odd goings-on, particularly at the extensive deep underground facility built on a part of the base that was exclusive American property to which even the RAF had no access.

According to local gossip this American facility, officially an oceanographic research station staffed by 600 U.S. personnel, was built to sustain a direct nuclear strike. It was known that the tiniest infringement of camp rules, even receiving a parking ticket offbase, was enough to trigger the offender's immediate repatriation to the US. For an establishment that claimed to be purely interested in oceanographic research, the UFOs seemed to take an inordinate interest in its activities.

It seems clear that Brawdy was under close observation. Russian trawlers were seen observing its installations. On the air traffic control map of southern Britain a specific area incorporating St Brides Bay was designated EGD111, marked "Danger, Restricted or Warning Area." 75% of all Welsh Triangle UFO sightings occurred within the EGD111 area, which includes Stack Rocks, Ripperston Farm, Broad Haven School and Herbrandston.

The last time that Pauline Coombs saw the "Silver Giant" was in February 1978. It was standing by her garden, this time without helmet visor. She described seeing long flowing, fair-coloured, shoulder-length hair. In the same month a fall of quartz-like crystals landed on St. Brides Bay. They were reddish-brown in colour and changed colour when picked up.

Intriguingly, the multiple sightings in Pembrokeshire took place over clean or dirty water or by effluence centres—the sewage works near Broad Haven School in which the visitors took such keen interest, and at the rubbish-strewn "beach" area of Herbrandston village; an underground water system and natural spring on Ripperston Farm; the nuclear shelter in the grounds of the Haven House Hotel and also over a tunnel linking the hotel cellars with the beach hundreds of yards away; and the chimneys of the Milford Haven oil complex. As Conan Doyle pointed out, fairies hate any kind of pollution in the natural world. Might this help to explain why the Dyfed visitors were particularly attracted to these precise localities?

That year Pembrokeshire's silver giants evidently decided to explore further afield. In September Pat Owen and her daughter were walking across a field in the village of Llanerchymedd on the island of Anglesey when they saw three men, 6-feet tall, wearing silver grey suits and a sort of head cap attached to the suits. The cows in the field were terrified. In the same period a grounded object and humanoids were seen in Ruabon, Wrexham, Colwyn Bay and Prestatyn, all in North Wales.

Some that encountered the Dyfed visitors suffered dermatological problems. In mediaeval times these kinds of effects were associated with coming into contact with fairies. The phenomenon was called "elf-burn" or "elf-disease." It took the form of a hardening of the epidermis called "elf-cake." The symptoms have been likened to radiation burns.

To all appearances, the "Silver Giant" phenomenon smacks of a typical UFO story. Bright lights, spaceships, tall silver-suited occupants that vanish before one's eyes, attempts at seizure, teleported cattle, Men in Black—these are archetypal components of NHE events that have been related routinely the world over in our modern times. But pause to look further back in human history and we see that these events, bizarre though they may seem, are simply old tales wearing new clothes.

Welsh folklore has much to say about Otherworldy visitors who seem intent on trying to find something that is evidently very important to them. Take, for example, the "Plant Rhys Dwfen," a colony of fairies reputed to dwell on an invisible island in Cardiganshire, roughly fifteen miles northeast of Stack Rocks. Dwfen is the root word for Annwfn, a variation on the name Annwn, the Otherworld. Annwfn is associated with hills and *islands*. In the tale of Pwyll in the Mabinogion Annfwn is a parallel world, very much like our Earth but populated with dangerous and magical beings.

In the poem *Prieddu Annwn*, Annfwn is a group of islands on which Arthur and his company search for a magical cauldron, a synonym for the Grail. Envisage a brave Knight of Camelot in his silver suit of armour. He is striding purposefully across a tiny island in a Welsh bay in search of his prize, his long fair hair flowing in the breeze. He and his fellows are seeking the magical cup.

Were Pauline Coombs, her family and neighbours granted the privilege of seeing through a unique window? Did they observe scenes taking place in a mystical world beyond human sentience, knowledge and sight of which is denied the greater part of humankind?

An account extracted under torture from the Knights Templars after their enforced dissolution was a revelation about Camelot. The Templars claimed that Camelot was not a place that could be reached by foot but was a separate region, a training dimension not bound by the laws of time and space and only accessible by those deemed sufficiently prepared for initiation into the higher mysteries. Tales about Camelot were spoken of by initiates that had "pierced the veil" (the root phrase expressed in the name Perceval) but who subsequently broke a bond of silence about the nature of their adventures. Consequently, a belief grew over the centuries that Arthur's Court was to be found in such and such physical place, be it Cornwall, Wales, Brittany, Scotland or any other that lay claim to its location.

A single moment in a timeless place passes like an eternity in our world. It follows that all of its affairs are always visible under certain circumstances. These special circumstances are triggered by something that lies buried deep within human consciousness. Perhaps, for a brief few months in 1977, a select group of percipients tapped into that secret unconscious reservoir, seeing neither fairies nor aliens but something far more mysterious and elusive. As if seen through gauze, a bold and handsome Knight appears to adopt a stiff-legged gait whose noble actions resemble jerky, random movements. In the absence of the "Silver Giants" making a convenient return to give an account of their repeated appearances, the Camelot explanation is as valid or as fanciful as any other.

Intriguingly, there is strong evidence to believe that thirteen years before arriving in Pembrokeshire the silver giant NHE, or a confederate, paid a visit to the Cumbrian coast 350 miles to the northeast.

On a sunny spring day, 24 May 1964, local fireman and keen photographer, Jim Templeton, and his family drove from their home in Carlisle to Burgh Marshes, which overlooks Solway Firth separating England from Scotland. Other than his wife Annie, his daughter Elizabeth, and two pensioners seated in a car, the Carlisle fireman maintained he saw no one else that day on Burgh Marsh.

Templeton wanted to take a photo of Elizabeth in her new dress. He looked across at Chapelcross atomic energy establishment situated on the Scottish side of the Firth and then turned his head and shoulders to the left to face Anthorn Radio Station and its VLF antennae. Having decided that this was the best position for a good shot, Templeton snapped Elizabeth.

He took the film into a local shop for developing and when he collected it the assistant said, "That's a marvellous colour film, but who's the big fellow?" Baffled by the remark, Jim looked at the photos and in one print was puzzled to see apparently standing just behind his daughter's head a large figure dressed in a "spaceman" suit. The image has become known worldwide as the Solway Firth Spaceman.

Knowing that there had been no one else standing in the vicinity at the time he took the photo, Jim had the negative tested by contacts in the police force and with the film's manufacturers, Kodak. Both said the image had not been tampered with.

Meanwhile, three journalists from local newspaper, *Cumberland News*, began their own investigation of the photo. They were in receipt of Kodak's review comments, which confirmed that the negative was untouched, that it was exactly the same as had gone through the camera and that what was on the negative was faithfully reproduced on the developed print. Unanimously, the journalists agreed that the figure looked exactly like a spaceman and accepted that no trickery had been involved.

Right up to his death in 2011, Jim Templeton said he was still seeking answers to the question: "Who is he and where is he from?"

There the story would have ended, a 50-year old unresolved mystery with believers and sceptics on both sides arguing their case. Today the Solway Firth Spaceman mystery remains unsolved but new aspects of the matter have recently been brought to public attention.

The BBC's *One Show* investigators interviewed in early 2018 Jim's friend, Steve Matthews, who revealed that Jim told him that in the summer of 1964 he was visited by "Men from the Ministry."

From Matthew's testimony and other sources it has been established that two men visited Jim at the Fire Station. They were dressed entirely in black and drove a brand new black Jaguar car. Both the clothing and the choice of vehicle car were very unusual for the times. The pair asked to be taken to the place where the photograph was taken. Jim asked for proof of identity and was shown a card bearing an official crest and the word "Security."

They told him, "We're from the Ministry but you don't need to know who we are. We go by numbers." During Jim's time with the men they referred to each other as Number 9 and Number 11.

The men's unfamiliarity with the area and their inability to pronounce place names told Templeton that the men were not locals.

On arrival at the marsh Jim said, "Pull up on here. This is where the photograph was taken."

"Can you take us to the exact spot?" they asked.

"Yes," said Jim walking to the spot. "This is where the photograph was taken."

The two exchanged looks and one asked Jim, "This is where you saw the large man, the alien?"

"No, we didn't see anybody...I never saw anybody," Jim corrected him.

"Thank you very much," the man said and walked away.

They asked Jim many more questions, especially about that day's weather conditions and, curiously, about the activities and behaviour of farm animals that grazed on the marsh. That day, Jim recalled, the animals were all uncharacteristically bunched together at the far end of the Marsh, unusual behaviour like that exhibited by Mrs Hewison's family pony.

The two men then adopted a more aggressive tone, accusing Jim of making the whole thing up, which Jim denied. They then returned to the parked Jaguar. Jim assumed that they were planning to reverse into a nearby road entrance to turn the car round before he could climb back in but they drove off leaving him to walk the ten mile trek back home.

The *One Show* commissioned photographers Paul Cordes and Jonathan Keys to test the theory that the spaceman was actually wife Annie who had wandered into shot, unseen by her husband who because of the bright sunshine was using an F16 camera setting that had the effect of darkening and lessening his overall field of view. Cordes and Keys created on the same spot on Burgh Sands a mock-up (reproduced below right) of the famous print, photographing a woman standing behind a seated girl and wearing a similar light coloured dress to Annie Templeton's, when, in fact, all that the photographer could see through his tiny F16 lens was the girl on the grass. However, as the *One Show* team readily conceded the result was not at all convincing and certainly could not explain away the enigmatic Spaceman figure in the original (below left).

Just as we have seen with regard to the Pembrokeshire Silver Giant, the figure in Templeton's photo has been associated with secret military activities and establishments. In this case, the photograph has been linked to an anomalous "figure" that is said to have appeared on a Blue Streak missile firing range at Woomera in south Australia.

The purported link with Solway is that Blue Streak missiles were developed and tested at RAF Spadeadam in Cumbria. They were part of a British missile system designed to be used as the first stage of a satellite launcher. Spadeadam was opened in the late 1950s as a test area for the British Intermediate Range Ballistic Missile (IRBM). The research program was split between Rolls Royce and Dehavilland (later Hawker Siddley).The British program was cancelled in 1958 after the deployment of American THOR missile sites in eastern England. Blue Streak was then adapted to be used as the first stage of the ELDOs (European Launcher Development Organisation) Europa satellite launcher.

According to a Wikipedia entry, a Blue Streak launch at the Woomera range had to be aborted on 25 May 1964 "because two large men [were] seen on the firing range…technicians at the time did not know about Templeton's sighting until it appeared on the front page of an Australian newspaper…and they said the figure in Cumbria looked the same as the ones they had seen on the monitor at Woomera."

Templeton repeated this story when interviewed by Jenny Randles for a BBC2 documentary on Tales of the Paranormal (1996). He said the Australian technicians had claimed the figures were "exactly the same type of man: same dress, same figure, same size as in the original photograph."

The mystery appeared to increase when, as part of the research for the programme, Randles searched UFO files from 1964 held by The National Archives. There she found letters from members of the public referring to both the "Cumberland spaceman" and to a "mysterious object" captured on film during the Woomera rocket launch. However, Randles found no trace of the can of film referred to in the archives. Had the Men in Black been busy getting rid of evidence?

In the next chapter we turn our attention to the quantum worlds where things are decidedly not what they seem. It is in these recondite spaces of high strangeness where we begin to attain a more complete understanding of the Wee Folk-UFOlk phenomenon.

Chapter 7

The Implicate Order

Much insight into non-human entities can be gained from a study of his ideas. He is on target with his concepts and our program is attempting, unfortunately, to exploit them...The concept of these events, real though they are, being the result of extraterrestrial beings is a masterful piece of disinformation to divert attention away from the real source of NHEs.[56]

—U.S. Dept. of Defense agents, 1994

New Mexico medical doctor, John J. Dalton,[57] encountered a grey creature with "overly long fingers, dull red eyes, a dank, acrid odour, mind to mind communication and ability to float above ground." It told Dalton:

We occupy all space, everywhere in the universe or any void in between. We are from a different dimension, a different plane of existence. We have no boundaries or limits...we are an anti-log of everything you see visually. We can travel in any dimension or space without being observed...

Physicists are divided in opinion about the existence of Dalton's grey's home within the "multiverse," a term that scientists use to describe the hypothetical set of possible universes or dimensions, including the universe in which we live. Many eminent UFO researchers have supported the notion of the multiverse. One such leading figure was Jacques Vallée who said that the UFO phenomenon is one way that alien intelligence is communicating with us symbolically from a multiverse that is all around us beyond space-time.

---

[56] Howe, L.M., *Glimpses of Other Realities - Vol II: High Strangeness,* p124
[57] Dalton, J.J., *The Cattle Mutilators*, Manor Books, Inc., NY, 1980

150

Unlike Secretary James Forrestal, Vallée believed that what we are experiencing is not an invasion but a sequence of actions arising from a spiritual system that acts on humans and uses humans.

One other physicist who had no doubts about the existence of multiple dimensions was the U.S. authorities' go-to quantum physicist, Professor David Bohm. Such was David Bohm's farsighted brilliance acknowledged in some quarters of the quantum science community that Einstein actually spoke of him as his successor. To advance one's understanding of how

David Bohm 1917-1992

there can even be a Magonia, a Tír Na nÓg, and an "Infernia," one is rewarded with a review of the work of Bohm and other pioneers in the field of quantum physics.

A consideration of Bohm's cutting edge thinking may also help to solve the fundamental paradox inherent in Jesus' statement: "In my Father's House are many mansions." How, one may ask, can even one mansion (dictionary definition: a large, impressive house—synonyms: stately home, seat, castle *et al.*) let alone many, fit inside a single house? If, as theologians suggest, Jesus used the word House to denote the heavens or Creation, the logical form of the sentence would be, "In my Father's Mansion are many houses" to illustrate all the planets, stars, nebulae, galaxies and other bodies (taken together: the "houses") that comprise our universe (the "mansion").

Instead, Jesus spoke it in the way He did, going on to make clear that this was precisely what He wanted to say by adding afterwards: "…if it were not so, I would have told you." However, the statement loses its seemingly contradictory sense if interpreted as a commentary on the existence of the multiverse, in which Creation not only comprises our universe but all other dimensions of reality that occupy Oxley's "space between spaces."

Esoteric Christian writer, A.P. Shepherd, quoted in Ken Wilber's 1982 work "The Holographic Paradigm and Other Paradoxes," said:

"These 'worlds' are dimensional levels and are not separate regions, spatially divided from one another, so that it would be

necessary to move in space in order to pass from one another. The highest worlds completely interpenetrate the lower worlds, which are fashioned and sustained by their activities."

One can imagine Bohm wrestling with this internal dialogue. The challenge he set himself was no less than to arrive at an understanding of the nature of reality in general and of consciousness in particular, seeing both as a coherent totality that is never static or complete but continually in a state of what he termed "unfoldment." Only 5% of the mass of our universe is accounted for. The remaining mass—dark matter and dark energy comprising 27% and 68% respectively—cannot (as yet) be detected. It should come as no surprise, therefore, that physicists have arrived at the mind-numbing calculation that every cubic centimetre of space contains more energy than the total energy of all the matter in the known universe. This remarkable fact infers the existence of an infinite ocean of energy, an inference in which Bohm invested an equally infinite quantity of belief. In this greater scheme of things our universe is dubbed the junior stepchild of something far larger, no more than a passing shadow in the infinitely greater cosmic order, which Bohm called the "Implicate Order." He also conceded that even beyond the vastness of the Implicate there might exist undreamed of orders representing infinite stages of further development. And so on, and so on, *ad nauseam*.

"Far away in the heavenly abode of the great god Indra, there is a wonderful net which has been hung by some cunning artificer in such a manner that it stretches out infinitely in all directions. In accordance with the extravagant tastes of deities, the artificer has hung a single glittering jewel in each 'eye' of the net, and since the net itself is infinite in dimension, the jewels are infinite in number. There hang the jewels, glittering 'like' stars in the first magnitude, a wonderful sight to behold. If we now arbitrarily select one of these jewels for inspection and look closely at it, we will discover that in its polished surface there are reflected all the other jewels in the net, infinite in number. Not only that, but each of the jewels reflected in this one jewel is also reflecting all the other jewels, so that there is an infinite reflecting process occurring."

Indra's net

William B. Smith, head of Project Magnet, a semi-official Canadian UFO study, arrived at the same conclusion. In 1958, towards the end of his life, Smith said that all his years of study of contactees and the UFO phenomena had taught him one valuable insight. Namely, he had come to comprehend the basic oneness of the universe and all that is in it. He understood that substance and energy are all facets of the same jewel and that before any one facet can be appreciated, the form of the jewel itself must be perceived.

U.S. government agents seeking access to Linda Moulton Howe's book contacted her in May 1994. They were given a copy and later provided Howe with a cassette tape of comments in which they said that the Department of Defense was seeking to exploit David Bohm's ideas. Disturbingly, they said that NHEs were carrying out human abductions and mutilating thousands of animals in a manner designed to create a grand smokescreen of deception. They explained that the motive behind these actions is to ensure that while fingers are being pointed into outer space for aliens and while public focus remains fixed on UFOs, secret government projects, satanic cults and the like no one is dwelling on a realisation that NHEs are dimensional in origin.

They also told Howe of a telepathic exchange between an elderly colleague and an NHE retrieved from a crashed disc in New Mexico. The NHE said:

> This is not the only universe. Imagine a large silver island of white sand and that each sand grain is a different universe separated from each other by an electromagnetic membrane. And surrounding the island is a cold, dark sea. [58]

Howe asked the agent about the cold dark sea. He said, "You don't want to know. It will change you forever." Visionary sci-fi writer H.P. Lovecraft said much the same thing.[59] In *The Call of Cthulhu* he said that because of an induced occluded vision humanity is wholly ignorant of the true nature of the universe, the disclosure of which would result in mass insanity and violence. Lovecraft described NHEs as ultraterrestrials, which are coterminous with all space and coexistent with all time

The agents went on to describe the dimensional NHEs, purportedly associated with ancient human civilisations, as neither benevolent nor neutral and are an integral element of a vastly bigger picture of the present day deception of mankind. NHEs, they added, have been industrious in building a foundation to establish themselves as the bringers of all that is good to humanity, while we continue to peer wistfully through rose-tinted spectacles to the far distant past in the "Golden Age" of ancient cultures. The agents suggested that Howe

---

[58] Howe, L.M., *Glimpses of Other Realities Volume 1: Facts and Eyewitnesses*, pXVII
[59] Lovecraft, H.P., *The Call of Cthulhu*, Weird Tales Magazine, 1928

should study Vallée's *Passport to Magonia* and the very close parallels between fairy culture and the appearance of NHEs, reminding her that while the scientist was correct in every other respect he was wrong to believe that the ultimate manifestations might be human. They are *not*, the agents told Howe emphatically.

Writer Bruce Rux has also referred to connections between UFO visitors and past civilisations. In *Architects of the Underworld*[60] Rux claims that following the Roswell incident in July 1947, the U.S. Government pursued a growing belief that the UFOlk were from a parallel race, variously known as the Watchers, the Anunnaki, Tuatha dé Dannan and the Elohim *et al*, which had its origins in human antiquity.

So who was this man, Bohm, whose thinking was held in such high esteem by U.S. government officials that they plundered his ideas to help deal with the thorny problem of NHEs, a threat to humankind connected with an ancient Earth race of technologically advanced reprobates?

David Bohm was born in Pennsylvania on 20 December 1917. Despite being raised in a Jewish family, he became an agnostic in his teenage years. Bohm graduated from Pennsylvania State College in 1939. He then studied for a year at the California Institute of Technology before transferring to the theoretical physics group directed by Robert Oppenheimer at the University of California, Berkeley Radiation Laboratory. Together with others among Oppenheimer's student group, Bohm became increasingly involved in Communist politics. Oppenheimer asked Bohm to work with him at Los Alamos on the Manhattan Project but Bohm's political leanings denied him the necessary security clearances. Bohm remained in Berkeley, teaching physics, until he completed his Ph.D. in 1943. After the war Bohm became an assistant professor at Princeton University where he worked closely with Albert Einstein.

In May 1949 Bohm invoked his Fifth Amendment rights and refused to testify against his colleagues before the House Un-American Activities Committee (HUAC). In 1950 Bohm was arrested for refusing to answer HUAC's questions and acquitted in May 1951 but Princeton had already suspended him. After the acquittal efforts to have Bohm reinstated at Princeton failed, a decision that disappointed Einstein who wanted Bohm to serve as his assistant. Bohm then left for Brazil to assume a professorship of physics at the University of São Paulo on

---

[60] Rux, B., *Architects of the Underworld*, Frog Ltd, Berkeley, 1996

Einstein and Oppenheimer's recommendations. After Bohm's arrival in Brazil the U.S. Consul in São Paulo confiscated his passport, informing him he could retrieve it only to return to his country. This dampened Bohm's spirits deeply. He applied for and received Brazilian citizenship but by law had to give up his U.S. citizenship and it was not until 1986 that he was able to reclaim it after mounting a lawsuit.

In 1957 Bohm relocated to the United Kingdom as a research fellow at the University of Bristol and four years later was made Professor of Theoretical Physics at the University of London's Birkbeck College, becoming emeritus in 1987, the year of his retirement. Thereafter, Bohm continued his work in quantum physics past his retirement. Not long afterwards Bohm began to experience a recurrence of the depression he had suffered earlier in life. He was admitted to the Maudsley Hospital in South London in May 1991 but his condition worsened and he was treated with electroconvulsive therapy. His symptoms showed a degree of improvement but he relapsed and was re-medicated. On 27 October 1992, aged 74, Bohm suffered a fatal heart attack while riding in a London black taxicab.

In *Wholeness and the Implicate Order*[61] Bohm introduced his audience to ontological concepts, which served to impart a metaphysical aspect to quantum theory. In this brilliant work Bohm imagined the universe as an infinite sea of space and energy out of which matter could be unfolded, which he called "explicating," and enfolded, which he called "implicating." The central underlying theme of Bohm's theory is the "unbroken wholeness of the totality of existence as an undivided flowing movement without borders."

Bohm's was not the first great mind to promulgate the existence of two distinct orders of reality. To illustrate the point that there are no new ideas, only a creative re-imagining of old ones Tibetan Buddhists long ago named Bohm's Implicate and Explicate Orders as the void and the nonvoid, the birthplace out of which pour like "boundless flux" all things in the universe. To Hindus, the Implicate is Brahman. In more recent times, mystic visionary poet William Yeats who was an enthusiastic supporter of Evans-Wentz's folklore studies was a proponent of the dual orders of existence theory. Nevertheless, it was Bohm that did the math and deep thinking and demonstrated to his peers that the concepts of the Implicate and Explicate Orders were sound.

In an ontological sense the Implicate Order can be seen as both a

---

[61] Bohm, Dr. J., *Wholeness and the Implicate Order*, Routledge, Great Britain, 1980

physical and metaphysical construction—a vast Intelligence which contains all things within itself and which enfolds or unfolds these things so that they emerge into the reality we experience as real.

(It is remarkable that it took nearly two thousand years before a brilliant scientific mind sought to explain in scientific terms the teachings of the 3rd century Buddhist Mahāyāna School. Using the metaphor of Indra's net, the school taught its students about the philosophical and metaphysical concepts of cosmic emptiness and interpenetration of existence.)

Bohm defined the Explicate Order as the order of the *physical world*, and the Implicate Order as the *source* of Explicate Order. He postulated that the Implicate Order behaves in an ultra-holistic fashion in that it connects everything with everything else and, in theory, any individual element could reveal information about every other element in the universe.

Bohm and Cambridge biophysicist Professor Rupert Sheldrake postulated an interacting universe whose tiniest element, like a hologram, contains the information of the entire universe. In this model it follows that there is no process of "chance," only a blueprint of evolution, which, via Sheldrake's principle of "morphic resonance,"[62] is transmitted throughout the entire universe. This means that creation can happen anywhere, not just here.

In a neat analogy designed to illustrate his theory of the Implicate and Explicate Orders, Bohm asked one to consider a pattern produced by making small cuts in a folded piece of paper and then, literally, unfolding it. Widely separated elements of the pattern are, in actuality, produced by the same original cut in the folded piece of paper. Here the cuts in the folded paper represent the Implicate Order and the unfolded pattern represents the Explicate Order.

Bohm regarded the Implicate Order as a deeper and more fundamental order of reality; whereas, in contrast, the Explicate Order includes the abstractions that humans normally perceive. In the words of F. David Peat, Bohm considered that what we regard as objective reality are "surface phenomena, explicate forms that have temporarily unfolded out of an underlying implicate order." That is, the Implicate Order is the ground from which reality *truly* emerges.

---

[62] Morphic resonance hypothesis posits that memory is inherent in nature and that natural systems such as termite colonies or insulin molecules inherit a collective memory from all previous things of their kind. Sheldrake proposes that morphic resonance is also responsible for psi-type interconnections between organisms such as precognition and telepathy.

At the very depths of this ground of all existence Bohm believed in the presence of an immense background of special energy, which Bohm termed the plenum. Bohm likened this ground to one whole and unbroken movement of continuous flux, which he called the "holomovement" (movement of the whole). It is the holomovement that carries the Implicate Order

Bohm believed that the Implicate Order has to be extended into a multidimensional reality, wherein the holomovement endlessly enfolds and unfolds into infinite dimensionality. One observes here the interplay between the Implicate and the Explicate Orders, the flow of matter, manifested and interdependent, towards consciousness. Within this milieu there are independent sub-totalities (such as physical elements and human entities) with relative autonomy. The layers of the Implicate Order can go deeper and deeper to the ultimately unknown.

The Implicate Order is not to be understood in terms of a regular arrangement of objects and events but, mirroring the inside-out geometry of Dr. Who's tardis, rather as total order contained in each region of space and time. In Bohm's framework of understanding the whole exists in every part (the infinite number of "mansions" of the Implicate occupying the explicate "house" of our physical universe, for example).

Bohm said that in classical physics reality is actually little particles that separate the world into its independent elements. He proposed the reverse: that the fundamental reality is the enfoldment and unfoldment and particles are abstractions from that process. We can picture the electron not as a particle that exists continuously but as something coming in and going out and then coming in again, the process repeating in endless cycles. If these condensations are close together, they approximate the track of a particle. Bohm said that the electron itself could never be separated from the whole of space, which is its *ground.*

Initially, Bohm developed his theory of the Implicate Order to help explain how two subatomic particles that have once interacted can instantaneously "respond to each other's motions thousands of years later when they are light-years apart." This kind of interconnectedness requires superluminal[63] signalling, which is faster than the speed of light. Bohm suspected that unobserved subquantum forces and particles lie at the heart of the paradox, believing that the apparent weirdness

---

[63] the apparently faster-than-light motion seen in some cosmic bodies such as radio galaxies and quasars

might be produced by hidden means—a deeper dimension of reality that poses no conflict with ordinary ideas of causality and reality.

"Fairyland exists as an invisible world within which the visible world [Bohm's Explicate Order] *is immersed like an island in an unexplored ocean* [Bohm's Implicate Order] *and which is peopled by more species of living beings than this world because incomparably more vast and varied are its possibilities."*

Walter Evans-Wentz

Indeed, Bohm had come to believe that space and time might be derived from the Implicate Order. He maintained that time is a projection of multidimensional reality from the Implicate Order into a sequence of moments. It follows that the flow of time is the product of a constant series of unfoldings and enfoldings; the enfolded present, becoming part of the past, returns to the present as a kind of Implicate Order. In this quantum model all possible realities co-exist in time and space.

Physicist David Finkelstein was of like mind when he asserted that: "space-time is a statistical construct from a deeper 'pre-geometric' quantum structure in which process is fundamental."[64] American theoretical physicist Richard Feynman also remarked on the illusory nature of time noting, for example, that a positron moving forward in time is actually an electron moving backward in time.

"What seest thou else in the dark and backward abysm of time?"

William Shakespeare, *The Tempest*

Advancing his thinking, Bohm went on to suggest that we actually construct space and time. He believed that the universe is "all thought," the inference being that it is consciousness alone that creates, maintains and sustains the physical universe, a postulate that presupposes that consciousness never dies. This was not a new idea. In 1932 English physicist, astronomer and mathematician Sir James Jeans said presciently,[65] "The universe begins to look more like a great thought than like a great machine."

Twenty years later David Bohm took these ideas to another level. Together with fellow scientist, Karl H. Pribram, Bohm proposed that

---

[64] Finkelstein, D., *The Space-Time Code*, Physical Review, 5D, no. 12 [15 June 1972]: 2922

[65] Jeans, J., *The Mysterious Universe*, E.P. Dutton, NY, 1932

158

the human brain mathematically constructs objective reality by interpreting frequencies that are projections from another dimension within the Implicate Order. Pribram coined the term "frequency domain" to refer to the interference patterns that comprise the Implicate Order. This domain is the border between mind and matter. This supposes that the brain is a hologram enfolded in a holographic universe. Writer Michael Talbot was a firm supporter of Bohm's concepts in this regard. He wrote poetically:[66]

> ...*just as every portion of the hologram contains the image of the whole, every portion of the universe enfolds the whole...if we knew how to access it we could find the Andromeda galaxy in the thumbnail of our left hand. We could also find Cleopatra meeting Caesar for the first time, for in principle the whole past and implications for the whole future are also enfolded in each small region of space and time. Every cell in our body enfolds the entire cosmos. So does every leaf, every raindrop, every dust mote...*

It follows from this line of reasoning that the physical body is a level of density in the total human energy field, a hologram that has coalesced out of the interference pattern of the aura, itself a subtle field of the Implicate Order. It is thought that the mind resides not in the brain but in the energy field that permeates both the brain and the physical body.

It took many years for physicists to begin to catch up with Bohm's ideas. Today quantum theory speculates that mind and matter are different vibrations or ripples in the same pond, precisely what Bohm was proposing forty years ago (and what Tantric philosophy taught two thousand years ago in stating that the universe is an emanation of the mind).

American physicist John A. Wheeler who helped develop the theory of nuclear fission asked: "May the universe in some strange sense be brought into being by the participation of those who participate?"

Theoretical physicist Jack Sarfatti believes that the structure of matter may not be independent of consciousness.[67] Sarfatti also believes that humankind's collective unconscious determines whether a particle decays or not. However, because we do not perceive that we are vital participants in the quantum universe our collective will is unfocused and chaotic, making quantum events appear random and problematic.

---

[66] Talbot, M., *The Holographic Universe*, 1991
[67] Sarfatti, J., *Implications of Meta-Physics for Psychoenergetic Systems*, in *Psychoenergetic Systems, Vol. 1*, Gordon and Breach: London, 1974

Talbot suggested[68] that new physics is increasingly accepting the premise that matter, space and time owe their existence to human consciousness, reality being a super-hologram created and maintained by consciousness.

Evan Harris Walker has suggested that consciousness is a "quantum mechanical tunnelling" process that takes place at the synapses between human nerve cells.[69] Sarfatti expounds on this observation in stating that the Swiss cheese-like wormhole connections (quantum foam) at the sub-atomic scale of 3-dimensional space connect every part of the universe directly with every other part, much like the "nervous system of a cosmic brain."

To avoid catastrophic psychic overload, a part of our consciousness that operates as a re-structuring mechanism edits out the realities that our minds cannot cope with. This action mirrors the remarkable conclusions of Aldous Huxley who after consuming mescaline and considering the nature of consciousness saw that the brain acts as a filter, a "reducing valve," of a vaster mind—consciousness—that he called the "Mind at Large." Bohm, working on his ideas at roughly the same time as Huxley wrote *The Doors of Perception* (1954), would go on to call this the Implicate Order.

Humans struggle to attain this level of realisation because of a lack of belief in the power of "seeing" what truly lies before one. Pribram reasoned that the objective world comprises a vast ocean of waves and frequencies. We see this as "concrete" because our brains can transmute this holographic blur into the sticks and stones that make up our world. The illusion of a seemingly smooth item of bone china is therefore equivalent to the phantom limb syndrome. If we could somehow unfilter the cup from our brain processes we would instead perceive an interference pattern, the cup and pattern at the same time being both real and unreal. Bohm said as much when he stated that the individual is in total contact with the Implicate Order. In that sense, the individual "is part of the whole of mankind and in another sense he can get beyond it." Bohm said that in the Implicate Order imagination and reality are one and the same.

Yaqui Indian Don Juan Matus when teaching Carlos Casteneda said essentially the same thing. In *Tales of Power* Don Juan explains, "The world doesn't yield to us directly, the description of the world stands in

[68] Talbot, M., *Mysticism and the New Physics*,
[69] Walker, H.E., *The Nature of Consciousness*, Mathematical Biosciences 7 [1970]: 138-197

between." In the absence of true *seeing* we remain blind to the true nature of creation and are condemned to yield to our preconceived notions such as the absolute truth of Euclid's theories (long since demonstrated as cannot be proven by Bolyai and Lobachevsky *et al.*).

More and more, Bohm began to sense a new development in which the individual is in total contact with the Implicate Order: a part of the whole of mankind but also the "focus for something beyond mankind." He reflected more deeply on this realisation when he advanced his concept of nonlocality in which a point in space becomes equal to all other points of space, an observation that connotes the presence of a single cosmic thought-form that is visualising the universe and thereby keeping it in place. Bohm himself said that the Implicate (enfolded) Order gives birth to all the objects and appearances of our physical world; that everything in the universe is part of a continuum.

Bohm felt that the cosmos has an inner life or quality (he used the term "interiority"), an underlying cosmic intelligence that is at work in the organisation of the Implicate and Explicate Orders. This cosmic intelligence, dubbed by Bohm "The Player," engages in endless experimentation and creativity, forever moving cyclically onward and onward, accruing an infinity of experienced being-ness.

Indeed, Bohm went further, equating the Implicate Order with the realm of the spirit when he observed that: "the (implicate) domain can equally be called Idealism, Spirit, Consciousness." The logical interpretation arising from these ideas that the Implicate Order is no less than the mind of the "The Player," encouraged the 1973 Nobel Prize winner in Physics, Brian Josephson, to state that Bohm's Implicate Order may one day lead to the inclusion of God or Mind within the framework of science.

Bohm considered a human being to be an "intrinsic feature of the universe, which would be incomplete in some fundamental sense" if the person did not exist. He believes that individuals participate in the whole and, consequently, give it meaning. Because of human participation the "Implicate Order is getting to know itself better." Bohm went so far as to suggest that consciousness is actually a subtle form of matter.

Bohm's mind-blowing ideas through which he proposed so much that was bold and new in quantum science, including the existence of cosmic intelligence, "The Player," evidently struck a chord in high circles. Those in the U.S. government dealing with the NHE issue saw in Bohm's theories possibilities to combat the increasing threat of NHE incursions, even possibly to exploit their technology to best advantage.

What precisely among the ingredients in Bohm's alembic of ideas became of specific interest has not been revealed. Fourteen years elapsed between Bohn publishing his work on the Implicate Order and the agents informing Linda Moulton Howe that his work was being exploited. By that time others in the quantum field had embraced Bohm's concepts but still it was the master's ideas which authority sought to turn to its best advantage in its dealings with NHEs. The enticing elements in Bohn's theories for government scientists would surely relate to what he had to say about the multi-dimensional nature of the Implicate Order. Let us remind ourselves of the agents' words: *"The causal source of the UFO and UFO abduction phenomena is not extraterrestrial...Dr. Vallée was so close to the truth of the situation, with the exception that the ultimate manipulators are not human."*

Contactee Linda Porter was told by her non-human abductors that the universe is built on sound patterns, which is why so many dimensions can exist in the same space. They described how each frequency is its own octave, which holds the particular dimension in place. Disrupt a dimension (by means of atomic tests, for example) to the extent that its carrier wave is compromised and there is a real risk of creating a hole that cannot support the dimensions that exist above and below it. This causes a domino effect with more and more dimensions collapsing into the sinkhole. One by one, other worlds and civilisations are destroyed and the corresponding effect on the gravitational field for parsecs around it provokes a chain reaction.

Porter was led to understand that atomic tests, left unchecked, would alter the density of matter to an extent that it will trigger this unstoppable chain reaction. One can imagine our dimensional neighbours with a vested interest in the protection of their world(s) as being very determined to prevent this from happening.

There is a belief in some quarters that one of the prime candidates for the true identity of NHEs, or at least a substantial element among them, is the Tuatha dé Dannan, the magical and decidedly human-like race that survived the Flood. This view rests on the belief that there has never been a time in human history when the Dannan were absent from the Earth and that today they maintain a closer watch on us than ever before. Folklore attributes the Tuatha dé Dannan with a mastery of the power of sound, knowledge that would make them especially sensitive to potential harm to their world caused by humankind's infringing actions.

Unable or unwilling to address humankind face to face on the issues, the Tuatha dé Dannan's communication is chiefly characterised by their skilful use of signs transmitted via dreams and riddles. (Consider physicist Fred Alan Wolf's remark that lucid dreams, if not all dreams, are actually visits to parallel universes, smaller holograms within the larger cosmic hologram.). On the occasions when they desire to communicate with humans directly they do so in accordance with the percipient's personal belief system (Arthur, Guinevere, Mother of God, "Jesus-type" Blond Tall, gnome, robot, Little Blue Man, grey and so forth). One senses that the objective sought through these various modes of communication is not basically altruistic but carried out to exert a degree of control and influence over humans. It is possible that the Dannan's strategy in this regard is also being pursued by subtler means and that it is Professor Bohm we can thank for lifting the lid on the hows and wherefores.

Bohm did not mention the UFO phenomenon in the course of his work on the Implicate, instead concentrating on the science that shines a light on whence non-human intelligence might originate. Others who subsequently found resonance in Bohm's thinking have discussed the phenomenon in terms of NHEs and offered valuable insights. American philosopher Carl Raschke, for example, believes that UFOs are a holographic materialisation from a conjugate dimension of the universe.[70]

Expanding on these reflections, American psychologist Lawrence LeShan has suggested[71] that our physical universe has a corresponding paranormal reality (Bohm's Implicate Order) whose resident entities are "functional" entities (as distinct from structural entities such as ourselves) that have no length, breadth nor depth. Not limited by the normal laws of space and time, they can move faster than light. They exist only when they are visualised or held in the mind and are thus like a mathematical point possessing no true reality in space-time. Whitley Strieber went further, adding the striking opinion that:

> UFO beings may be our first true quantum discovery in the large-scale world. The very act of observing it may be creating it as a concrete actuality, with sense, definition and a consciousness of its own.[72]

Strieber's insights suggest that the more we observe, the more we add substance to energies emerging from the Implicate purely by virtue

[70] Stillings, D., (Ed)., *Cyberbiological Studies of the Imaginal Component in the UFO Contact Experience*, Archaeus Project, 1989, p24
[71] LeShan, L., *The Medium, The Mystic and the Physicist*, Viking Press, NY, 1974
[72] Strieber, W., *Communion: A True Story*, Harper. New York, 2008

of the power of our conscious minds. By this process, understood by technologically advanced neighbours, the Tuatha dé Dannan or other such advanced NHE life forms may be seeking to capitalise on this quantum phenomenon to strengthen their powers to influence human behaviour. If true, our own thoughts risk making us captive to a process of manipulation and control about whose outcome we are wholly ignorant.

But, of course, things are never so one-sided as to obviate all sense of balance and potential for positive action. Walter Evans-Wentz, a true early visionary, posed the question: does man's consciousness continue to exist in an unmanifest state after death? He asked what happens to the willing, the thinking, the remembering and the directing force (soul / spirit) that fed and maintained these activities in life.

Seeing that matter and energy can neither be created nor destroyed, Evans-Wentz held that the soul has always existed as an indestructible unity of energy, the permanent principle that is relative to an even higher power. He regarded this psychic power as a vast reservoir of consciousness ever-seeking to force itself through the illusory walls of matter such that in the future time of this fully evolved man the reservoir will burst the banks of the physical, transmuting our consciousness into a higher order of reality. This pre-existent psychic power is continually striving to express itself through dense matter.

Fifty years later, David Bohm, reflecting on similar panpsychic themes, using the analogy of the transformation of the atom ultimately into a power and chain reaction, made some startling observations. He believed that the individual who uses inner energy and intelligence and transmutes their consciousness into a higher force could transform mankind.

"My love is stronger than the universe"

"Heartbreaker," the Gibb Brothers, 1982

Moreover, Bohm proposed that the collectivity of individuals has reached the "principle of the consciousness of mankind." However, individuals have not quite the "energy to reach the whole, to put it all on fire." He said that those who have shaken off the "pollution of the ages" (wrong worldviews that propagate ignorance) and who come together in close and trusting relationships can begin to generate the immense power needed to ignite the whole consciousness of the world. In the depths of the Implicate Order, Bohm said, there is a "consciousness, deep down, of the whole of mankind."

Bohm's study of the Implicate Order had inspired him to voice these remarkable insights. He understood that humans possess all of the unlimited powers of the "Player," a gift that puts each individual on a par with their Creator. In short, the implicate cosmic spark, the Godforce, that resides deep within makes each of us in principle stronger than the universe, which is merely one emanation among an infinite number arising from the special plenum energy of the holomovement.

By this measure of thinking, humans possess unlimited power to transcend illusory attempts at control and subversion by external forces, no matter from where they may hail. What stops us from properly "seeing" our unlimited potential and exercising our cosmic powers is our stubborn refusal to slough off the "pollution of the ages."

David Bohm's belief that the human collective has reached the "principle of the consciousness of mankind," is comforting but one look at the daily headlines demonstrates that we still have a long way to go before, with one mind, we can light up the heavens and see what truly lies within and around us.

Chapter 8

Mars—an Atlantean Outpost

"That I am in direct mind-to-mind touch with extraterrestrial intelligence systems has been obvious to me for some time, but what this means is not in any way obvious...These are new words to describe ancient experiences...Basically this is a religious experience, but also it is more because we are no longer a religious world."

—Philip K. Dick, letter to Claudia Bush, 26 November, 1974

The briefing papers contained in the 35mm film sent to Jaime Shanders included a comment about the New Mexico UFOs' point of origin. A consensus appeared to be emerging among MJ-12's investigating elite that identified Mars as the UFOs' likely home base. Dr. Donald H. Menzel, regarded as an archsceptic of the UFO phenomenon, was a dissenting voice in nominating Venus, a relative stone's throw from Mars, as his favoured planet. Mars or Venus—the point about both candidates is that they are Earth's near planetary neighbours.

Other top scientists connected to the "unholy thirteen" shared the same view. In answering British-Armenian researcher Henry Azadehdel's question about the objects having a base on one of our solar system planets, Professor Robert I. Sarbacher, one time scientific consultant to the Research and Development Board at the U.S. Defense Department with his own office at the Pentagon, said, "Well, we can make a point of all these, but they did not tell us." The meaning was clear. The suspicion of a near planetary origin was strong among the investigators but none of the recovered greys had given the game away.

One should reflect on this in conjunction with a number of other observations that emerged from the papers, which indicated that UFOs (certainly those of the type that crashed in New Mexico) appear to be short-range reconnaissance craft piloted by advanced robotic constructs.

Sarbacher told nuclear physicist Stanton Friedman that his colleagues (in MJ-12) had been convinced that the UFO crews were biological robots. Seemingly keen to continue disseminating his knowledge, Sarbacher then told investigator Wilbert Smith that the "aliens were constructed like certain insects, wherein because of the low mass the inertial forces involved in operating the craft's instruments would be quite low." In another letter to Smith, Sarbacher referred to UFO occupants as "instruments," constructed from very lightweight materials to facilitate operating the machines.

A professor of chemistry from Florida whom American ufologist Leonard Stringfield gave the pseudonym "Edith Simpson" was an assistant to Einstein in the summer of 1947 between semesters. She accompanied Einstein to attend a crisis conference of top scientists at an Air Force Base in a "southwestern State." There they saw NHEs for the first time. There were five of them: 5-feet tall, no hair, big head, enormous dark eyes, skin grey with greenish tinge. The bodies were dressed in tight fitting suits. They were told the beings had neither a naval nor genitalia. An aspect of appearance that indicated artificial contruction was the presence of a bilious green fluid that oozed from the nose, the ooze gradually becoming bluish, suggestive of a copper or cobalt base.

The physiologist who autopsied the aliens at Wright Patterson AFB told Stringfield in 1978 that the aliens' absence of a digestive system, gastro-intestinal tract, intestinal or alimentary canal, rectal area (no food was found on the crashed craft), or a reproductive organ suggested that their bodies were produced by means of a cloning process or had been formed out of a mould.

Looking at these opinions in the round, it appears that the majority of the Majestic membership and its allies in the scientific community believed that the Roswell visitors made a relatively short hop from the Red Planet, parked their mothership in our orbit and despatched much smaller vehicles crewed by remotely controlled androids to Earth's surface.

It is reported that abductees taken on board craft are often shown film of a desert planet with a dark sky, where its life forms live only in subterranean spaces. Abductees are alerted to the ecological damage to our Earth and the degree of over-population, as if to warn them about a potential recurrence of identical past problems due to present day human activity. It is as if they are saying, "Do not repeat the mistakes we made when once we called Earth our home." On first consideration it might seem ridiculous to seriously suggest that Earth has been experiencing a barrage of UFO visits from a race of beings whose home is the Red Planet. But is the possibility really so farfetched?

In this narrative we are not speaking of the residents of Magonia who may only be observed by invitation, by serendipity or by exercising special gifts of perception that allow one to peer into interpenetrating dimensions. One did not require a psychic key in 1947 to see the robots that were propelled from crashed reconnaissance vehicles. Nor was one needed by MJ-12 and its representatives in order to meet with the greys' masters and to engage in dialogue. In this chapter we enter into the territory of "Infernium" and its hostile inhabitants. Once they walked the Earth; in fact, they walked on it in four successive civilisations. On each occasion their actions brought about their undoing, the last occurring approximately 12,000 years ago.

Full trance communications workshops held in the U.S.A and in Europe in the early 1970s revealed startling insights about Earth's antediluvian civilisations. Ancient and mythological histories are full of references that hint at the existence of pre-Flood peoples. Sumerian history, for example, relates that their race was of non-human origin, whose purpose was to instruct mankind. They took steps to preserve the newly introduced knowledge into men prior to the Flood.

Zecharia Sitchin says that the Sumerian "gods" were an advanced NHE civilisation, which eons earlier used genetic manipulation in already-evolving primates to create primitive workers for mining and other physical labour on Earth. Thereafter, the Sumerian culture developed as a result of an interactive relationship between the primitive homosapiens and the NHEs. The Sumerians were a dark-haired people that spoke an agglutinative language resembling ancient Turkish (Turanian). The southern Mesopotamians had big, long narrow heads with *prominent noses*. Perhaps one does not have to look too far to identify the source of the physical characteristics of the big-nose grey.

The trance workshops spoke specifically about the Atlantean civilisations. It emerged that over a period of tens of thousands of years there was not one but four Atlantean races, each eliminated by successive cataclysms. Previous gifted psychics had made similar statements. Edgar Cayce (1877-1945) who began his channelling in 1901 when he was a fundamental Christian said in readings that the last three destructions occurred in 50,000 B.C., 28,000 B.C., and 10,000 B.C. He said that on each occasion the few that fled and survived migrated to diverse locations, including the Americas, in line with legends from local natives.

In recent years, research has shown that Cayce's accounts are consistent with archaeological evidence. Moreover, recent research on a form of DNA recovered from ancient remains has matched Cayce's account perfectly. In particular, what genetic scientists call the "Haplogroup X" has been found in ancient remains in every location in the world stipulated in the Cayce readings. Incredibly, Haplogroup X has not been found in other places in the world.

The Atlanteans' technological prowess was far in advance of ours today. Celebrated British medium Margaret Lumley Brown described the Atlanteans' mastery of nuclear physics, the use of "firestones" that harnessed cosmic forces and of crystal technologies that utilised both solar and geothermal power. Through their understanding of certain concentrated energy points in space and time, the Atlanteans were also able to interface with other realities and communicate with dimensional neighbours.

Medium James Merrill (1926-1990) said that the Atlanteans built a hugely ambitious new atomically powered world in the stratosphere, comprising a network of antigravitated platforms anchored to Earth at 14 points by glowing radioactive stones.

But all was not well. Atlantis in 10,000 B.C. had become a morass of violence and depravity. The trance communications explained that what finally undid the fourth and final race was its exploitation of genetics, one of the most powerful means of control in the black magic practices of the Sons of Belial, otherwise known as the Lords of Material Existence who denied the existence of God and instead worshipped themselves.

In a massive programme of social engineering, newborn children were implanted with a crystal in the base of the spine by which their behaviour, wants and moods were remotely controlled. (Significantly, during the Roswell autopsy an object described as a kind of chestnut-sized "crystal" was cut out of the belly area.) Man-animal hybrids were bred for sexual gratification. Human sacrifice was rampant.

Worse was to follow. Tasked by power-crazed rulers to manufacture the perfect man, scientists grew laboratory-bred humans. The NHEs held prisoner at the Ice Cave in Los Alamos claimed that they created man as a hybrid and established religious belief to control the human race.

In Atlantis no one understood the metaphysical consequences of making superperfect human clones free from disease and physical impediment. No spirit would choose such a vehicle for its next incarnation because evolutionary growth may only be achieved through experiencing a degree of physical imbalance. This left the door open for earthbound souls (of suicides, murderers and so forth) and negative energies from the astral dimensions to inhabit the immaculate host bodies. There was no turning back from this.

Those in power were not entirely blind to the consequences of their actions. The leaders of the fourth Atlantean race, a civilisation that occupied ten continents, knew what was coming and also knew that it could not be stopped. The extent to which the Atlanteans' science, technology and occult practices infringed upon the natural world and so alarmed the cosmic powers that caretake our planet had, just as on previous occasions, commenced an irreversible countdown.

Systems scientist, Paul LaViolette, believes that activity in the centre of our galaxy intermittently causes newly created matter formed out of etheric prematerial to spew out, creating "superwaves" that reverberate throughout the solar system. It is reasoned that the superwave of circa 12,700 B.C. was a contributory factor that caused multiple impacts of cometlike objects that struck the Northern Hemisphere causing climate change, earthquakes, fires, magnetic oscillations and increased radiation. An ensuing crustal shift, followed by an instant switch of the poles in which in moments North became South, triggered cataclysm.

As Plato described in *Timaeus,* Atlantis was consumed "in a single dreadful day and night." There were survivors. Channeling sources indicate that between 20,000 and 30,000 people situated in the right place at the right time were on safe ground when the waves struck.

The trance workshops then introduced an amazing new element to the Atlantean story. Not all of those that fled the waves survived by moving to new lands above the floodwaters; a few made for the heavens. With what little time remaining, they put into effect a bold contingency plan.

Recently, I watched a BBC television documentary about developments in robotics technologies. Presenters visited NASA's research labs and were proudly shown a new robot being put through its paces. Valkyrie is a very sophisticated looking "female" robot, which is being designed to undertake an unmanned mission to Mars in 2030 to prepare the way for eventual human settlement. To the embarrassment of her NASA handlers, in several attempts Valkyrie was not able to step over a half-inch high lip on the floor without stumbling.

Nonetheless, it is a sobering thought that we are approximately at the same point in time relative to when the fourth civilisation Atlantean technologists were toiling over their own version of Valkyrie in the decades prior to their attempt to save their species by taking off for a nearby sanctuary in space.

The leaders knew that their cumulative actions had once again brought them to a point of no return, knew that they were powerless to dampen the imminent wrath of Gaia and its cataclysmic consequences, and knew with equal certainty that they were royally screwed if they couldn't find a way to get an Ark into the dark skies and head for a viable planet. They had done this before and urgently needed to do it again.

Before the Earth's weather systems wreaked their unimaginable destruction a boat-shaped, space ship was launched. On board were as many specimens of fauna and flora as could be accommodated before the first waves hit Atlantis' population centres. Nine thousand years later the account of the Vaivasvata Manu's rescue by "Vishnu" in the form of a fish was written as the story of Noah and his Ark.

Reflect on British medium William Scott-Elliott, 10th Laird of Arkleton's description of the Atlanteans' airships in the year of its destruction, 9,564 B.C. With the aid of his wife, Mary, an acclaimed trance medium, Scott-Elliott described the Atlanteans' "air-boats" as made of an "alloy" of two white-coloured metals and one red one that was "even lighter than aluminium." The outside surface was "apparently seamless and perfectly smooth," and they "shone in the dark" as if coated with luminous paint. They were "boat-shaped but invariably decked over" with propelling and steering gear at both ends.

Their motive power was an "etheric force" (Bulmer–Lytton's "Vril power," discussed later) made in a generator and passed through adjustable tubes which then operated like a modern jet. The course of flight was never straight but in "long waves." Readers will, of course, note the uncanny similarities between Scott-Elliott's description and modern UFO accounts. Rudolph Steiner also supported Scott-Elliott's Atlantis commentary, adding from his own insights that the airships' power was derived from tapping the energy within "growing things."

Dr Silas Newton, who accompanied the Roswell retrieval team, echoed Scott-Elliott's description telling American journalist Frank Scully that UFOs seem to fly along geomagnetic lines of force. Insider Richard Doty said that when alien craft visit our planet they literally swim on the Earth's gravity field.

Where did the Atlanteans go in their boat-shaped space-ark? Well-known abductee Howard Mengel had photos of Mars, which he claimed to have taken while travelling in a UFO in August 1956.

In one of his photos is a huge crater identified now as the Schiaperelli, which was not officially discovered and photographed until Viking I's voyage in 1976. Contactee, author, channel and close friend of celebrated abductee George Adamski, George Hunt Williamson (1926-1986), also was in no doubt that they made for the Red Planet.

It is evident that U.S. scientists were in broad agreement. The production of sci-fi movies in the 1950s such as *Invaders from Mars* in 1952, show that by then the Government knew that UFOs were operated by robots guided by a race based on Mars that abducted humans and implanted them.

By 1958 the U.S. Government was investigating the premise that the race behind the UFOs was connected with an ancient human civilisation. NASA was established around this time and the Brookings Report[73] speculated that the discovery of alien artefacts on Venus, Mars and the Moon was inevitable. In fact, in the same year, on 29 September, Dr. Kenzahuro Toyoda of Japan's Menjii University discovered actual letters on the Moon's surface, so large and black that he could easily read them: "PYAX JWA." There are many noted instances of formations and features on the Moon's surface that accord with definite geometric laws.

Evidence increasingly suggested the presence of habitations below the lunar surface. By 1966 the suspicion became a certainty with the discovery in photographs taken by Soviet probes of regular structures in the Sea of Storms and the Blair Cuspids in the Moon's Sea of Tranquility, the latter being the site of the first Apollo mission landings.

Apollo astronauts saw evidence of an alien base on the dark side of the moon ("Luna"). They saw large machines believed to be for mining activity. Also seen at Luna were very large mother ships.

Viking I dropped a robot probe on the Martian surface on 20 July 1976. On its 35th orbit it photographed something from 1,000 feet up, approx 41 degrees north of the equator in the Cydonia region. Imaging team member Toby Owen found on frame 35A72 a mesa more than 1 mile across, 2 miles long and a half-mile high, which looked exactly like a human face. 35 days later frame 70A13 showed a photo of the same area with a lighting change of 20 degrees. It showed the same thing but clearer this time. Three years later two scientists using

---

[73] *Proposed Studies on the Implications of Peaceful Space Activities for Human Affairs*: a 1960 report commissioned by NASA and created by the Brookings Institution in collaboration with NASA's Committee on Long-Range Studies.

advanced computer graphic techniques ascertained that the face was bisymmetrical. They set about creating a 3-D computer facsimile. At that time, though, no one was really that interested in the findings.

Further heightened detail was later found with the assistance of the Analytic Science Corporation, including the pupil in the Face's eye, teeth in its mouth, cheekbone delineations and darkened bands on its Egyptian-style headdress or helmet (believed up to then to have been facial hair). They also discovered a giant pyramid, approximately 1 mile by 1.6 miles, 10 miles southwest of the Face, its four faces aligned to the spin axis of Mars, just as the pyramids of Giza are to the Earth's cardinal points. Other smaller pyramids were also identified in the same area.

Investigator Richard Hoagland met the team behind the findings in 1981 and together using more photos from the Viking mission they identified a city of intelligent construction. The entire construction complex conforms to Fibonacci proportions: the e/pi ratio 0.865, just as in the Giza complex. The e/pi ratio has been called the "tetrehedral Message of Cydonis," and is also found in crop circles. For example, the celebrated formation at Barbury Castle in 2008 in Wiltshire, England, showed a 3-D representation of Cydonia geometry.

Bruce Rux[74] believes that the Cydonia Face is that of a hawk representing Ra, a second face found in a nearby cliff area portraying a baboon (Thoth). The Ra Face has also been identified to include a five-pointed human-faced diadem in the centre of Ra's helmet. Hoagland believes the Ra Face to be an image of Homo erectus, the theoretical evolutionary stage of man from approx 450,000 years ago. The datings of Babylonian historian Berossus and the evidence of the Cydonia complex on Mars indicate that Mars and the Moon have been bases for ancient earth "gods" for between 450,000 and 500,000 years.

According to Rux, the likely identity of this intelligent race is the ancient "gods" (Annunaki, Elohim, Nefilim, Watchers, Tuatha dé Dannan and so forth). Rux points out that the Anu is the connecting force between ancient civilisations and the Tuatha dé Dannan (which means "children of the Goddess Anu.") In Sumerian mythology Ani is the progenitor of all the other gods. Anu also means "the waters of heaven or space" (the Implicate). In Egyption mythology Nu is the primal waters of chaos, suggestive of the "cold dark sea surrounding the universe." The Dannan's enemy was the Fomorians, a name that derives from two Gaelic words meaning "under the sea." They were a

---

[74] Rux, B. ibid

race of hideous, malformed giants (the Nefilim of the Bible). These mythological factors speak of a time in the far distant past when Atlantis was destroyed for making monsters for occult purposes.

Strip away the esoteric and metaphysical hyperbole and what is left? What does inhabit the subterranean spaces beneath our neighbouring planetary and satellite bodies? The answer appears to be the descendants of an Earth-based human race that preceded ours by tens, even hundreds of millennia. In the post-1947 dialogue between the U.S. authorities and these beings it was learned that they are 50,000 years ahead of us, precisely the period when the second Atlantean civilisation was destroyed by cataclysm.

Perhaps these ancient exiles once truly loved this planet and treated it with respect but ultimately a lust for power and dominion by the few over the many provoked the cosmic powers to take defensive action. The result was that a surviving phalanx of technologically advanced humans with a wholly negative mindset took to the skies. On the Moon and on Mars, and possibly as Menzel believed, on other neighbouring bodies such as Venus, the Atlantean elite found a way for it and its descendants to survive, perhaps by creating and sustaining a protective dimensional bubble, all the while exercising an infringing and manipulative interest in the Earth they left behind.

Professor Robert Carr at the University of South Florida heard from a colleague in 1952 that alien bodies held at Hangar 18 at Wright Patterson AFB had also been autopsied. These procedures revealed a Type-O blood circulatory system. Their blood could easily have been used for human transfusion purposes. All their organs were in the right place anatomically. When they opened the skull they saw the brain of a man several hundreds of years old, yet the body suggested a much younger man of between 20-30 years old.

Naively, the USA struck an agreement because our ancient brethren said that they were intrinsically benevolent and had created the human race through crossbreeding with a primitive ape-like creature (Cro-Magnon man). The Americans believed this because the NHEs could show in an octagonal crystal various holographic pictures of past periods of Earth's history. The pilot exchange at the end of *Close Encounters of the Third Kind* is regarded as close to the truth. The U.S. Government did set up an exchange program, exchanging humans for two NHEs.

Ultimately, the Americans came to believe that these beings were lying and deceitful. They were mutilating humans, implanting devices in their brain and not returning them to earth. Ronald Reagan's

Strategic Defense Initiative "Star Wars" programme was designed and constructed to tackle those that appear in our skies, destroy our communications with EMP bursts, colonise our lunar surface and mutilate our cattle and citizens for medical tests and hybridization of the species. However, evidence suggests that the U.S. authorities were not the first state power to collaborate with our ancient human cousins.

Researchers claim that senior members of Germany's Thule-Gesellschaft ("Thule Society") believed that a master race of alien beings was living in underground caverns on Earth. The occultist and völkisch Thule Society, named after a mythical northern country in Greek legend, was founded in Munich by Rudolf von Sebottendorf in 1918. It was originally known as the Studiengruppe für Germanisches Altertum ("Study Group for Germanic Antiquity.") It was a key sponsor of the Deutsche Arbeiterpartei (German Workers' Party), later reorganized by Adolf Hitler into the National Socialist German Workers' Party (the NSDAP or Nazi Party). The Thule Society believed in an esoteric history of mankind, knowledge of which is preserved in Tibetan monastary archives. It is claimed that a secret manuscript relating to the history of Atlantis is kept in the Vatican library with a copy placed in a Tibetan monastery.

The Thule-Gesellschaft was actually preceded by the establishment of a decidedly more sinister body known as the Vril Society or the Luminous Lodge of Light, an order whose occult principles lay at the heart and soul of Nazi occult doctrine. News of this society was first revealed to the western world by Willi Ley, the rocket scientist who fled Germany in 1933. Vril is a term that derives from Baron Edward Bulmer-Lytton's 19th century novel *The Coming Race*. In it Bulmer-Lytton, said to have been an adept of German occult lodge the Rising Dawn describes a subterranean race that has developed an all-powerful energy termed Vril.

The Luminous Lodge was formed in the late nineteenth century by Berlin-based Rosicrucians after attending a lecture by anti-Christian Louis Jacolliot. Jacolliot was inspired by eminent figures such as eighteenth century mystical Christian Emmanuel Swedenborg and sixteenth century theologist Jacob Boehme, the latter being a co-founder of Rosicrucianism. The Lodge forged close links with like-minded theosophical centres, among them the British Golden Dawn Society. Golden Dawn members engaged in "spiritual" exercises to harness the Vril force, seeking in its attempts to make contact with supernatural beings in the centre of the world with whom to make alliances to rule the surface and its inhabitants. This subterranean society of the "Vril-ya," the descendants of an ancient race driven long ago from the surface by the threat of a cataclysmic event, was believed to have developed futuristic technology far beyond the capability of surface humans. While Vril could power machines and heal living creatures it also had enormous destructive power, sufficient to reduce an entire city to rubble. Many believe that it was this Vril power that the Nazis sought so avidly.

Some suggest that the Vril-ya are not and never were confined to their subterranean redoubt. Sensationally, the Fars News Agency, the English-language news service of Iran, reported that documents leaked by whistleblower Edward Snowden indicate that the United States is in the thrall of a race of tall, white NHEs that assisted the rise of Nazi Germany in the 1930s.

The report goes on to say that these beings arrived on Earth and helped the Nazis to build a fleet of advanced submarines in the 1930s before going on to meet in 1954 with President Eisenhower, a dialogue that heralded the beginnings of an "alien/extraterrestrial intelligence agenda" that is driving U.S. domestic and international policy. The inference one is encouraged to draw from these extraordinary accounts is that the beings behind the New Mexico UFO crashes, the Vril-ya and the "tall white NHEs" are one and the same, their true identity being the race of humans that once populated Earth, and which was expelled from it for the fourth and final time for unspeakable crimes against nature and the Cosmic Powers 12,000 years ago.

This scenario casts fantastical reports of successful early twentieth century manned missions to the Moon and to Mars in a new light. One persistent rumour has it that the Nazis travelled to both bodies in the 1940s. Vladimir Terziski, president of the American Academy of Dissident Sciences, is among those researchers who support the remarkable claim. Terziski is a Bulgarian born engineer and physicist who graduated Cum Laude from the Master of Science programme of Tokai University in Tokyo in 1980. He served as a solar energy researcher in the Bulgarian Academy of Sciences before emigrating to the U.S. in 1984.

Terziski claims that by 1942 the Germans landed on the Moon, utilizing rocket saucers of the Miethe and Schriever type. He further claims that a joint Japanese-German program culminated in April 1945 in a journey to Mars using craft of the Haunebu-3 type, manned by a volunteer suicide crew. The implication behind these claims is that the Axis forces were assisted in these endeavours by an "alien" intelligence, which imparted to them highly advanced technological know-how. We are encouraged to believe that the identity of this intelligence is the Atlantean Vril-ya line of descent whose members reside both beneath our world and under the surface of nearby space bodies.

A lot of hooey? These photos in NASA's Mars Curiosity Image Gallery taken Saturday, 18 May 2013 at 12:58 show a mysterious object that casts a shadow on the rocky Martian surface. On close inspection it looks like a Nazi helmet. Another photo reveals what appear to be the remains of a human rib cage. NASA has not yet made any official comment about these images.

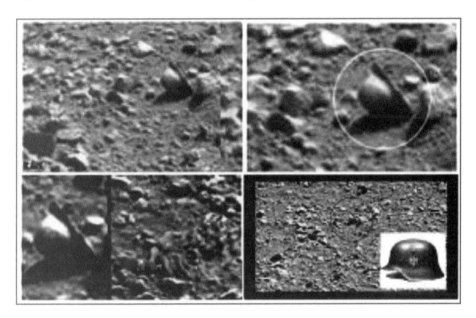

Mars. Atlantis. Secret bases. Dimensions. Air-boats. Energy points in space and time. Antigravity. Geomagnetic lines of force. Ancient "gods." Cydonia. Aliens with Type-O blood. Thule Society. Vril power. Nazi rocket technology. Vril-ya. The Coming Race. Tall, white NHEs. Helmets on the Martian surface…

Chewing over these seemingly disparate elements encouraged me to review the research material I gathered in the 1990s for my work on Otto Rahn. There I rediscovered fresh insights that shine a little more light on the Atlantis story.

In my book I noted the relationship between Reichsführer-SS Heinrich Himmler's office and Rahn's research colleague, Paris-based mathematician, alchemist and occultist Gaston de Mengel. De Mengel conducted scientific research for Himmler in the 1930s. In February

1936 Rahn participated in a report on de Mengel who was visiting Berlin to present certain research conclusions. At this time de Mengel was focusing his research efforts on pre-Christian Indian, Persian and Chinese religious matters but the topic under discussion in Berlin was of a very different kind. Over the following months de Mengel's conclusions were to be checked by mathematician SS-Sturmbannführer Schmid.

Early in 1937 Himmler and de Mengel, then well into his sixties and described in SS correspondence as a "private scholar," had a closed-door meeting in Berlin with Rahn in attendance as interpreter. There are no extant records of the meeting but a key topic that exercised the minds of both Himmler and de Mengel in this period was the search for Atlantis. The meeting reportedly went well and was followed by further conversations between de Mengel and Himmler's subordinates. A copy of de Mengel's written works was subsequently copied and secured in a safe at 33 Caspar-Theyß-Straße in Berlin.

"Coincidentally," de Mengel's private chat with Himmler took place a few months after a reported UFO crash in the Schwarzwald (Black Forest) near Freiburg in 1936. Crucially, Freiburg was a location very familiar to Otto Rahn. It was while living there in 1935 that Rahn was commissioned by Himmler's office to travel extensively in furtherance of the Nazis' obsession with gathering evidence on the Aryan race's genesis in the Golden Age of Hyperborea. A few months later, at approximately the time of the crash event, Rahn wrote to his friend Dr. Alfred Schmid, describing seeing things that others couldn't, an easy feat for people "who are on good terms with imps and other cave-men." What might have Rahn meant by this curious remark? What had he seen?

The Freiburg disc is reported to have been immediately removed to Himmler's Wewelsburg Castle. Wewelsburg was dedicated to the discovery and application of pioneering advanced and alternative technologies and the harnessing of superpowerful energies that could later be used in the war effort.

While the Vril and Thule Societies had experimented with "otherworldly" flight machines in the 1920s, the concept of inter-dimensional space flight was not considered viable despite the channeling efforts of the Alldeutsche Gesellschaft für Metaphysik (All German Society for Metaphysics), a female circle of mediums formed in the early twentieth century led by Zagreb-born Maria Orsitsch (Oršić, pictured opposite).

The society was later renamed the "Vril Gesellschaft" or "Society of Vrilerinnen Women." The group, whose work was taken very seriously by Himmler and his circle, claimed to be in contact with Aryan beings living on Alpha Centauri in the Aldebaran system. Allegedly, these extraterrestrials had visited Earth and settled in Sumeria, the word "Vril" deriving from an ancient Sumerian word "Vri-ll" ("like god or God-like.") It is alleged that in collaboration with the SS Technical Branch E-IV Unit (Entwicklungsstelle 4), the Thule Society and the Luminous Lodge became possibly the first groups in  history to attempt the reverse engineering of a non-terrestrial spacecraft when it meticulously dissected the Freiburg craft to extract maximum military value. In addition to the SS occult and metaphysical research input, the project team also incorporated German quantum theory and the works of Nikola Tesla into the disc development programs.

Some believe that the Nazis also enlisted the assistance of negative entities in the astral dimension. Out-of-body investigator Robert A. Monroe[75] spoke of the whereabouts of Locale II, the astral region that is composed of our deepest desires and fears. Its location is founded on the wave-vibration concept, which presumes the existence of an infinite number of worlds all operating at different frequencies, one of which is the physical world. Each plane in the infinite web of worlds occupies the same area as our physical earth. In his celebrated Space Trilogy (*Out of the Silent Planet*, *Perelandra* and *That Hideous Strength*), C.S. Lewis referred to the astral entities as the "eldils," energies that represent dark chaos.

Jan von Helsing[76] claims that the outcome of this partnership was the development of a new form of propulsion based on the Luminous Lodge's obsession with the concept of power derived from the "Black Sun," an invisible eternal light with infinite power not visible to the human eye but existing in anti-matter (the Implicate Order.) It was

[75] Monroe, R., *Journeys Out Of The Body*, Anchor Press, New York, 1973
[76] Helsing, J., *Secret Societies and their Power in the 20th Century*, Ewertverlag S.L., Gran Canaria, 1995

180

called at that time "The Light of the Godhead."

Ultimately, these combined efforts led to the establishment of a project, the H-Gerät, to build a flying saucer craft named the Haunebu disc machine. The Thule Society financed the effort, the Vril Society provided overall project management and the SS Technical Branch built the machine under the highest security.

German aircraft historian Henry Stevens states[77] that Haunebu 1 was allegedly the first of the Flugscheiben (Flight Discs) developed in Germany. Plans allegedly obtained from SS files describe the Haunebu 1 as a flying saucer approximately seventy-five feet in diameter and powered by an electro-magnetic-gravitic type Tachyonator 7 drive. Stevens believes that it probably lifted off for the first time in August 1939.

Writer and academic, Joscelyn Godwin, has suggested that the Thule Society is linked with the work of Dr. John Dee, Queen Elizabeth I's astrologer and magician. Dee believed that specially constructed mirrors could be used to draw magical power from the sun to transmit messages and objects to the stars and distant planets. He said that a mirror propelled into space at a speed faster than light would reveal to man all the events of the past by reflection. Dee also believed in a system of a multitude of planes of existence, all occupying the same space but not interfering with one another. Dee's extraordinarily prescient ideas evidently presaged David Bohm's theories on the Implicate Order by four centuries.

In earlier pages I mentioned the Kecksburg, Pennsylvania, event of 1965. The topic has been comprehensively discussed elsewhere, not least by fellow AUP author Joseph P. Farrell and in the *Ancient Aliens* series of films. I will add only this fascinating adjunct. Henry Stevens mentions[78] German scientist Otto Cerny who spoke of a special Third Reich technology that utilized a concave mirror atop a device believed to be a reference to the Nazi Bell. The device was said to have been capable of generating images from the past. It would appear that the Nazis' much vaunted technological prowess was playing second fiddle to the incredible 400-year old space-time theories postulated by Elizabeth I's magus, Dr. Dee. Plus ça change.

In March 1937 Schmid finally delivered his opinion of de Mengel's research work. Schmid told Himmler[79] that in his professional opinion

[77] Stevens, H., *Hitler's Suppressed and Still-Secret Weapons, Science and Technology*, Adventures Unlimited Press, Illinois, 2007
[78] ibid
[79] Wegener, F., *Heinrich Himmler: German Spiritualism, French Occultism and the*

de Mengel's magnetic calculations were built on ancient insights and were correct but added that they would unfortunately be hardly understood by those who did not believe in the metaphysical aspects of the hard sciences. He concluded his report by saying that de Mengel's observations shed light on the profundity of thought of the Atlanteans and the Germanic and Indo-Germanic peoples, described by Schmid as the "Arian-Atlantisers World Circle."

Twelve weeks later Himmler's favourite: Brigadeführer Karl Maria Weisthor (formerly Wiligut), head of Section VIII, archives, of RuSHA (Rasse- und Siedlungshauptamt, principal race and population bureau of the SS), reported under "strictly confidential" to Himmler the text of a letter dated 23 June 1937. The letter, mailed from Helsinki, was from Gaston de Mengel who wrote:

"The axis, which is north east of Paris, works very well. But the axis is neither near Berlin nor Helsinki. I was able to calculate the origin of the forces from the average of the axis. It is in Murmansk (Lapland) approximately 35 degrees eastern length and 68 degrees northern breadth in the vicinity of Lowosereo (Lovozero) in Russia. I have also located the place of the big black centre. It is within the big triangle that is formed by Kobdo, Urumtschi and Bakul near Sinkinag in western Mongolia."

Significantly, Gaston de Mengel's co-ordinates tally closely with one of the favoured areas for the location of the mythical world of Shamballah.

Weisthor signed off his report to Himmler with this telling statement: *"In my opinion the Russians, after agreement with France and Britain, set up air bases there. The SD* (Sicherheitsdienst des Reichsführers-SS, the intelligence agency of the SS and the Nazi Party) *could try to find out if I am right."* Clearly, one obvious strategic reason for the three nations to establish air bases in a remote Mongolian location would have been the necessity to provide a stronghold from which to monitor and, possibly, to take defensive actions against uninvited extraterrestrial visitors.

Lovozero lies northwest of the Ural Mountains. I referred in the Rahn work to the 2002 Pravda report on the scientific findings at Bashkir State University in 1999 of a stone slab etched with a 3-D relief map of the Ufa region in the Republic of Bashkortostan between the Volga River and the Urals. The scientists believed that the map proves the existence of an extremely ancient and highly developed civilisation.

Tests indicated that the map was machined by precision tools and that it shows a view which could only have been plotted by aerial survey. It also shows precise details of massive civil engineering undertakings including irrigation and dams that would have required the removal of more than a "quadrillion" cubic metres of earth to construct. The scientists believe that the map is only a fragment of a much larger one that would have shown the entire surface of the planet.

At my request, earth energy science expert Captain Bruce Cathie kindly analysed de Mengel's co-ordinates. In successive studies Cathie had demonstrated that there exists on Earth an all-encompassing grid whose interlocking lines correspond to the lines of flight of UFO appearances. The grid is directly linked to ancient master artefacts, including the Great Pyramid, Stonehenge and the Aztec Pyramids. (Evans-Wentz was told by an Irish seer mystic that "fairy passes and paths are actual arteries...through which circulate the Earth's magnetism.")

The leyline structure of the grid has been likened to the Earth's etheric body. Cathie showed that the values of the grid reflect harmonic relationships with the speed of light, gravity and the mass of the earth. His studies indicate that volcanic activity, atomic disruption (nuclear bomb blasts) and earthquakes are all connected to the grid structure. The main plank of Cathie's work rests upon his observation that all major changes of physical state are caused by harmonic interactions of light, gravity and the mass of electrical and magnetic forces. The controlled manipulation of these resonant factors makes it possible to move mass from one point to another in space-time. Similarly, time can also be controlled by these manipulations of harmonic pulsations due to time's relationship to the speed of light.

Cathie subsequently reported to me his astonishing findings:

"It appears that the SS did have some knowledge of the grid and harmonic maths. The latitude and longitude you gave has connections with the harmonic 288 (twice the speed of light), and also the answer to one of the unified equations. They were getting close to the truth. Much is being kept hidden."

Mixing in Berlin's social circles, Otto Rahn became friendly with Russian Grigol Robakidse. Robakidse was a member of the Schwannen—the Order of the Black Swan. The Order was inaugurated in the eleventh century and was also known as the Guardian Order of the Grail. The Order is in existence today but in a form reconstituted in 1982 as The Order of the Noble Companions of the Swan, consisting of Knights from various Orders of Chivalry.

Among the religious leaders who have bestowed apostolic blessings on the Order is His Beatitude Maximos V, Patriarch of Antioch. This introduces us to a significant element of synchronicity because it is from within the U.S. based Catholic Apostolic Church of Antioch that information emerged purporting to add new levels of insight concerning the true agenda of Hitler and his backers.[80] The Antioch ministry is a little known but influential source for students of mystical ("new paradigm") Christianity, earth energies and associated esoteric history topics.

The source reports on the work of scientist Dr. Karl Obermayer. It relates that Obermayer was determined to repair a rip in the fabric of time brought about in 1923 by the Nazis' occult activities. The source claims that with the aid of Rudolph Steiner and Nikola Tesla, Obermayer set up a project in the Urals under the auspices of his Prometheus Foundation (an area that links geographically with Gaston de Mengel's triangle coordinates and its black centre.) The source reported that Obermayer's plan entailed opening a time window to the eleventh century and enlisting the aid of the Guardian Order of the Grail initiates. According to the source, Obermayer and his twentieth century allies and the eleventh century Black Swan initiates strove to prevent Hitler from opening a threshold by which negative forces from other dimensions could enter this world to help the Nazis secure their military and occult objectives.

All this sounds bizarre and utterly fantastical but one detects a thin thread of something real and profoundly disturbing running through the patchwork weave of these frankly crazy tales.

The villains of the piece are not the fairy folk of Magonia who, for the most part, are not inimical to humans even though their sense of mischief can often appear cruel. Here, the bad guys are jointly the "Inferniums," which derive from two camps.

In one are the negative and self-serving human cockroach types that had their beginnings here on Earth in the distant past, having been forced off the surface by self-induced cataclysmic upheaval as recently as 9,500 B.C. according to Edgar Cayce.

---

[80] *Temple Doors* and *Koala* publications 1995-1999, formerly accessible at: http://www.spiritmythos.org/misc/archives/archive-zips.html

The other camp is non-human in nature and hails from the astral and etheric soul-worlds. Metaphysical philosophers such as Manly P. Hall[81] have suggested that these planes are inhabited by energy forms fed and sustained by negative mass-conscious emanations streamed moment by moment by billions of humans.

The Nazis' esoteric and technological work on flying discs and the circumstances of numerous global instances of UFO crashes, particularly from the time of the Freiburg event, emphasise the baleful influence and presence of human and non-human agencies.

My belief is that their "infernal" liaison represents a very real and ongoing threat to humankind but one nevertheless that is monitored by powers vastly superior to either faction. More and more, I feel, we should be keeping an eye on the weather.

---

[81] Hall, M., *The Secret Teachings of All Ages,* The Philosophical Research Society, Inc., Los Angeles, 1928

"Oumuamua"—the mysterious object in our solar system that is exciting astronomers in 2017

Chapter 9

Psi-Fi

"The UFO phenomenon exists. It has been with us throughout history. It is physical in nature and it remains unexplained in terms of contemporary science. It represents a level of consciousness that we have not yet recognised and which is able to manipulate dimensions beyond time and space, as we understand them. It affects our own consciousness in ways that we do not fully grasp and it generally behaves as a control system."

—Jacques Vallée, *Forbidden Science*

Psychoanalytical interpretation of NHE activity provides an invaluable opportunity to peer several layers deeper into the phenomenon in one's quest for new insights.

Even in the very early days of UFO research astute minds were ascribing a psychic component to the phenomenon. The British science writer Gerald Heard in *Is Another World Watching* (1950) proposed his "bee" theory, in which UFOs represent a mindless order organised and controlled by a larger intelligence. Arthur C. Clarke said much the same thing, arriving at the conclusion that UFOs were paraphysical and not from other planets.

In his response to a letter from Randall Pugh and Frederick Holiday, John Keel said also that UFOs are related to psychic phenomena.[82] Keel believed that history, psychiatry, religion and the occult are far more important for an understanding of the flying saucer mystery than the publication of book after book that simply recount sightings.

Michael Gosso, too, advanced the idea that despite their encroachment into the world of matter UFOs are more akin to a psychic

[82] Keel, J. *Operation Trojan Horse*, Anomalist Books, San Antonio, 1970

projection than non-human intelligence. He said, "UFOs and other extraordinary phenomena are manifestations of a disturbance in the collective unconscious of the human species."[83]

To many analysts, the observed behaviour of UFOs indicates that they are evidently not constructed of solid matter and, hence, are paraphysical in nature. They move at incredible speeds but create no sonic booms. They perform impossible manoeuvres that defy the laws of inertia and appear and disappear instantly like phantoms.

In 1955, eight years after seeing a string of nine, shiny unidentified flying objects flying past Mount Rainier at speeds of 1,200 miles per hour, private pilot Kenneth Arnold expressed his view that spaceships were a form of living energy. Also in 1955, Air Marshall Lord Dowding (the man who directed the Battle of Britain in 1940) made the astonishing statement in a public lecture that the phenomenon was paraphysical, declaring that not only were UFO occupants immortal but also could make themselves invisible to human sight, take on human form and walk and work among us unnoticed.

In 1957 Ray Palmer, founder of *Flying Saucers* magazine, said that in his opinion UFOs hailed from civilisations with paraphysical ties to the human race. Earlier, in 1949, Palmer had already said that he believed UFOs to be extra-dimensional, not extra-terrestrial.

Engineer Bryant Reeve in his 1965 book *The Advent of the Cosmic Viewpoint* concluded that UFO sightings in themselves are irrelevant, subordinate in importance to the far more fundamental recognition that they are actually a part of a larger paraphysical phenomenon.

What is the paraphysical hypothesis? It is stated succinctly by RAF Air-Marshal Sir Victor Goddard, KCB, CBE, MA. On 3 May 1969 he delivered a public lecture in which he said:

"That while it may be that some operators of UFO are normally the paraphysical denizens of a planet other than Earth, there is no logical need for this to be so. For, if the materiality of UFO is paraphysical (and consequently normally invisible), UFO could more plausibly be creations of an invisible world coincident with the space of our physical Earth planet than creations in the paraphysical realms of any other planet in the solar system...Given that real UFO are paraphysical, capable of reflecting light like ghosts; and given also that, according to many observers, they remain visible as they

---

[83] Grosso, M., *"UFOs and the Myth of the New Age,"* in *Cyberbiological Studies of the Imaginal Component in the UFO Contact Experience*, ed. Dennis Stillings [St. Paul, Minnesota Archaeus Project, 1989], P. 81

change position at ultrahigh speeds from one point to another, it follows that those that remain visible in transition do not dematerialize for that swift transition and therefore, their mass must be of a diaphanous, very diffuse nature, and their substance relatively etheric...The observed validity of this supports the paraphysical assertion and makes the likelihood of UFO being Earth-created greater than the likelihood of their creation on another planet...The astral world of illusion, which (on psychical evidence) is greatly inhabited by illusion-prone spirits, is well known for its multifarious imaginative activities and exhortations. Seemingly, some of its denizens are eager to exemplify principalities and powers. Others pronounce upon morality, spirituality, Deity, et cetera. All of these astral components who invoke human consciousness may be sincere but many of their theses may be framed to propagate some special phantasm, perhaps of an earlier incarnation, or to indulge an inveterate and continuing technological urge toward materialistic progress, or simply to astonish and disturb the gullible for the devil of it."

In this remarkable statement Goddard (pictured below), a senior British establishment figure, astutely outlined the paraphysical hypothesis. Moreover, in describing the unholy alliance between the astral worlds and Nazi Germany Goddard broached what in his day was the taboo subject of the Hitler regime's preoccupation with occult matters.

The late John Napier, distinguished anthropologist and one time Visiting Professor of Primate Biology at London University and

Director of the Primate Biology Programme at the Smithsonian Institute, gave an opinion to Pugh and Holiday (a seemingly inveterate pair of letter-writers) on the humanoid format of UFO entities. Professor Napier said that as a result of the natural inclination of human reason to deny the existence of UFO humanoid types the only alternative explanation, if the establishment is intent on preserving the illusion of non-existence, is the "Great Conspiracy" theory. For Napier this latter option was equally unacceptable as it ignored the testimony of countless eyewitnesses or, absurdly, made them party to the "Great Conspiracy." Napier said that this must open the door to a third hypothesis, which is neither a matter of reason nor fakery, namely one that is unreasonable in human terms but entirely rational from the perspective of what Napier termed the "Goblin Universe." In this context, Napier observed, the third explanation must concern the minds of men.

In *Operation Trojan Horse* John Keel advanced the idea that somewhere in the vast electromagnetic spectrum there is an omnipotent intelligence able to manipulate energy, one that literally can bring phenomena into existence in this plane.

In contemplating the same topic, Paul Devereux suggested[84] that this manipulative energy is here on our doorstep. He believes that the Gaia energy of Earth is the source of input for the UFO form, wherein the entire planet is a single self-monitoring organism that enables the planet to dream forms into existence. During the Dyfed wave, for example, the silver robotic-looking entities at times appeared solid; at others they faded away as if they were components of someone's dream being dispelled upon waking.

Keel went on to ask: are there really UFOs at all? UFOs were being variously described as triangles, spheres, hexagons, flying cubes, cigar shapes and doughnuts dressed in dazzling arrays of colours and light formations. Keel reflected on this and decided that hard objects such as the disc and cigar shapes, for example, existed merely as "temporary transmogrifications." They would land, could be seen and touched and leave markings where they set down. Keel became convinced that these illusory forms are intended as decoys for the soft objects such as the dirigibles seen in the 1897 flap and the mysterious "Ghost Planes" observed over Scandinavia in the 1940s.

The "soft" crafts' abilities to exhibit bizarre forms of behaviour, make impossible turns and reach unheard of speeds lead some investigators to believe they that are in some sense sentient, maybe even alive. Keel concluded that the immense breadth of the phenomenon and the sheer number of sightings serves only to give the lie to its validity and makes it far more likely that UFOs are temporary extrusions from exotic energies originating in the higher bands of the electromagnetic spectrum.

Devereux believes that UFO entities are not travellers within a separate aeroform structure but that they are formed in the same way as the UFO shape itself and that they share the same substance, the one

---

[84] Devereaux, P., *Spirit Roads*, Collins & Brown, London, 2003

being merely a different aspect of one common phenomenon

In a similar vein, Jacques Vallée proposed[85] that UFOs are neither extraterrestrial nor the result of hoaxes or delusions but rather are a control system, which is intended to stabilise the relationship between man's conscious needs and the rapidly evolving complexities of living in the physical world. He believes that UFOs have both a visible reality (with mass, volume, inertia and so on) and a window to other planes of reality. Its occupants, he suggests, are creations from the dreamscape, a reality (Magonia) that intersects ours at right angles where we encounter and witness UFOs in the psychic planes of perception.

In Vallée's opinion UFOs neither fly nor are they objects; they materialise and dematerialise, violating in the process all known laws of motion. Vallée maintains that they are not necessarily an aspect of some form of an unknowable higher order of life but are products of a well defined and regulated technology, seemingly utterly bizarre by human standards. He suggests that the same power imputed to saucer people of influencing human events was once the exclusive property of fairies. He believes that the UFO phenomenon could be an "instance of a still undiscovered natural occurrence."

Vallée pondered on the oft-asked question as to whether it is necessarily true that we would detect meaningful patterns (by our objective standards) in the behaviour of a superior race. In his opinion, the inferior race would by necessity translate the seemingly absurd actions of the other as random impressions. For humankind's collective conscious to be able to see the underlying patterns in the superior race's actions would require a quantum leap in our evolutionary journey as a smart species. Understanding this, the superior race compensates for our lack of perceptive ability by limiting its communications to the level of signs and symbols and in the case of crop circles, for example, to pictographic and mathematical symmetry.

Keel believed also that, innately, humankind has always been aware of these special energies, largely by virtue of the ufonauts' practice to tailor their appearances in accordance with witnesses's personal beliefs and subconscious mores. This sleight of hand practice suggests that the objective of the UFO entities is to sew confusion. This "now you see it, now you don't" trickery ensures that observers never identify what cup is covering the ball. In the face of such powerful psychological control it is little wonder that man has always worshipped visiting gods.

It has long been observed that UFOs tend to form on or close to the

---

[85] Vallée, J., *UFOs: The Psychic Solution,* Panther Books Ltd, St. Albans, 1977

ground, the period of visibility rarely lasting longer than fifteen minutes or so. They can build up an inner shape and rise up into the atmosphere. During the Egryn Lights wave of 1904-1905 oval UFOs grew out of balls of fire with two brilliant arms protruding towards the earth. Between the arms were more lights, resembling a quivering star cluster.

The ability of UFOs to harden into the finally recognised form—spaceship, EBE Type I and II robots, little green man, big nose *et al*—demonstrates that the craft and their occupants can shapeshift, a phenomenon parallel to Jung's thinking that "there exists a yet unknown substrate possessing material and at the same time psychic qualities." In WWII observers reported that German foo fighters responded to their thoughts, suggesting that UFOs are sentient energies able to respond to percipients' mental processes.

Jacques Vallée made the observation[86] that many if not all materialisations of UFOs and their occupants are three-dimensional holograms projected through space, time and other dimensions, the same hypothesis applying to fairy-folk appearances. Moreover, he believes that materialisations are deliberately exposed to observers so that they will record their details and transmit them to others. This line of thinking suggests that the mechanisms underlying the phenomena and our belief in them derive from a single source.

John Michell, too, reflected on this topic. He remarked[87] that ufonauts' appearances as humanoids complete with spacesuits, breathing apparatus, radios, aerials and the like is a relatively new phenomenon. He pointed out that fairy witnesses see no such thing and that it is presumably something passed off by UFOlk convincingly for show. Michell noted the success of this trickery, which has been instrumental in spawning cultist beliefs about how we are visited by godlike men and angels from space.

Because fairies inhabit a different dimension contact has been likened to the operation of a short-wave radio that may crackle and then suddenly become clear for a few moments. It is believed that there are doorways to such realms located at special points throughout nature, such as exemplified in the Narnia stories.

In *The Coming of the Fairies*[88] Arthur Conan Doyle reflected upon the humanoid appearance of elemental spirits. He said that it was not clear what determines the shape observed by humans and how the

---

[86] Vallée, J., *Passport to Magonia*, Daily Grail Publishing, Brisbane, 2014.

[87] Michell, J., *The New View Over Atlantis*, Thames and Hudson, London, 1983

[88] Conan Doyle, A., *The Coming of the Fairies*, Hodder & Stoughton Ltd., London, 1922

transformation from their usual working body (small, hazy, luminous clouds of colour with a brighter spark-like nucleus) is affected. However, he suggested that human thought, either individually or in the mass, plays a key part in determining what percipients see.

Michael Talbot suggests[89] that UFO and fairy sightings are neither objective nor subjective but what he terms "omnijective," a concept mindful of the Hindu Tantric tradition, for example, that recognises no distinction between the mind and reality and between the observer and the observed.

Vallée spoke of the medium in which human dreams can be implemented and which serves as the mechanism that generates UFO events. He posited the existence of a natural phenomenon / field of consciousness, whose manifestations border on both the physical and the mental, "which serves as the mechanism that generates UFO events, obviating the requirement for a superior intelligence to trigger them."

It follows from these striking lines of thought that the task before one is not so much to seek to understand what UFOs are made of but rather to comprehend the phenomenon's effect on one's psychological and metaphysical states of being.

Jenny Randles and Peter Warrington[90] distinguished between "true" UFOs and "real" UFOs. The former are the lights in the sky seen from a distance, while the latter are those in which witnesses see much more detail or report greater contact. In the case of "real" UFOs, it is striking how many percipients display psychic tendencies; that other people present do not always see the same thing; and that such witnesses have a history of repeated UFO encounters or of poltergeist and other psychic manifestations. For example, Maureen Puddy of Australia swore she was being taken aboard a UFO even though she was in a car with two investigators during the whole time she was reporting the event! These kinds of experiences encouraged Randles and Warrington to propose replacing the term UFO to UAP—Unidentified Atmospheric Phenomenon.

One logical conclusion that can be drawn from these insights is that there may be no such thing as an objective UFO phenomenon. In this context the entire matter is a purely subjective process in which UFO forms and entities are drawn forth from the Implicate Order into the Explicate Order by the power of the mind.

---

[89] Talbot, M., *Mysticism and the New Physics*, Arkana, London, 1993
[90] Randles, J. & Warrington, P., *UFOs-A British Viewpoint*, Robert Hale Limited, London, 1979

Devereux proposes something different, suggesting, like Vallée, that there *is* an objective component but one that derives from a form of natural phenomenon not yet identified as such by present day science.

By 1950 Dr. Meade Layne, a proponent of an interdimensional hypothesis to explain flying saucer sightings, was directing his research efforts on the paraphysicality of UFOs and the parapsychological elements of the contactee syndrome.[91] Before founding Borderland Sciences Research Associates (BSRA) in San Diego Layne was professor at the University of Southern California, and English department head at Illinois Wesleyan University and Florida Southern College.

Layne's research bears a distinctly esoteric flavour. He believed that the separation of science from metaphysics and occultism is arbitrary and must be understood if one is to arrive at a totality of understanding on UFO matters and associated phenomena. In Layne's thinking the concepts of "here" and "there" are solely determined by frequencies, densities and wavelengths and not by spatial, three-dimensional considerations. He proposed that there are an infinite number of etheric planes or fields whose vibratory rates respond to finer forces such as those of mind and thought. He said that any thoughtform can be materialised in etheric matter and can be seen and touched at the appropriate rate of vibration. The discs are one such thoughtform, he maintained.

Layne believed that spacetime is manufactured by the self (by consciousness) and projected from it in extremely minute pulses. On the earth plane these impulses are chemical particles. Deep within the gross matter field (Bohm's Explicate Order) there exists a subtler field, the etheric plane (Bohm's Implicate Order.) It is from this latter order, Layne held, that solidified matter draws its maintenance energy in the physical world.

BSRA sought information from diverse sources, including trance mediums. From these came the disclosure that the release of atomic forces has greatly disturbed the etheric planes from which UFOs originate; hence, the purpose of their visits is to force our attention upon our infringing actions. The entities populating these planes (the "Ethereans" as Layne called them) belong to the human order of evolution but are vastly our superiors in science and intelligence. They

---

[91] Layne, M., *MAT and DEMAT: Etheric Aspects of the UFO*, Flying Saucer Review, Vol. 1, No. 4, 1955

are appearing in ever-larger numbers because our civilisation is on the point of collapse. They come also to make an examination and a final record in an anthropological sense.

Layne believed that the etheric regions (home to devas, elementals, fairies and the like) are the regions of life. There flourish civilizations and cultures (such as the Tuatha dé Dannan). They have knowledge of our world and can and do penetrate it.

The astral regions are the waiting-hall of the death and transition experiences. Negative energies on the astral plane and beings of lower intelligence that inhabit the cavern homes of the ancient Elder races and have use of electronic apparatus abandoned there are collaborating with negative-oriented humans.

UFOs and other strange emergent phenomena, Layne said, are simply the result of one form of matter merging with another with which it shares an affinity, the process sometimes taking place at such a high speed that an explosion occurs. A sudden explosion is but one way in which a dimension may merge with another, instantly regrouping to form new substance.

Aeroforms are the living bodies of etheric entities. The "vehicle" of an Etherian, whether this be his body or his "ship," is a thoughtform and a thoughtform can be positioned anywhere. All the aeroforms can pass through each other and through our dwellings at will and are (and always have been) invisibly present in great numbers.

Layne explained that the problems of space travel as we conceive them do not exist for the Etherian. By altering his vibratory rates the Etherian penetrates our seas and the substance of our globe as easily as he does our atmosphere. The "ship" and its "crew" become light waves or frequencies from the ether, all the while consciousness continuing to abide in the entities.

They are extradimensional "emergents"; that is, they extrude into our plane of perception from a spacetime frame of reference, which is different from ours. This process is marked by a conversion of energy and a change of vibratory rates. When the energy conversion takes place, the aeroform becomes visible and tangible. It appears as solid substance and remains so until the vibratory rate is again converted.

The "steel" of a landed disc is etheric steel and its "copper" is etheric copper, since the prototypes of all our metals exist equally in etheric matter. The conversion process is one of materialisation and dematerialisation (terms truncated by Layne to "mat and demat.") Layne emphasised that in the mat and demat processes there is *no* "crossing of space" involved at any time. There is simply a change of location, equivalent to a change of frequency or conversion of vibratory rates.

From Layne's channelling sessions came the message that there will come an "ether-quake," which shall be characterised by great disruption of magnetic and etheric fields. The sky will seem filled with fire. Landmasses will be displaced and great inundations will occur. After cataclysm the Ethereans will, as on many previous occasions, begin to hand down to Earth people the knowledge from before to assist in the gradual rebuilding of civilisation.

Remarkably, among the most profound insights on the UFO phenomenon are those that came from the founder of analytical psychology, Carl Gustav Jung.[92] Jung (pictured) concluded that myths, dreams, hallucinations and visions emanate from the same source. The reason why we are not all walking encyclopaedias is that we can only tap into the implicate order for information that is of direct relevance to our personal memories and which conforms to a system of personal resonance. Jung was greatly concerned that UFOs are powerful portents of rapidly approaching great changes and turned his attention to the phenomena to warn humanity of them. He described those things seen in the sky as "long-lasting transformations of the collective psyche."

If it were the case that UFOs are a psychological projection, Jung posited, there must be a powerful psychic cause for it because it is obviously an issue of great importance due to the thousands of sightings. He felt that the projection and cause must have a basis in an "emotional tension," having its cause in a situation of collective distress or danger, one that was very obvious at the time that Jung was writing in the Cold War era. Developing his thinking, Jung regarded UFOs as a "visionary rumour," akin to the collective visions such as those experienced by the crusaders of Jerusalem, the Fátima witnesses and the troops at Mons. He understood that visions are often given greater credence because oftentimes those who are least

---

[92] Jung, C.G., *Flying Saucers-A Modern Myth of Things Seen in the Skies*, Ark Paperbacks edition, London, 1987

credulous or most indifferent claim to see them most. Jung did not discount witnesses' reports of UFOs; in fact, he fully accepted that something was definitely seen. This led Jung to postulate the existence of a "yet unknown substrate possessing material and at the same time psychic qualities," a statement which may have inspired Vallée's recognition that UFOs emanate from the "medium in which human dreams are implemented."

> *"Precisely as in a dream it is our own will that unconsciously appears as inexorable objective destiny, everything in it proceeding out of ourselves and each of us being the secret theatre-manager of our own dreams, so also…our fate may be the product of our inmost selves, of our wills, and we are actually bringing about what seems to be happening to us."* Thomas Mann

The late British visionary, John Michell (pictured), enlarged on these remarkable aspects of Jung's thinking. In *The Flying Saucer Vision*[93] Michell suggested that it is probable that UFOs, having a nature and meaning outside our experience belong, like ghosts, to another order of matter and that their coming is a part of some approaching vision with which we shall soon be confronted. Michell also observed how often UFOs appear to percipients as if they are moving in their natural element like fish or fireflies rather than as mechanical craft. This supports the notion that we are visited by energies of other elements or dimensions, appearing in a way that conforms to what we expect of

them and related to the psychological condition of percipients. Jung associated UFOs with changes in the constellation of psychic dominants, of the archetypes or "gods" as they were once called which bring about or accompany long lasting transformations of the collective psyche. These changes take place in the mind as the sun comes under a new sign of the zodiac every 2,160 years (one Platonic Month) and portend great seasonal changes in mental attitudes and perceptions. Our entrance into the Age of Aquarius is, Jung said, provoking such

---

[93] Michell, J., *The Flying Saucer Vision*, Abacus, London, 1974

psychic changes. Michell agreed, saying:[94]

> *Maybe our hope of development and survival seems to lie in the achievement of a new, higher vision...It may be that flying saucers...are a portent of a future evolutionary step to be brought about through the working of some influence from outside the earth.*

Jung said that UFOs are an involuntary archetype or mythological conception of an unconscious content, a "rotundem" as the Renaissance alchemists called it, which expresses the totality of an individual. He was struck by the UFO discs' resemblance to the mandala, a magic circle that organises and encloses the psychic totality. In this symbology it is expressive of the archetype of the self, which comprises both the conscious and unconscious minds (the soul) and not merely the ego. He compared this notion to the Platonic belief that the soul is spherical, symbolic of the heavenly spheres. Plato spoke of the "supra-celestial place" where the "Ideas" of all things are stored up. Esoteric philosophy describes this spirit storehouse or library as the Akashic Record.

Ultimately, Jung arrived at what for him personally was an uncomfortable possibility. He speculated that UFOs might actually be living creatures of an unfathomable kind, one that is both a psychic projection and also an exteriorisation that assumes material attributes: a "materialised psychism." This exteriorisation comes not from physical space but rather from a mechanism in which an internal projection from the unconscious emerges onto conscious awareness.

This concept was developed very powerfully in the classic 1956 movie, *Forbidden Planet*, whose storyline also shares analogues with Shakespeare's *"The Tempest."* In the movie Dr. Edward Morbius (played by Walter Pidgeon) and his daughter Altaira (Ann Francis), the sole survivors of an expedition from Earth to the distant world Altair IV, are visited by 23rd century starship C-57D. Is mission is to determine the fate of the expedition's scientists. The investigation team, led by Commander John J. Adams (Leslie Nielson), faces a terrifying invisible intruder that kills a number of crewmembers.

Adams learns that Morbius has spent the past twenty years studying the technology of the Krells, Altair IV's former indigenous race. The Krells had developed the capacity to bring into physical existence anything that their minds could imagine. It turns out that in developing this technology the Krells had forgotten the one crucial thing that ultimately will always rob one of the power to control the thing created: the "Monsters from the Id."

---

[94] ibid

Mobius at first denies that his own mind is the source of the invisible entity's power but finally is forced to concede that his imagination is the murderous cuplrit. Mobius confronts and disowns his self-made Monster of the Id, which in a final act of vengeance turns on its creator and kills him.

Jung analysed many dreams that featured UFOs. In one case he commented on a woman's dream in which she saw a teardrop shaped UFO. He remarked that the drop was akin to the "aqua permanens" ("permanent water") of alchemic science and symbolised the "quinta essentia."

In ancient times the Greeks believed that all matter beneath the moon was made of varying combinations of the four elements: Earth, Water, Fire and Air. Above the moon, matter was made up of a fifth element they called *aither* or *pempte ousia*, in Latin the *quinta essentia*. The alchemists called it the Philosopher's Stone, which cures all illness, extends life and turns base metals into gold (the transmutation of day-to-day consciousness into a spiritual oneness with God). This process is mindful of Bohm's visualisation of something emerging from the Implicate.

On another occasion Jung remarked on a dream in which the UFOs were reminiscent of insects. This led him to speculate that nature could implement her "knowledge' in any number of ways, including evolving creatures capable of anti-gravity.

Evans-Wentz had already considered this topic. From his conversations with villagers who provided diverse descriptions of the Wee Folk and their archaic appearance, Evans-Wentz came to believe that nature herself has a memory. He held that there is a psychic element in the earth's atmosphere upon which human actions and phenomena are impressed like photographs on film. These imprints upon the invisible fabric of nature correspond to mental impressions, which under certain conditions one may play back like moving pictures. Evans-Wentz proposed that:

> *"the fairy Folk belong to a doctrine of souls; that it is to say it is a state of condition, realm or place very much like, if not the same, as that where men place the souls of the dead, in company with other invisible beings such as gods, daemons and all sorts of good and bad spirits."*

Jung was impressed by Orfeo Angelucci's book "The Secrets of the Saucers."[95] In it Orfeo meets with a man and a woman ("our older

---

[95] Angelucci, O., *The Secrets of the Saucers*, Amherst Press, 1955

brothers") who tell him they have a deep sense of brotherhood with Earthlings of whom they record details and vital statistics of every individual's life using crystal disks. They said that their craft was remotely controlled by a mothership but in reality they needed no such vessels as they were etheric entities and used them solely to manifest themselves materially to man. They said, "The speed of light is the speed of truth." Cosmic law forbids spectacular landings on Earth, which is threatened by greater dangers than was realised. They had been monitoring us for centuries but that we have only recently been entirely re-surveyed.

On 23 July 1952 Orfeo saw a huge igloo-shaped, misty soap bubble. He stepped inside into a vaulted room. There he was told that Earth is a purgatorial world among the planets in which there is evolving intelligent life but that every being on Earth was divinely created. Man had not kept pace morally and psychologically with his technological development so other planetary inhabitants were trying to instil a better understanding of their present predicament and to help them, especially in the art of healing.

Orfeo was encouraged to understand that everyone on Earth has a spiritual, unknown self that transcends the material world and consciousness and dwells eternally outside of the Time dimension in spiritual perfection within the unity of the Oversoul of Mankind. The sole purpose of human existence is to attain reunion with our "immortal consciousness." That Jung was in empathy with Agelucci's experience is suggested by the fact that he made very little comment on Orfeo's testimony, apparently happy in the epilogue of his work to let it speak for itself.

Angelucci's "older brothers" are portrayed as avuncular types with only our best interests at heart. Charles Fort struck a more cynical; some might say more realistic tone when he suggested that the human race may be no more than an alien civilisation's property that is the subject of a study rapidly reaching its climax.

Jung asked the fundamental question. If UFOs are something psychic that is equipped with certain physical properties, where do they come from? He said that the notion of a "materialised psychism opens a bottomless void under our feet" but he didn't go on to rule out the extraordinary proposition that the human mind is capable of creating and manifesting form. Subconsciously, Jung evidently accepted the existence of an implicate order and its etheric constituencies.

Compare Jung's remarks with Bohm's thinking on consciousness. As we have seen, Bohm believed that those who have shaken off the "pollution of the ages" could begin to generate the immense power needed to ignite the whole consciousness of the world. Bohm believed that in the depths of the Implicate Order there is a "consciousness, deep down…of the whole of mankind."

It is this collective consciousness of mankind that is truly significant for Bohm. He regarded it as truly one and indivisible, it being the responsibility of each human person to contribute towards the building of this consciousness of mankind, which he dubbed the "noosphere"—the sphere of human thought. In Bohm's opinion there is truly no other viable course of action. Bohm said, "There's nothing else to do; there is no other way out. That is absolutely what has to be done and nothing else can work."

Indicating that he was in tune with past inspirational philosophers, in particular visionary Jesuit priest, Teilhard de Chardin, Bohm also believed that the individual would eventually be fulfilled upon the completion of cosmic noogenesis, a term that refers to the inexorable movement of all the elements of the cosmos, including the biological human, toward ultimate totality. Referring to this principle of cosmic noogenesis, Bohm noted that as a "human being takes part in the process of this totality, he is fundamentally changed in the very activity in which his aim is to change that reality, which is the content of his consciousness." Here Bohm was intuiting that the human person and mankind collectively, upon accomplishing a successful noogenesis, will come to fullness within that greater dimension of reality termed the Cosmic Apex—the ground of all existence.

Bohm referred to this ultimate level—the source of the nonmanifest—as the Subtle Nonmanifest, something akin to spirit, a mover, but still matter in the sense that it is a part of the Implicate Order. For Bohm, the Subtle Nonmanifest is an "active intelligence" beyond any of the "energies defined in thought." Attempting to describe the Subtle Nonmanifest, Bohm stated that the "subtle is what is basic and the manifest is its result." Active intelligence, he posited, "directly transforms matter."

And, finally, Bohm told it straight: "There's a truth, an actuality, a being beyond what can be grasped in thought, and this is intelligence, the sacred, the holy," he wrote. For Bohm, the Cosmic Apex is a Holy Intelligence, the ultimate architect of the Implicate Order, the "Player"—the Godforce in mystical-metaphysical terminology.

We can finish on no higher authority. I see truth and insight in each of these experts' opinions. I concur with the essential thrust of their well formed arguments that "UFOs" and, by "Implicat(e)ion," their occupants, the citizens of Magonia whom in our present state of ignorance we label as fairies or ETs, are essentially a product of the Universal Mind, of which our individual minds are no less an integral part and no less powerful.

Bohm's ideas, and to an extent Jung's, suggest that the human mind not only occupies all dimensions of existence simultaneously but also, if required, could reconstruct them provided one had a manual. We already have the requisite tool—our consciousness. It follows from this recognition that the implicate part of our mind (of which we are wholly unaware under normal circumstances) creates and maintains the etheric worlds from which our aeroform friends originate. To my mind, UFOs and other unworldly visitations are, in a very real sense, materialisations from humankind's collective unconscious.

Our human mind exists in both the Explicate and Implicate Orders of reality. We are aware of the presence and the workings of that part of our mind that inhabits the Explicate. It is the part we use to traverse the physical, mental and emotional pathways our journey through life demands each and every moment between successive births and deaths.

In life we become dimly aware in dreams and visions of the part of the mind that resides in a sub-folder labelled "the Implicate," where there is complete and perfect understanding of the Magonia dimension and what UFOs and their occupants really are, for example. In the normal course of day-to-day living we are unable to access the information stored in this "anti-matter" cabinet but I believe that there are techniques available which, once mastered, may reveal how to turn a hidden eye upon its contents.

Ancient wisdom teaches that at the other end of the axis of mortal life, the moment of death, one's unlimited spirit sight sees the Implicate and Explicate orders for what they really are: two artificial divisions of the One Universal Mind.

We may dwell no longer on the Wee Folk and the UFOlk. In acknowledgement of Johnny Nash's immortal statement: "There are more questions than answers," it is time we turned to loftier topics.

Chapter 10

High Spirits

"Before the starry threshold of Joves Court
My mansion is, where those immortal shapes
Of bright aëreal Spirits live insphear'd
In Regions milde of calm and serene Ayr,
Above the smoak and stirr of this dim spot,
Which men call Earth..."

— John Milton, *Comus*

In this chapter we turn to a higher class of beings without whose invisible presence the natural world and, hence, humankind cannot exist. I refer to the Elementals. An Irish mystic told Evans-Wentz that the Elementals draw their power out of the "Soul of the World."

What is an Elemental? They have been called the pulse or lifeforce of God, the Universal Mind, the Godforce, Jehovah and countless other names. They flow through the unseen veins of nature. Ancient wisdom described them as nature's living essence, through whose portals men and women find their spirit and a corresponding sense of immortality and universality. It taught that the Elementals are the caretakers of nature. They are always near us but one must have a daily, reverential immersion in nature to begin to feel and perceive their magical presence. Throughout history men have mistaken nature spirits for angels, demons and other supernatural forms.

"The Minstrel crossed his right ankle over the left and spread his arms outwards in the shape of a cross. With eyes closed, he relaxed and listened to the silence. At length, after what seemed like hours, he felt something on his right hand. He opened his eyes but saw nothing. He closed his eyes once more and adopted his relaxation posture. Presently, he felt something soft upon his left hand. This time he barely

opened his eyes and squinted through his eyelashes. He was amazed to see small balls of light moving up his left arm. Moments later he saw the same wispy movement on his right arm and then up both of his legs. Just as he about to open his eyes wide the movement stopped. He thought to himself, "Who or what are these things?"

"We are Elementals, Minstrel," came the immediate mental reply.

"Oh, my God, they can read my thoughts," the Minstrel said to himself. "How do I censor them?"

"We do not read your thoughts, Minstrel! Thoughts are energy. Thoughts create words. You may think that your thoughts are private, known only to you. To us, the Elementals, and those that are bonded to the inner powers of nature, thoughts have sound and are like the spoken word."

"That means I have no privacy, I am not an individ..."

The Elementals cut in. "If you are in physical balance, then you will have contact with the Elementals. Your thoughts will be pure and filled with the truths of the universe. What you think will not be harmful, infringing, spiteful or judging. Only then will you be able to see us and to communicate with us."

"Frankly, that would be a very boring world," countered the Minstrel. "What would I find to sing about?"

"The observer sees, hears, smells, tastes and touches but does not allow themselves to have a negative reaction to their senses. You can sing of what you see and hear but you do not have to judge it."

"This is getting scary. I'm having a conversation with a bunch of lights without using my voice. I must be losing my mind!"

"We are the pulse of your God, whoever or whatever you feel your God is," said the Elementals. "As blood flows through veins, so we flow through the unseen veins of nature. The beauty you see in a woman is enhanced a thousandfold when you see her through the subtle power of nature."

The Minstrel opened his eyes. There, standing on his chest, was a small elf-like man. Flashing a broad smile and twinkling eyes, he stood there completely naked. "Who are you, where did all the lights go and why are you naked?" the Minstrel asked in alarm.

"I am those lights," explained the elf-man, "and I am the composite of what your mind wants me to be in order that it can begin to comprehend a reality behind the physical and the five senses. I am the wind, rain, earth and fire all in one. Although I am an Elemental, my energy or my essence is in the form that you want it to be. You sing of the little people of the Celts who live in the forest and dance and sing. You have heard of the sprites of the water and the sylphs of the air...I am a composite of those. It is because you mind doesn't know how to clothe me that I am naked!"

The Minstrel felt a slight shift in movement. Opening his eyes once more he saw sitting cross-legged on his chest the most beautiful maiden he had ever seen. She, too, was naked. "Oh no, I'm in trouble now. I can't concentrate with someone so beautiful and nude sitting on my chest. I want the little man back!"

"Pure powerful energy has no form," said the Elemental. "It is only when your mind tries to put form to it that energy loses its power. When you play your lute the music is energy...there is no form. When you walk or move you create energy...there is no form. Minstrel, pure, powerful energy is God. It is through the pulse of God—the Elementals—that you reach the heights within yourself.

"We are the spirit that pulsates through nature. Your spirit pulsates through the body that you have chosen for this lifetime. Our elemental spirit and your spirit are related, something like brother and sister. You have come to this earth to feel, express and project your spirit. When you do that you will discover that your God is actually you. We are neutral and, as a human, your neutrality will lead to personal control. It will free you from the spectacle of seeing yourself the way you feel others want you to be."

A Languedoc Minstrel's Solstice adventure, Winter 999 A.D.

The story of the Minstrel's adventure has been handed down to storytellers through the generations. Whether it is a parable or a true tale is immaterial, although I like to think that it is not beyond the bounds of possibility for one to communicate directly with the nature spirits. There have been accounts from people drowning who have been saved by the intervention of brightly coloured balls of light that have literally pulled them out of the waves and propelled them to safety.

This extract from the Minstrel's millennial tale is impressive because it provides an insight, one thousand years before Bohm, into the workings of the Implicate Order and of the Architect that brought it into existence before the beginning of "Explicate" time.

The elf man and his analog, the beautiful maiden, teach the Minstrel of the unlimited power of the mind, of the strength of being an observer rather than remaining a slave to the senses and of the vital understanding that humans and the higher powers are divine sibling energies, which flow together through the Subtle Nonmanifest form of the Cosmic Player.

In alchemic philosophy the substance of the Implicate Order was termed the "ether." It is that part of the body of the universal logos out of which are extracted the four creative principles: physical (earthly),

206

etheric (watery), astral (fiery) and mental (airy).

In his study of "Unseen Forces"[96] acclaimed twentieth century mystical-metaphysical philosopher, Manly P. Hall (1901-1990), explained that the ancients symbolised these four principles or vehicles as the arms of the cross representing the major crossing points of the vital forces in the human body. These intersecting points of the etheric world have their seat in the solar plexus and spleen. The etheric world is often referred to as the molten sea for in its depths the soul must ultimately be washed and purified. As each kingdom of nature in the outer world of earth life has diverse lives evolving through it, so the four divisions of ether inhabited by intelligent life forms are evolving through the four elemental essences.

In the West, serious study of the Elementals did not fully emerge until the time of Swiss physician, alchemist and astrologer, "Paracelsus," born Philippus Aureolus Theophrastus Bombastus von Hohenheim (1493-1541, illustrated below). A giant figure of the German Renaissance, Paracelsus immersed himself in the study of occult pneumatology: the branch of philosophy that deals with spiritual substances. Paracelsus believed that each of the four primary elements (earth, fire, air, and water) consists of two parts: a subtle, vaporous etheric (Implicate) principle and a gross corporeal (Explicate) substance.

In this analogy Air is twofold in nature, comprising a tangible atmosphere and an intangible, volatile substratum that may be termed spiritual air. Fire's visible nature also has an indiscernible quality in the

form of a spiritual, ethereal flame. Water consists of a dense fluid and a potential essence of a fluidic nature. Earth's twofold nature comprises a lower part, which is fixed, terreous and immobile, and a higher that is rarefied, mobile, and virtual. Ancient doctrine taught that the four Elements are under the rulership of the great body-building Devas, the Lords of Form, also known as the four-headed Cherubim that stood at the gates of the Garden of Eden and which also knelt upon the mercy seat of the Ark of the Covenant. Matter was believed to be the

---

[96] Hall, M., *Unseen Forces*, Philosophical Research Society, Inc., Los Angeles, 1978

product of the geometrical outpourings of the Lords of Form. Minerals, plants, animals and men live in a world composed of the gross part of the four elements. From various combinations each element constructs their living organisms.

According to Paracelsus, just as visible nature is populated by a vast number of living creatures its invisible spiritual etheric counterpart is similarly populated by unique life forms. He gave these forms the name Elementals. Later, they became known more widely as nature spirits. Paracelsus divided these beings of the elements into four distinct groups: gnomes (of the Earth), undines (Water), sylphs (Air) and salamanders (Fire). Crucially, Paracelsus taught that they are living entities, many resembling human beings.

Members of each group are fashioned out of the corresponding ether in which they exist. It is believed that the sylphs, salamanders and nymphs had much to do with the oracles of the ancients; that, in fact, they were the ones who spoke from the depths of the earth and from the air above.

Paracelsus said that the Earth is not just our visible spinning ball but that it comprises other, more subtle dimensions that are home to the higher powers of Nature.

It is these invisible "mansions" in the "house" of the Earth that accommodate, in the words of the Minstrel's elf man, "*the Elementals and those that are bonded to the inner powers of nature.*" Paracelsus explained that we are unable to see these higher dimensions because our undeveloped senses are incapable of functioning beyond the limitations of the grosser parts of the elements.

The Elementals' individual kingdoms dwell at the four corners of the Earth: the gnomes in the North, the undines in the West, the salamanders in the South and the sylphs in the East.

The wood beings are a shiny, silvery colour with a tinge of blue or pale violet and dark purple coloured hair.[97]

The king of the water beings sits on a throne under a lake in the West of Ireland. He is coloured blue and orange. Under his throne is a fountain of mystical fire. With him under the lake by his throne are pale grey beings. They place their head and lips near the elemental king and in touching him become plumed and radiant, shooting upwards as if given new life by their king.[98]

---

[97] Evans-Wentz, ibid
[98] ibid

Theosophist Edward L. Gardner described the life, work and appearance of the Nature Spirits:[99]

> *The life of the nature spirit, nearly the lowest or outermost of all, is active in woodland, meadow and garden, in fact with vegetation everywhere, for its function is to furnish the vital connecting link between the stimulating energy of the sun and the raw material of the form-to-be. The growth of a plant from seed, which we regard as the "natural" result of its being placed in a warm and moist soil, could not happen unless nature's builders played their part. Just as music from an organ is not produced by merely bringing wind-pressure and a composer's score together, but needs also the vital link supplied by the organist, so must nature's craftsmen be present to weave and convert the constituents of the soil into the structure of a plant. The normal working body of the sprites, used when they are engaged in assisting growth processes, is not of human nor of any other definite form...They have no clear-cut shape and their working bodies can be described only as clouds of colour, rather hazy, somewhat luminous, with a bright spark-like nucleus...Although the nature spirit must be regarded as irresponsible, living seemingly a gladsome, joyous and untroubled life, with an eager enjoyment of its work, it occasionally leaves that work and steps out of the plant, as it were and instantly changes shape into that of a dimunitive human being, not necessarily then visible to ordinary sight but quite near to the range of visibility. Assumed in a flash, it may disappear as quickly.*

According to Paracelsus the *gnomes* (female gnomes are called gnomides) live in a world the Norse people call Elfheim. Their king is Gob. They are able to penetrate into the very core of the earth. They have charge over the solids, bones and other tissues of the human body. No bone could set without them. Some work with the stones, gems, and metals and are supposed to be the guardians of hidden treasures. Gnomes build houses of substances resembling alabaster, marble and cement but only the gnomes know the true nature of these materials, which have no counterpart in physical nature. They live in caves, far down in what the Scandinavians called the Land of the Nibelungen. In Wagner's opera cycle, The Ring of the Nibelungen, Alberich makes himself King of the Pygmies and forces these little creatures to gather for him the treasures concealed beneath the surface of the earth.

---

[99] Gardner, L.E., *Fairies: A Book of Real Fairies*, The Theosophical Publishing House, London, 1945

Tree and forest sprites also belong to the company of the gnomes. Here one finds the sylvestres, satyrs, pans, dryads, hamadryads, durdalis, elves, brownies and little old men of the woods. Some families of gnomes gather in communities, while others are indigenous to the substances with which they work. For example, the hamadryads live and die with the plants or trees of which they are a part.

Every shrub and flower is said to have its own Nature spirit, which often uses the physical body of the plant as its home. The archetypal form of gnome most frequently seen is the brownie, or elf, a mischievous little creature from twelve to eighteen inches high, usually dressed in green or russet brown. Most of them appear as very aged, often with long white beards, their figures inclined to rotundity. They can be seen scampering out of holes in the stumps of trees and sometimes they vanish by actually dissolving into the tree itself. Most of them are of a miserly temperament, fond of storing things away in secret places.

There is abundant evidence that children, retaining a degree of attachment to the invisible worlds in their early years, often see the gnomes, such as during the occasions of the Little Blue Man of Studham and the Gnomes of Wollaton.

The *undines* comprise the limoniades, nymphs, niaids, mermaids, oreades, sirens, oceanids, potamides, harpies, sea-daughters and sea-goddesses of ancient lore. Their ruler is Necksa. Beauty is the cornerstone and key feature of their power. They govern the liquids and vital forces in plants, animals and human beings. There are many groups of undines such as the Naga-Maidens of the Hindus that dwell in pools and streams.

The water spirits do not establish homes in the same way that the gnomes do but live in coral caves under the ocean or among the reeds growing on the banks of rivers. Some inhabit waterfalls where they can be seen in the spray; others are indigenous to swiftly moving rivers; some have their habitat in dripping, oozing fens or marshes, while other

groups dwell in clear mountain lakes. Diminutive undines live under lily pads and in little houses of moss sprayed by waterfalls. According to the philosophers of antiquity, every fountain had its nymph; every oceanwave its oceanid. Often the water nymphs derived their names from the streams, lakes or seas in which they dwelt.

In describing the undines, the ancients agreed on certain common features. In general, nearly all the undines closely resemble human beings in appearance and size, though the ones inhabiting small streams and fountains are of correspondingly lesser proportions. It was believed that these water spirits are occasionally capable of assuming the appearance of normal human beings and actually associating with men and women. When seen, the undines generally resemble the goddesses of Greek statuary. There are many legends about these spirits and their adoption by the families of fishermen but in nearly every case the undines heard the call of the waters and returned to the realm of Neptune, the King of the Sea.

Among the Celts there is a legend that Ireland was once peopled by a strange race of semi-divine creatures. With the coming of the modem Celts they retired into the marshes and fens, where they remain even to this day as Elemental undines.

The *salamanders* are the strongest and most powerful of the elementals. Their ruler is a magnificent flaming spirit called Djin, terrible and awe-inspiring in appearance. In both animals and men, the salamanders work through the emotional nature by means of the body heat, the liver and the blood stream. Without their assistance there would be no warmth.

Philosophers were of the opinion that the most common form of salamander is lizard-like in shape, a foot or more in length, and glows fiercely as it twists and crawls in the midst of the fire. Another group was described as huge flaming giants in flowing robes, protected with sheets of fiery armour. One important subdivision of the salamanders was the Acthnici. These creatures appear only as indistinct globes.

Arthur Rackham's Undine figure

Paracelsus' representation of a Salamander Elemental

They float over water at night and occasionally appear as forks of flame on the masts and rigging of ships (St. Elmo's fire).

The *sylphs* are composed from the finest ether of the four elements. Female sylphs (represented below) are called sylphids. Among their many appellations, the sylphs are the riders of the night, the wind-born, the storm angels and the air-devas. Their leader is Paralda who is said to dwell on the highest mountain of the earth. To the sylphs were given the eastern corner of creation. Their temperament is mirthful, changeable and eccentric. They have no fixed domicile but wander about from place to place in the manner of elemental nomads, invisible but ever-present powers in the intelligent activity of the universe. They move from castle to castle built out of the ether of the air element, which is the reflection of the mental plane.

The sylphs sometimes assume human form but for only short periods of time. Their size varies but in the majority of cases they are no larger than human beings and often considerably smaller. It is said that the sylphs have accepted human beings into their communities and have permitted them to live there for a considerable period. They are always busy and work with the thoughts of living creatures. They work directly with the airy elementals of man's body such as the gases and ethers that have gathered within the body and indirectly with the nervous system. To the sylphs the ancients gave the labour of modeling the snowflakes and gathering clouds, accomplishing the latter with the help of the undines who supply the moisture. The sylphs are the highest form out of all the elementals, their native element being the highest in vibratory rate. They live hundreds of years, often attaining to a thousand years and never seeming to grow old. The Greek Muses are believed to have been sylphs for these spirits are said to gather around the mind of the dreamer, the poet and the artist and inspire one with their intimate knowledge of the beauties and workings of Nature. The peculiar qualities common to men and women of genius are supposedly the result of the cooperation of sylphs. The sylphs wield a powerful influence over things where the air is an

important factor. Hence, during the air-age of the next 2,000 years their influence will be keenly felt.

In the Welsh tale of Kulhwch and Olwen, Kulhwch discovers Camelot to be a fairy court where there is much feasting and carousing. Among Arthur's retinue was Henbedestyr, a sylph with whom no one could keep pace either on horseback or on foot, and Sgilti Yscawndroed, another spirit of the air who never had to find a path to deliver a message to his king but instead ran over the tops of trees. Never once in his whole life did he bend a blade of reed-grass beneath his feet.

Another of Arthur's subjects in the fairy court was Gwynn ab Nudd, the ruler of the devils of Annwn, known in Irish folklore as Nuada of the Silver Hand, king of the Tuatha dé Dannan and ruler of the Fairies and the Elves. It is evident that long ago Arthur was regarded not as a material person but as a highborn personage who lived in the fabled land of the Elementals. As the Once and Future King he resides there still, continuing to teach seekers of the truth the secrets of Nature and of Creation.

Among the mooted locations for Arthur's fairy court is the Scottish Isle of Arran, identified with Annwyn, a name for the Otherworld and the home of the Cauldron of Plenty. 6th century Welsh bard Taliesin, said to be the reincarnation of Merlin, wrote that The Nine Ladies of the Lake who travelled with Arthur on his funeral barge were the guardians of the magic cauldron of the Grail. The Nine were a secret sisterhood, each of whom embodied different characteristics of the Sacred Feminine, which are at the core of the Arthurian mysteries. Geoffrey of Monmouth said that Avalon was ruled by nine sisters, three of whom were Arthur's mother Igraine (of fairy blood), Gwenhwyvar and enchantress Morgan le Fay.

The Welsh poem "Preiddeu Annwyn" describes the Celtic Otherworld as having three regions. One is the Land of the Silent Dead where the Lost Ones are kept in a glass fort known as Caer Wydyr or Nennius, according with the stories of gold and crystal palaces in Fairyland. A second is Caer Feddwidd, the Fort of Carousa ruled by Arianrhod, Goddess of Time, Karma and Destiny. Caer Feddwidd is blessed with a mystical mountain of wine, which offers eternal youth for whose who elect to spend their immortality in the afterlife. The third region is Avalon, the most divine realm, known as the Vale of Apples. Only those that had made great sacrifices could enter here, its most illustrious inhabitant being Arthur.

Christian mystic Emmanual Swedenborg (1688-1772) was

214

renowned for his ability to journey in full consciousness into the spirit worlds. He spoke of the elemental balls of light, describing them as (holographic) thought balls that the angels use to communicate. He remarked that these thought-balls are no different from the portrayals he could see in the "wave-substance" (the aura) that surrounds a person. He described these telepathic bursts of knowledge as a picture language so dense with information that each image contains a thousand ideas.

Swedenborg made many astonishing remarks that pre-empted Bohm and Pibram's theories by more than two hundred years. He said that although human beings appear to be separate from one another, we are all connected in a cosmic unity. Moreover, each of us is a heaven in miniature and every person, indeed the entire physical universe, is a microcosm of the greater divine reality. He also believed that underlying visible reality is a wave-substance.

In fact, several Swedenborg scholars have commented on the many parallels between Swedenborg's concepts and Bohm and Pribram's theories. Dr. George F. Dole, a professor of theology at the Swedenborg School of Religion in Newton, Massachusetts, and with degrees from Yale, Oxford and Harvard, notes that a basic tenet of Swedenborg's thinking is that our universe is constantly created and sustained by two wavelike flows, one from heaven and one coming from our own soul or spirit. Dole remarks upon these images' striking resemblance to a hologram.

Remarkably, Swedenborg believed that, despite its ghostlike and ephemeral qualities, heaven is actually a more fundamental level of reality than our own physical world. It is, he said, the archetypal source from which all earthly forms originate and to which all forms return, a concept very close to Bohm's idea of the Implicate and Explicate Orders.

In addition Swedenborg believed that the afterlife realm and physical reality are different in degree but not in kind, and that the material world is just a frozen version of the thought-built reality of heaven. The matter that comprises both heaven and earth "flows in by stages" from the Divine, said Swedenborg, and "at each new stage it becomes more general and, therefore, coarser and hazier and it becomes slower, colder and more viscous."

Manly P. Hall enlarged upon the descriptions of the energies that inhabit these stages of Creation. He explained[100] that in addition to the Elementals there are two additional classes of elemental spirit: the

---

[100] Hall, ibid

Dweller at the Threshold—a person's individual elemental, and the man-created elementals of the astral and mental planes: ghosts, revenants, shades, spectres, and larvae. The larvae are the etheric shells of individuals that after death drift into the astral plane and very gradually disintegrate. While not imaginary beings, the larvae are the offspring of the imagination.

Differing widely from the elementals is the vampire, which is defined by Paracelsus as the astral body of a person either living or dead (usually the latter state). The vampire seeks to prolong existence upon the physical plane by robbing the living of their vital energies and misappropriating such energies to its own ends.

The beast that blocks the way of the ascending spirit to the higher planes is a concentrated energy of unpaid karma. It is the Dweller or Guardian of the Threshold that after death we must confront and go beyond. The price of entry into the higher Temple world is the conquest of our own lower nature.

Hall also expounds on the concept of an invisible patron spirit of man known as the *natal daemon*, an entity analogous to the totem of the North American Indian. The natal daemon is coexistent with the soul of the individual. Philosophers regarded it as the personified aggregate of past experiences in all past lives and synonymous with man's instinctive impulse-nature. It is the composite self: the transcendental by-product of a man's temporal experiences in the physical world.

The Egyptians believed that the natal daemon is created at the time of birth through the convergence of celestial rays. Plato believed that this daemon or familiar is allotted to every human to serve as patron saint and guide of one's outer life. It is one's consciousness born of experience. The natal daemon is regarded as the supreme flower of the soul, which is the garment woven from the threads of everyday living. This supra-physical entity is a perfect guardian and speaks with us in dreams, signs and symbols and, when occasion demands, *in manifestation* to redirect one to the positive path in life.

Slaying the Jabberwocky, symbol for the "Dweller at the Threshold"?

The Elementals are the makers of the circles in the fields. On 7 June 1999, Dutch teenager Robbert saw a light making a circle near his home in the village of Hoeven in Holland. During the previous two years Robbert had seen unusual lights in his neighbourhood. In 1997, while riding his bike through a crop field, he saw hundreds of glowing spheres the sizes of tennis balls and grapefruit. Some approached and began circling him. The next thing he knew, he was waking up on the ground in the middle of a new circle.

On that early summer day in 1999 Robbert saw a small, misty, pinkish-purple light, more (American) football shaped than a sphere but slightly smaller. It was entering the field at a height of about 10 feet. It came to a spot 150 feet behind his house where it hung in the air before elongating, becoming thinner and thinner until it resembled a disc. He saw electrical discharges emitted from the bottom of the disc. After these ceased he went to look and saw two circles in the wheat, one of 30-feet diameter and another nearby of 10-feet diameter.

Robbert received mental impressions from the lights: the circle makers. He understood that the formations are very, very important and are somehow connected to what he thinks are angels. Humans should be paying attention to them. The circles have something to do with problems in the environment and with deceit. The crop circles, he says, are like an antidote but he has absolutely no idea what that means or why he is involved. Robbert described seeing or sensing a female figure associated with one of the lights or that was transformed from one of the lights.

There is much speculation that the advanced intelligence making the crop circles is trying to wake us up to our past and present so that we will have a future.

Interestingly, 20% of all circles are preceded by a UFO sighting. John Michell told Michael Hesemann[101] that crop circles are not just connected to the UFO phenomenon; both are expressions of the same phenomenon. The mysterious lights in the sky, the peculiar noises and the strange effects and things which people experience in connection with crop circles indicate this.

Abductee Linda Porter poses a radical notion. She believes that crop circles are subliminal messages; that they are harbingers for the arrival of huge alien, city ships that will appear and then dematerialise certain people on Earth and take them aboard just prior to cataclysm. That is as maybe.

---

[101] Hesemann, M., *The Cosmic Connection*, Gateway Books, Bath, 1996

The overlapping arcs in the Cherhill Down formation in Wiltshire in August 1993 are mindful of the Old European script symbol called "lu" that means light. This sacred writing was used in Goddess worship between 5,300 and 4,300 BC to inscribe religious objects and to communicate between man and the gods. It would appear that the Elementals are seeking to enlighten mankind and direct its focus on taking actions that honour the Earth and not advance its destruction.

Some have wondered if crop circles, created by the Elemental balls of light in one powerful movement, are intended to provide mathematical insight, which, once understood, will help mankind to restore its reverence for the Earth. Linda Moulton Howe poses the question: "Could something out there be trying to reinforce the idea that our universe and all its energy and mass are defined by a repeating feedback loop that is mathematical in evolution and powered by consciousness?"

Much of the language of "Lu" is mathematically oriented. Patterns in circles identified by Professor Gerald Hawking that display alphanumeric codes correspond to diatonic ratios (white piano keys): C 1, D 9/8, E 5/4, F 4/3, G 3/2, A 5/3, B 15/8, H 2, I 9/4… Hawking calculated that the probability of random occurrence is 1:25,000. He describes it as "frozen music," which is how the Ancient Greeks defined geometry.

In March 1987 Medium Isabelle Kingston received a communication at Ogbourne St George in Wiltshire in connection with Silbury Hill at Avebury. The Watchers, she was told, are the Universal Powers, the guardians of this planet. They told Kingston that they instigated the construction of Silbury Hill for the purposes of helping humankind in the future. Avebury, they said, is energetically linked with places of worldwide power. It is their present task to prepare Earth for the New Jerusalem, a New Age. Kingston understood that the circles in the fields have a multi-layered meaning, comprising many components in which many types of energy are coming together from the earth and from the universe. The Nature realms and spiritual spheres are creating formations with a profound effect on those people who see and explore them. They are created in an energy form, a form of consciousness, *possibly out of our own self, possibly from other spheres and dimensions* (my italics). The Watchers explained that England is located at the centre of a great pyramid of light, which they had established long ago. Silbury means "Hill of the Shining Ones." It is the very centre of activity, a vibrant energy centre, the *axis mundi* (the world centre).

218

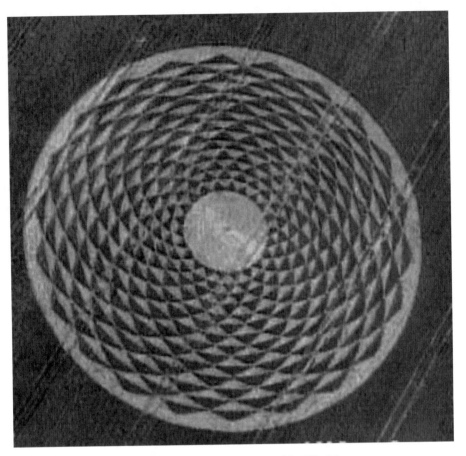

"Flower of Life," Woodborough Hill, Wiltshire

For this purpose they are "charging" the "ley lines" at various points, visible as the patterns of circles in the fields. The Watchers said:

"This old country (England) holds the balance. It is the key to the world. The pyramid power is the key, in your understanding a button that must be pressed for activation. You are your planet's immune system, the healing system, which will create the changes but there are other keys that must be activated.

"This country is a test area. It has to be right before the whole can be lined up with the other dimensions. Things are changing at Stonehenge, an energy field is above the stones. Some circles are the exact dimensions of Stonehenge. Circles have appeared as a blueprint for humankind to mark that place as a place of power. It is as if these places are being unlocked. Centres are being awakened; it is part of the plan."

Later, in 1991, Isabelle was told:

"Go to the hills and call for the Brethren. Link yourselves wth the Cosmos and draw the energies in to help. Become lightning conductors. Channel the light into the very soil. Transfer it into pure love and wait for the explosion."

The Watcher's advice to Isabelle Kingston to "go to the hills and call for the brethren" is as relevant today as it was in 1987, in fact much more so. The Elementals are not shirking their toil in the fields to prise open our eyes, nor should we let up on our efforts to understand the signs in the circles. So much rests on our ability to interpret the messages and to act accordingly.

*

"Don't be lazy, look you, but get out of bed, and let's go out into the fields dressed as shepherds, as we decided to. Perhaps we shall find the lady Dulcinea behind some hedge, disenchanted and as pretty as a picture."

Cervantes, *Don Quixote*

It is between the lines of comical passages such as Don Quixote's tilting at windmills that one begins to get a true sense of what Cervantes was really seeking to convey to his readers. The Knight of the Rueful Countenance dared to dream the impossible dream. He saw beauty where others could not. He recognized in Aldonza Lorenzo not an unattractive, overweight farm girl but a Goddess, Dulcinea, his "queen and lady, her beauty superhuman, all the impossible and fanciful attributes of beauty which the poets apply to their ladies, verified in her." Cervantes' masterpiece is a parable of a unique man's quest to journey to his inner worlds of enchantment and to find the Goddess Queen in her Castle.

The pathway to our Lady, to our Knight, is to be found in the labyrinths in the fields. We should not take the geometry and fractal elegance of the circles at face value but, instead, perceive them in a new way in order to unlock the "frozen music" and add some compositional flare of our own. This music is etheric in frequency and form. It is an emanation of the Implicate. I believe that little by little its powerful vibrations are opening a corridor to higher dimensions of nature

("Magonia plus") through which light from the Cosmic Apex may flow to reinvigorate a planet that is in dire need of healing.

If we stand back and observe carefully, the little balls of Elemental energy shall light the way for those whose capacity to dream is undiminished.

Chapter 11

"Once Upon a Time..."

"To see a World in a Grain of Sand
And a Heaven in a Wild Flower,
Hold Infinity in the palm of your hand
And Eternity in an hour."

—William Blake, *Auguries of Innocence*

We conclude *The Landing Lights of Magonia* with a handful of enchanting "once upon a time" tales. Some have been handed down through the generations; others are accounts of more recent events. What binds them in common is that they each tell of a person's remarkable encounter with a special figure, energy or consciousness from a higher dimension of reality: for want of a better phrase—the "heaven world" or Tír Na nÓg. We begin with the 5th century tale that was a favourite of Otto Rahn's.

Legend of the Knight of Bern
One day, a knight belonging to the retinue of Dietrich de Bern (a German appellation for Theodoric the Great, 454-526) was out riding in the Tyrol along the ancient Troj de Reses, the pathway strewn with roses, which goes from the Karrer Pass northward to the Tierser valley. He was seeking an access to the Kingdom of Laurin.

King Laurin was the ruler of a race of dwarfs who mined the mountains for precious jewels and valuable ores. Laurin possessed a subterranean palace made of sparkling quartz but his pride and joy was the great garden located in front of his underground crystal castle. Countless wonderful roses with enchanting scents blossomed in this garden. Woe to those who might attempt to pick one! Laurin would order that his left hand and right foot be chopped off. He exercised the same punishment on those who tore the silken thread that formed a magical enclosure around his cherished rose garden.

Each time the knight believed he had found a way into Laurin's kingdom insurmountable walls would rise up in the mountains around him. Eventually, he came to a gorge and passed through. Close by a stream he heard the marvellous singing of a multitude of birds. He stopped to listen.

The knight then saw a shepherdess in a sunny meadow. He asked her if the birds always sang in such a delightful manner. She replied that she had not heard them sing for a very long time but now that they were she thought it might be possible to rediscover the windmill and again put it to work for the good of men.

"What sort of windmill is it?" asked the knight.

"It is an enchanted windmill," the shepherdess replied. "In the past, it was dwarfs who worked the mill on behalf of Laurin who owned it and milled flour for the poor. But there were those among the dwarfs who had become greedy and one day one of them was tossed in the water because he had nt given enough flour. Since then the mill had stopped and no one knew where it was. It would be thus until the birds sang again. The windmill will be found at the bottom of a gorge. It is well concealed and even its wheel turns no longer. People call it the windmill of roses because it is covered in wild roses."

The knight finds the mill. It is covered in moss, its wooden sides blackened with age, its wheel stuck. The roses form a thicket around the mill such that a passer-by could not see it.

The knight tries to open the door but it will not budge. In the wall he sees a tiny window. The knight climbs on his horse's back and peers through. Inside are seven dwarfs stretched out, sleeping. The knight calls and taps on the window but there is no response.

Defeated, the knight returns to the meadow and sleeps for the night. The following day he climbs on a high point overlooking the gorge. Three rose bushes are in bloom before him. The knight picks a rose from the first bush.

An elf cries out from the foliage, "Bring me a rose from the good old days!"

"Willingly" replies the knight, "but how will I find it?"

The elf disappears in lament.

The knight approaches the second bush and picks a flower. Again, an elf appears, asks the same question, gets the same answer and withdraws lamenting.

The knight then picks a bloom from the third bush and another elf asks, "Why do you knock at our door?"

"I wish to enter the garden of roses of King Laurin, for I seek the fiancée of the Month of May!" he said

"Only the child and the poet may enter the garden of roses," said the elf. "If you can sing a beautiful ballad then the way will be open to you."

"I can do it," affirmed the knight.

"Then come with me," said the elf who picks some wild roses and descends into the gorge followed by the knight. They reach the windmill. Its door opens. The dwarfs sleep still. The elf brushes them with the roses, crying: "Awaken, sleepers, the young roses are in flower!"

The dwarfs wake from their enchanted sleep, open their eyes and commence to mill. The elf shows the mill cellar to the knight. From there runs a gallery deep into the mountain and finishes in a dazzling light. With his happy eye the knight sees the garden paradise of King Laurin with its multi-coloured flowerbeds, exquisite groves and resplendent roses. The knight sees also the web of woven silk covering its entrance and which encompasses everything.

"Now, begin your song," says the elf.

The knight then sings the song of Love and of the Month of May. The paradise of roses opens to admit him forever and the knight steps into Eternity.

The knight's story is a classic allegory of initiation in which one pursuing a quest under the protection of ancient guardians must fashion a skeleton key (*dietrich*) to their Higher Self, unlock the door and enter the worlds within. The web of woven silk alludes to the timeless thread of order that is ever-present in the midst of chaos. It is the guide between this world and the Otherworld, personified in mythology by Ariadne, Circe, Ceridwen and Hecate

Western mysticism also describes this story as a Rosicrucian allegory. The song is a mantram: an incantation of prayer. The mill cellar is the lowest chakra of the body: the sacral plexus. The passage leading into the mountain is the spine. The sushumna nadi (chakra) runs down the central axis of the body, through the spinal cord and is the most important nadi of the emotional body. The Rose Paradise is the Kingdom of Heaven, in the human body the Sanskrit 1,000-petalled crown chakra. The woven silk is the Homeric chain of correspondences and reciprocal effects. The act of stepping into eternity is not passing over but the attaining of cosmic consciousness.

Gothic King Theoderic the Great, known in legend as Dietrich von Bern

Roderick U. Sayce, Museum of Archaeology and Anthropology, University of Cambridge, remarked upon the similarities between the legend of Robert Kirk Sr.'s death and the legend of Dietrich von Bern who in one version of the tale was taken away by a dwarf when he died. According to Sayce both share a theme common to ancestral spirit cults—the departed are taken away to fairyland.

The Crusader Knight and the Rose Queen of the Pyrenees, Winter Solstice, 1110 A.D.

Raoul the Crusader Knight was a friend of the Minstrel so perhaps it is little wonder that he also attracted his share of amazing adventures.

Raoul was more fatigued than he thought it possible for a man to be. He clutched the starboard rail as hard as his dwindling strength would allow, the ropes binding him to the timbers twisting and heaving in the mounting gale. He vomited for the tenth time in as many minutes. Another wave, a giant one, struck the weathered Genoese galleon and knocked the knight unconscious.

A fresh ripple of pain coursing though Raoul's body soon brought him round. The sea was now rising and falling a little more gently and a pink light in the east heralded a new dawn. Impressed by its beauty even as his body continued to be racked by wave after wave of agonising pain, Raoul wondered out loud how the hell of a cold and unforgiving sea could so quickly become a paradise almost too beautiful to behold.

The galleon's captain joined the knight on deck with cups of hot mulled wine. The old seadog untied the ropes, safe in the knowledge that the storm had passed. Together the men toasted the beauty of a new day. The captain went below, leaving Raoul to enjoy the sun's warming rays as it rose anew over the coast of southern France.

Suddenly, Raoul saw a figure walking with arms outstretched across the waves. The striking female was tall with blonde, braided hair that hung loose over her left shoulder. She held out an arm and pulled him up from the deck into an enormous room.

"Welcome, Sir Knight, to the Castle of the Rose!" she said brightly.

At that instant Raoul swiftly returned to consciousness like sand flowing rapidly through an hourglass. At the same time he heard the call from the cabin boy that they were approaching land and that passengers should prepare to disembark.

With a gargantuan effort Raoul dressed himself in his armour and saddled his horse and dearest companion, Véronique, all the while pondering his strange dream. He knew that he did not have the reserves of strength to withstand the one hundred mile journey to his home in the Pyrenees. Nevertheless, he drew on his training and discipline to go through the mechanics of traversing the arduous terrain.

Hail, snow, sleet and biting winds conspired to bring the knight ever closer to death by the elements. Raoul had been travelling for more than a week and was passing though a dense forest. Véronique stumbled on the root of a giant pine sending the knight crashing to the snow-covered forest floor.

Raoul knew by the impossible angle of his bloodied leg that it was badly broken. In a way he felt relieved that it was in this beautiful forest where he would die. He was beyond exhaustion and knew that even if by some miracle he managed to heave himself back onto his horse he would be dead within minutes.

Raoul resigned himself to his certain fate.

Suddenly, Véronique pawed the ground and nuzzled her master excitedly. Raoul, mistaking the significance of her actions, patted her lovingly on the neck and wished her a fond farewell. Véronique redoubled her nuzzling actions and this time the knight saw a glimmer of light through the trees. In an agony of pain, Raoul managed to pull himself upright and hang on to Véronique's rein while he half hobbled and was half dragged towards the ever-brightening light that was glimmering through the snowy pines.

After a few minutes, horse and master reached the edge of the forest and saw, to their amazement, a beautiful castle sparkling with lights. Its lowered drawbridge provided a pathway over the castle's wide moat. Raoul was very familiar with this part of the world and knew with certainty that there was no castle within fifty miles of where they stood.

With gritted teeth Raoul staggered the last fifty yards to the drawbridge. No sooner had Véronique placed a front hoof upon the wooden planking than Raoul fell into a dead faint upon the drawbridge. Inside the castle the Queen, witnessing Raoul's desperate plight, put her knuckles to her lips and thought quickly.

Mystical tradition demanded that if Raoul was to enter the castle and learn of its secrets he must do so under his own steam; none inside were permitted to assist his passage into its enchanted walls. She knew what must be done. The Queen summoned her squire and told him to raise the drawbridge with all haste. The slimly built squire heaved and tugged for what seemed like an eternity but finally he found hidden reserves of strength to raise both the drawbridge and Raoul's unconscious body.

Véronique scrambled down the drawbridge into the castle courtyard while Raoul slid unceremoniously down the planking to land at the feet of the Queen. The squire and three female courtiers hurriedly picked up Raoul, by now deep in coma, put him on a makeshift stretcher and took him to his quarters.

Throughout the night the women recited special healing prayers. Three times the Queen came to check on the knight's condition, departing on each occasion increasingly optimistic and satisfied. Just before dawn Raoul was carried from his room into a great hall and seated on a chair. The Queen snapped her fingers and Raoul awoke from his coma. His leg hurt terribly.

"Welcome, Sir Knight, to the Castle of the Order of the Rose. I am Queen Ros Niveus and together we will celebrate the Winter Solstice."

Raoul gasped.

The Queen was the same figure he had seen upon the waves during his spell of delirium upon the boat. The Queen approached Raoul and lightly touched his broken leg. Instantly, his leg went icy cold then back to warm. All pain vanished and the bones were once again whole and strong. The squire brought Raoul a steaming goblet of mulled wine, which Raoul sipped eagerly. The Queen explained to Raoul that it was his inner strength that had brought him to her castle drawbridge. Now that he had succeeded in his journey he was now to be initiated into the Order of the Rose, an experience that would fertilise the divine seed that dwelt deep within him.

During his initiation Raoul was confronted by robed and hooded figures. The Queen introduced them as the Lords of Form who between them give Voice to the Light from which the world is composed. They teach Raoul of the energies of CHALLENGE, which he repeated in turn aloud:

1. OPPORTUNITY is the energy of unlimitedness. I have no limits in my life.

2. COMRADESHIP is the energy of deep interpersonal understanding. I accept unconditionally the realities of others, embracing neutrality rather than interference.

3. CELEBRATION is the energy of joy, humour and hopefulness. Through celebration I bring adventure into my life, daily.

4. FORCE AND STRENGTH is the energy of personal stability. This energy is not forceful but the essence of force. Through it I express my inner power while going beyond intimidation and fear.

5. BALANCE is the energy of rejuvenation. I renew my energies every hour, refocussing myself so that I move positively into the future.

6. TEMPERANCE is the energy of understanding strengths and weaknesses and is the companion to BALANCE. Within this energy I learn to enjoy all aspects of life. In this, I must learn to persist for the when, where and how will be in a temperate manner.

7. INTUITION is the energy of instinct. I allow myself to listen to my inner voice more and more daily.

8. PATIENCE is the energy of the neutral observer. I am open and more observant each and every day, allowing a positive perception of all living things.

9. REVOLUTION is the energy of complete change: a change to the opposite pole or idea. Through REVOLUTION I step into a no-return energy and literally change my life.

Raoul listens intently as the Lords of Form explain that the world is made up of many powerful beliefs and traditions. Some call themselves religions, secret societies, philosophical societies, political movements or ancient mystical teachings.

He learns that those in the Castle of the White Rose and the Lords of Form are the bonding energies that interconnect between all beliefs, quietly and secretly.

The Lords of Form draw on the ancient wisdom, which teaches that despite the confusion from nation to nation and people to people there is one all-powerful energy. It does not see or recognise evil; it is neutral. It teaches that neutrality is omnipotent, that there are no gods in any form, just unlimited power through the use of energy: positive and negative, attracting and repulsing.

They speak to Raoul of the secret powers that nourish the earth plane and its vital role as the University of the Physical, revealing that, although the world is a humanities classroom, it is also home for other energies that experience the world on other levels and of which humankind is wholly unaware.

They describe the many evolutions on this planet: that of animal, plant, of man; the evolution of atoms and molecules; the evolution of the four elements; the evolution of many other spiritual beings and vibrations; the evolution of colour and sounds in their respective vibrations.

The Lords of Form speak of the poly-dimensional worlds in which we have existences before we incarnate into this world to experience in a series of lifetimes every aspect, both positive and negative, of living in a physical world. They explain that earth, plant, insect, birds and animals create the equilibrium that one might describe as a classroom into which an energy called humanity enters in order to learn. The Lords of Form teach Raoul that humankind is the only class of life on earth that can create something through a creative thought process, a magnificent power.

Raoul learns that in this classroom one is taught the curriculum of the earth experience, comprising twelve elemental teaching units that one must study and master before evolving beyond it: Fire—religion, war and government; Earth—creativity, famine and agriculture; Air—wealth, science and philosophy; and Water—teaching, disease and femininity.

Finally, Raoul understands that as a man he is a Guardian. First and foremost, he will realise that he is God; all power lies within and comes from within. He learns that the physical symbol that connects his outer form to his inner God-seed is the Cross: head held high, arms outstretched and feet planted solidly on the earth.

The knight's initiation draws to an end. Queen Ros Niveus dubs Raoul on each shoulder with a double-edged sword, one edge for justice, the other for chivalry. Raoul rises as a Knight of the Order of the Rose, understanding that as he steps forward on his life's new Journey the inner power of this magical-mystical Order gradually will be released to him. Finally, he is told that the Castle is his sanctuary and that wherever he is in the world he would always be able to return for sanctuary, replenishment and renewal. Raoul and Véronique make their departure. As soon as he crossed the drawbridge and stepped into the forest Raoul looked back and saw the castle disappearing before his eyes.

Shortly after this adventure in the Castle of the Order of the Rose, Raoul arrived in Vienna where he was invited to join eight men in the formation of a new mystical-military brotherhood that the world in future years would call the Knights Templar. Raoul declined the invitation because his newly expanded inner sight had given him the understanding that visible, ostensible power is only ever a protective force for a far greater power that works best invisibly, silently and secretly. Instead, Raoul chose to dedicate his life to protect and serve the legacy of the Mystical Christian power that Mary Magdalene had brought to the South of France eleven hundred years earlier.

Such is the personal story handed down through generations of storytellers of a Crusader Knight and his remarkable Solstice journey to the Castle of the Rose where he met a magical Queen and the higher spirits that give Voice to the Light of the World.

The story of Juan Diego, 9 December 1531

Aztec Indian Juan Diego was on his way to church when he heard the most amazing company of singing birds. It was bitterly cold; birds would not normally be heard singing in such conditions. A woman's voice called out his name. It came from a nearby hilltop, its origin hidden "in a frosty mist, a brightening cloud." He climbed the hill to see her. Although the sun had not yet risen, Diego saw the golden beams that illuminated her from head to foot. She was a young Mexican girl, around fourteen years old and very beautiful.

In the conversation that followed the girl said she was Mary and she desired that a temple should be built on this spot. She urged Diego to run to Tenochtitlan (Mexico City) to tell the Lord Bishop of what he had seen and heard.

The bishop didn't believe a word of Diego's foolish story so the Indian returned to the hilltop at Tlaltelolco and suggested the girl send a more credible messenger. She demurred, insisting that he was her chosen messenger. She told him to return to the bishop and tell him that it was the Virgin Mary who sent him to state her desire for a church.

Diego met with the bishop the next day. This time the bishop, sensing something genuine in Diego's story, asked him to bring back a more tangible sign. On hearing of this, the girl asked Diego to return on the following daybreak. The next day he couldn't come; his uncle, his only relative, was dying.

While he was running to Tlaltelolco to fetch a priest to administer to his uncle the apparition barred his way. Gently, she admonished him asking him was she not his Mother under her shadow and protection? She said that it was not the uncle's time to die.

She told Juan to climb to the top of the hill. Cut the flowers growing there and bring them to me, she said. Diego did so even though he knew that in the middle of December he would find no flowers growing there. To his amazement he found beautiful Castilian roses in bloom, "their petals wet with dew."

After cutting them he wrapped them in his cape, his *tilma*, to protect them. The girl arranged the flowers in the wrap and tied the lower corners of the *tilma* behind Diego's neck so that he wouldn't lose any of the blooms. After advising Diego to show no one but the bishop the sign, she disappeared. He never saw her again.

Back at the bishop's palace some of the officials, making fun at Diego, tried to grab the flowers but they instantly dissolved at their touch. Astonished, they let Diego go on. To Diego's dismay the *tilma* came loose and the flowers fell to the floor in disarray before he could approach the bishop.

Seconds later the bishop was kneeling at Diego's feet because there, imprinted in the fabric of the *tilma*, was a lovely figure, fifty-six inches tall, surrounded by golden rays emerging as from a shell of light. The head was slightly and very gracefully tilting to the right. The mantel that covered the head was greenish blue with a border of purest gold and scattered through with golden stars. The tunic was rose-coloured, patterned with a lace-like design of golden flowers. Below was a crescent moon and beneath it the head and arms of a cherub.

Clergy identified the imprint in the *tilma* with these lines in Revelation: *"And there appeared a great sign in heaven; a woman clothed with the sun, and the moon was under her feet, and upon her head a crown of twelve stars."*

The *tilma* has been seen by millions as the faithful file past the high altar in the basilica of Our Lady of Guadalupe in Mexico City. Diego's uncle was cured. He saw his room fill with a luminous light. The figure of a young woman appeared, told him of his nephew's mission and asked that her image be known as Santa Maria de Guadalupe.

The Apparition of the Lady at Fátima

The remarkable story of Lúcia Santos and her cousins, Jacinta and Francisco Marto, and their visions of the Lady at Fátima did not in fact begin in 1917, the famous year of the apparitions that shook the Catholic Church and its faithful.

It began two years earlier. In April 1915 while reciting her rosary at a spot near Fátima, a village in the municipality of Ourém in Portugal's Santarém District, eight-year old Lúcia Santos saw a transparent white cloud and a human figure. The same scene occurred twice more that year.

The following year events took a dramatic turn. One day in springtime, the three shepherd girls were herding sheep at the Cova da Iria (the cave of St. Irene, an ancient sacred spot) near Fátima. It had been raining hard and they had sheltered in a cave. The rain stopped and the children heard the rumble of a strong wind whipping up (incidentally, a common precursor to UFO activity). Suddenly, a white light appeared around the nearby treetops. Inside the light was a youth of startling beauty.

He told them, "I am an Angel of Peace." He taught the children a prayer and departed. The children, awestruck by the encounter and seemingly in a trance-state, stood there reciting the prayer until they fell to the ground in exhaustion. During the midsummer period the angel re-appeared to the children and challenged them.

"What are you doing? Pray! Pray a great deal! Offer prayers and sacrifices continually."

Lúcia asked how to make sacrifices.

Lúcia Santos and Jacinta and Francisco Marto

The angel said, "Make a sacrifice of everything you possibly can. Above all, accept and bear with submission the suffering that the Lord shall send you." The Angel then vanished leaving the children paralyzed. In the autumn he appeared for a third time, this time at the cave of Cabeso, and gave the children Communion.

In 1917 events really took off. On 13 May the three children saw a globe of light above a small tree. Inside the globe stood a lady of small stature. She wore a white mantle edged with gold and held a rosary in her hand (mindful of the figure in Diego's sixteenth century vision). She was "brighter than the sun, shedding rays of light clearer and stronger than a crystal goblet filled with the most sparkling water and pierced by the burning rays of the sun."

The woman did not give a name or otherwise describe her identity, except to say that she came from heaven. Coming from devout Catholic families, the children perceived her as the Virgin Mary. She left them with a message of consolation.

Jacinta told her family about seeing the brightly lit woman, despite Lúcia having said earlier to her companions that the three should keep their experience private. Jacinta's disbelieving mother told gossipy neighbours about it as a joke and within a day the whole village knew of the children's vision.

The children said the woman had told them to return to the Cova da Iria five more times in successive months, the first occasion to be the 13 June (the feast of St. Anthony, patron of the local parish church). Lúcia told parish priest, Father Ferreira that the lady had said that before the thirteenth she should learn to read in order to understand what she wanted of her. Lúcia's mother sought counsel from Father Ferreira who suggested she allow her to go. He asked to have Lúcia brought to him afterward so that he could question her.

On 13 June the children went to the designated spot accompanied by a group of people from neighbouring villagers to witness the second vision. The lady returned as promised. While she spoke with Lúcia the villagers could only hear a noise like the buzzing of a bee. The lady told Lúcia that Francisco and Jacinta would be taken to Heaven soon, but Lúcia would live longer in order to spread her message and devotion to the Immaculate Heart. The lady also asked the children to devote themselves to the Holy Trinity and to pray "the Rosary every day, to bring peace to the world and an end to the war." At the conclusion of the dialogue the fifty or so onlookers heard an explosion and saw a small cloud rising from a tree.

On the second of the five occasions, 13 July, there were 4,500 people present to witness the next phase of the apparitions. They heard a buzzing noise, saw and felt a decrease in the Sun's glow and heat and saw a small cloud by the tree where the apparition appeared to the girls.

A lady clothed in light then revealed to the girls a secret in three parts. First, she let the children see a brief vision of hell:

"We saw something like an ocean of fire. Immersed in the fire were the demons and the souls (of the damned), that were like transparent embers, black or bronze, that had human forms."

In the second secret Our Lady told the girls that World War I would soon end but another world war would break out if people did not stop offending God and if Russia was not converted. The lady then took Lúcia aside and revealed to her a third secret, which she promised never to reveal. (The first two secrets were made public in 1941.) At the conclusion of the apparition onlookers heard a loud noise signalling the lady's departure.

By the time of the due date for the girls' next meeting with the lady, 13 August, they were unable to keep the appointment because they had been thrown in jail! The provincial administrator and anticlerical Freemason, Artur Santos (no relation), believing that the events were politically disruptive, arrested the children before they could reach the Cova da Iria that day. Other prisoners later testified that the children, while upset, were consoled by the inmates and led them in saying the Rosary. The administrator interrogated the children and unsuccessfully attempted to get them to divulge the content of the secrets. In the process he tried, hatefully, to convince the children that he would boil them one by one in a pot of oil unless they confessed the secrets. The children, however, resisted.

Meanwhile, in the girls' absence, onlookers at the Cova da Iria heard a clap of thunder and saw a bright flash. The white cloud hovered by the tree, rose up and dissipated. The clouds turned a crimson red, then successively pink, yellow and blue. Witnesses among the 18,000-strong gathering saw falling flowers, reminiscent of the "angel hair" phenomenon. One observer, Manuel Pedro Marto, saw a luminous globe spinning in the clouds.

On 19 August the children, having been released, reported seeing the Virgin Mary at Valinhos. The temperature dropped and they saw the colours of the rainbow fill the countryside and then a bright flash of light. A female figure came as a glowing light by a tree. She asked them again to pray the rosary daily, spoke about a miracle coming on 13 October and asked them "to pray a lot, a lot for the sinners and sacrifice a lot, as many souls perish in hell because nobody is praying or making sacrifices for them." Her departure was accompanied by a roaring sound towards the east.

On the day of the fifth appointment, 3 September, roughly 30,000 gathered at Cova da Iria. At noon the sun dimmed in a cloudless sky. Thousands cried, "There she is!"

A globe of light was approaching from east to west along the valley towards the three children. Out of a white cloud came a fall of shiny white petals, which, when onlookers tried to grasp them, melted away. The children saw the lady in the globe and were promised a miracle on the 13 October meeting. The globe then rose and disappeared into the sun

70,000 people, including reporters and photographers, gathered to see the final vision on 13 October. What happened then became known as the "Miracle of the Sun." Various claims have been made as to what actually took place.

According to accounts, at noon, after a period of rain, there was a flash of light accompanied by the pervading scent of a sweet perfume. The clouds parted and the sun then appeared as an opaque, spinning flat disc in the sky that was easily gazed at with the naked eye. It was said to be significantly duller than normal and to cast multicoloured lights across the landscape, the people, and the surrounding clouds.

Witnesses reported seeing the sun turn on its axis and dance across the sky "like a globe of snow revolving on itself."

Two onlookers peering at the disk through binoculars later reported seeing a ladder and two entities. As it spun, a red glow appeared on its rim.

The sky was lit up and the faces of onlookers shone with brilliance. Other colours followed: green, red, orange, blue and violet. Spinning rapidly, the sun careened towards the earth, hanging motionless in the air for several minutes before zigzagging back to its normal position.

Finally, the disk disappeared into the "sun," the real sun fixed in position and shining dazzlingly in the sky. Witnesses reported that their previously wet clothes became "suddenly and completely dry, as well as the wet and muddy ground that had been soaked because of the rain that had been falling."

Not all witnesses reported seeing the sun "dance." Some people only saw the radiant colours while others, including some believers, saw nothing at all. The only known picture of the sun taken during the event does not show anything unusual. None of the 70,000 could report that they definitely saw the lady.

On 3 January 1944 Carmelite nun, Lúcia, confided to Bishop Silva "by order of His Excellency the Bishop of Leiria and the Most Holy Mother" the content of the Third Secret. Therafter, rumours persisted that it contained information about the Apocalypse, apostasy and satanic infiltration of the Church.

In 1960 Pope John XXIII invited the most senior members of the Church into his office to hear the text of the secret part of the prophecies. One of the Pope's secretaries confided that through an open door he saw looks of absolute horror upon the faces of the Cardinals as the secret was disclosed. As they filed out the secretary, knowing one of the cardinals well, asked him about the meeting. The Cardinal said nothing and hurried out ashen-faced. The Cardinals looked as if they had seen a ghost.

In a 1980 interview for the German magazine *Stimme des Glaubens* published in October 1981, John Paul II was asked explicitly to speak about the Third Secret. He said:

> *"Because of the seriousness of its contents, in order not to encourage the worldwide power of Communism to carry out certain coups, my predecessors in the chair of Peter have diplomatically preferred to withhold its publication. On the other hand, it should be sufficient for all Christians to know this much: if there is a message in which it is said that the oceans will flood entire sections of the earth; that, from one moment to the other, millions of people will perish... there is no longer any point in really wanting to publish this secret message. Many want to know merely out of curiosity, or because of their taste for sensationalism, but they forget that "to know" implies for them a responsibility. It is dangerous to want to satisfy one's curiosity only, if one is convinced that we can do nothing against a catastrophe that has been predicted."*

The Pope then held up his rosary and stated,

> *"Here is the remedy against this evil. Pray, pray and ask for nothing else. Put everything in the hands of the Mother of God."*

Asked what would happen in the Church, John Paul II said:

> *"We must be prepared to undergo great trials in the not-too-distant future; trials that will require us to be ready to give up even our lives, and a total gift of self to Christ and for Christ. Through your prayers and mine, it is possible to alleviate this tribulation, but it is no longer possible to avert it, because it is only in this way that the Church can be effectively renewed. How many times, indeed, has the renewal of the Church been effected in blood? This time, again, it will not be otherwise. We must be strong....we must entrust ourselves to Christ and to His holy Mother, and we must be attentive, very attentive, to the prayer of the Rosary."*

Lúcia herself was reported to state explicitly that the Third Secret carries Apocalyptic content. When asked one time about this, she said it was "in the Gospels and in the Apocalypse," specifying Apocalypse chapters 8 through 13, a range that includes Apocalypse 12:4,[102] the chapter and verse cited by Pope John Paul II in the homily that he delivered in Fátima, 13 May 2000.

---

[102] *"Its tail swept a third of the stars out of the sky and flung them to the earth. The dragon stood in front of the woman who was about to give birth, so that it might devour her child the moment he was born."*

In an interview published 11 November 1984 in *Jesus Magazine*, Cardinal Ratzinger was asked whether he had read the text of the Third Secret and why it had not been revealed. Ratzinger acknowledged that he had read the Third Secret and stated in part that it involves the "importance of the novissimi" (the eschaton, end of days, Apocalypse), and "dangers threatening the faith and the life of the Christian and therefore (the life) of the world." Ratzinger also commented that, "If it is not made public, at least for the time being, it is in order to prevent religious prophecy from being mistaken for a quest for the sensational."

Additionally, a news article quoted former Philippine ambassador to the Vatican, Howard Dee. Dee was remarking on comments made to him by Ratzinger in connection with the content of the third secret and the messages of Our Lady of Akita. The latter is associated with a wooden statue venerated by Japanese Catholic faithful who hold it to be miraculous. The image is known due to the Marian apparitions reported in 1973 by Sister Agnes Katsuko Sasagawa in the remote area of Yuzawadai, in the suburbs of Akita.

The messages emphasize prayer (especially recitation of the Holy Rosary) and penance in combination with cryptic visions prophesying sacerdotal persecution and heresy within the Catholic Church. Ratzinger told Dee that the Fátima and Akita messages are "essentially the same." The Akita prophecy includes the following:

"The work of the devil will infiltrate even into the Church in such a way that one will see cardinals opposing cardinals, bishops against bishops...churches and altars sacked..."

In a syndicated radio broadcast, Fr. Malachi Martin stated that the Third Secret "doesn't make any sense unless we accept that there will be, or that there is in progress, a wholesale apostasy amongst clerics and laity in the Catholic Church."

The Vatican's "official" text of the third secret was published on June 26, 2000 after Lúcia had been pressed by her superiors to reveal it before she died: She wrote:

"I write in obedience to you, my God, who command me to do so through his Excellency the Bishop of Leiria and through your Most Holy Mother and mine. After the two parts which I have already explained, at the left of Our Lady and a little above, we saw an Angel with a flaming sword in his left hand; flashing, it gave out flames that looked as though they would set the world on fire; but they died out in contact with the splendour that Our Lady radiated towards him from her right hand: pointing to the earth with his right hand, the Angel

cried out in a loud voice: 'Penance, Penance, Penance!' And we saw in an immense light, that is God, something similar to how people appear in a mirror when they pass in front of it: a Bishop dressed in White. We had the impression that it was the Holy Father.

"Other Bishops, Priests, men and women Religious going up a steep mountain, at the top of which there was a big Cross of rough-hewn trunks as of a cork-tree with the bark; before reaching there the Holy Father passed through a big city half in ruins and half trembling with halting step, afflicted with pain and sorrow, he prayed for the souls of the corpses he met on his way; having reached the top of the mountain, on his knees at the foot of the big Cross he was killed by a group of soldiers who fired bullets and arrows at him, and in the same way there died one after another the other Bishops, Priests, men and women Religious, and various lay people of different ranks and positions. Beneath the two arms of the Cross there were two Angels each with a crystal aspersorium [a vessel for holy water] in his hand, in which they gathered up the blood of the Martyrs and with it sprinkled the souls that were making their way to God."

From these remarks it is clear that the Third Secret, delivered to the three girls during what appeared to be a series of classic UFO-style visitations, is a statement of intent that God will put humanity on the Cross and sweep the stables clean. The unambiguous inference is that this cataclysmic event will take place in the not too distant future. John Paul II made clear his belief that this Apocalyptic action could be alleviated but not averted. The content and mode of delivery of the messages to Lúcia and her cousins conforms closely to many other NHE phenomena in which repeated warnings have been made about the dire consequences of humankind's continuing and rapidly accelerating negative actions.

Grace Cooke and the White Eagle Lodge

Grace Cooke (1892-1979) was a British medium who wrote of the teachings she received from a spirit in the higher worlds named White Eagle. She began her calling as a medium in 1913 and used her phenomenal gifts to demonstrate evidence of survival after death. British Prime Minister, Ramsay MacDonald, vouched for the accuracy of her spirit communications.

Grace and her husband, Ivan, founded the White Eagle Lodge in 1936. Personally, I find that there is a sincere depth and authority of insight in White Eagle's commentaries that distinguish Grace Cooke's mediumship from many other channelling sources. In two excellent books[103] in particular, White Eagle provides a remarkable spiritual perspective into humankind's ancient past in the light of present day society.

White Eagle said that long, long ago humans descended from their original "god-man" form (then a lot finer, White Eagle explained, for man's spirit-consciousness was more outside than within the body) in accordance with a divine plan. Gradually, thereafter, man underwent a process of descent in order to inhabit a physical vehicle, which, in its turn, had evolved from a lower state of life, stage by stage, until the brain had developed to such a degree that it could begin to comprehend the power and beauty of the Godforce within. This process entailed not just a development of the physical body but also the development of the subtler bodies that clothe the spirit of man. This was the divine plan and process of man's fall (the Adam and Eve story) brought into play in order that in time there would be awakened in man his self-conscious, which would lead in time to God consciousness.

The "evil," the serpent, was man's love of power, a mental craving that asserts itself in the lower aspect of man. But at the same time, the fall (the "evil") also caused development and growth of man's individual soul and mind. Therefore, in accordance with the principle of reciprocity, "evil" produced individualisation, a very necessary part of man's evolutionary growth, without which there would be no stimulus or desire in man to grow to become a more complete, perfected son of God.

In developing his message, White Eagle explained that there is a world composed of finer ethers just within our own "solid" world. Long ago the ancient masters taught that the heaven world is not beyond the stars but is a plane that is here, around us all the time, interpenetrating all physical life. White Eagle reiterated this teaching, clarifying that this world of "finer ethers" is not the spirit world after death but a realm or dimension closer to Earth. Here the ancient Brethren of the Sun live and worship in the Sun temples and Sun cities.

The Brethren of the Sun, the "Sun-Men," arrived in this world after the fall, coming to a land submerged by the waters so very long ago, long before Atlantis. They came to this planet in the form of an indescribably beautiful light: the spiritual Sun. White Eagle explained that the Sun-Men were messengers from the Brotherhood of the Cross

[103] Cooke, G. & Cooke, I., *The Light in Britain*, The White eagle Publishing Trust, 1971; and Cooke, G., *Sun Men of the Americas*, The White Eagle Publishing Trust, 1983

of Light within the Circle of Light: the Great White Brotherhood, which since the beginning of life on Earth has had mankind in its care. Their purpose was to bring wisdom to a young humanity so that it might learn the Law of God and to eventually break the bondage of physical matter and return to full spiritual awareness and consciousness with the Godforce. In the distant past White Eagle (then known as Hah Wah-Tah) had been an initiate of this Brotherhood.

White Eagle spoke many times on the role of Britain in the continual battles between the forces of Light and Darkness.

"Throughout the ages the light of the sun brothers has been centred within...this mystic isle, a sacred domain, thousands and thousands years since. They travelled all over the earth but this isle was their home. They had great knowledge...of physics, of the proportions of matter. This knowledge and influence still lingers, hidden; we (Britons) are the inheritors of an ancient wisdom, a great light."

He said that in the Atlantean period there was a tremendous battle on the etheric plane between these forces. The dark priests of Atlantis gained knowledge of a destructive power that would have destroyed the earth. A great battle took place at Dragon Hill in Britain (situated immediately below the Uffington White Horse in Oxfordshire), which manifested right through to the physical plane. The forces of darkness were defeated.

Subsequently, the Dragon Hill area became a principal centre for the enactment of powerful ceremonies in which the forces of nature played a vital part. Cooke's spirit sight observed one such ceremony in which was gathered in the amphitheatre below Dragon Hill a great assembly for a grand ceremony of sun worship.

Twelve high priests standing on the top of the hill summoned the great angels of the White Light. Among the celestial beings present were representatives of the four orders of the Elemental nature spirits. An ever-rising spiral of golden light filled the amphitheatre, its radiation appearing as a fountain of light that cascaded brilliantly over the earth. A great being, a cosmic Christ-form, appeared in the light. Then appeared another figure, a king wearing a crown of gold and robed in light, the points of his crown emitting rays of great brilliance. This was King Ar-Thor, the ancient King of Hyperborea who had come to bring blessings for a ceremony convened to show people how to overcome man's material self (the slaying of the dragon within). White Eagle said of the God-Men of Hyperborea":

"These were the perfect sons of God who came as guardians of a young race on a young planet. These god-men impregnated the very stones with the light of their being from the upper worlds. From the great Sun Brotherhood, Britain was once a part of Hyperborea and, later, Atlantis. Because many ancient peoples journeyed here and established mystery centres of great light and power, in Britain today is a great spiritual power which can and will wake in the future through all the people of these islands.

"Britain was the first home of the ancient white brothers of the Hyperborea regions. Centres of the ancient brotherhood have been established in many countries but invisible because they occupy a higher dimension. They are engaged in slowing down the vibration of the etheric plane in which they exist until they can once again come amongst humanity to impart their knowledge to those willing to listen and to understand.

"The age of Earth's humanity is beyond man's calculation; many, many civilisations and continents now submerged of which we know nothing. The human race is not highly evolved but will be when the secret ancient spiritual power in Britain is released and the whole vibration of the earth is raised accordingly. Dragon Hill is one area where the god-men left their blessings for future races of men."

White Eagle spoke at length about the power of the stone circles in Britain. They played a vital role in the enactment of rituals to bring about the physical manifestation of life from the etheric world. The Avebury Temple was a great creative centre on this planet, the heart of ancient and powerful ceremonies. The communities in the surrounding hills, peopled by a race that White Eagle said originated in the Greek part of the world, came to the temple to witness and participate in extraordinary marvels.

Avebury was associated with the moon and with obeisance to the moon goddess. The goddess was enthroned upon Silbury Hill. The ancient mother-ritual, which eventually brought about the creation of life in physical form, came from Mu, the Motherland. The rituals invoked the invisible power of the gods and then concentrated upon the movement of the cells and the building up of form.

The stones themselves came into physical manifestation from the etheric forms created by ritual, all the stone temples in Britain being created in this manner. All things created in the Avebury Temple were steeped in music and harmony (the Music of the Spheres) and reflected the harmony of the cosmos, the whole interacting with higher intelligences and the Universal Powers. Avebury and Stonehenge, entrances into the inner, higher worlds, served also as temples of magic.

Fairies, Elementals and all other constituents of etheric life united with the Sun-priests to perform inconceivable acts of power. In these rituals the bluestones brought from the fairy-ruled mountains of Prescelly played a vital role. These stones had the power to draw forth the fairies and the souls of the stones. The Sun-priests were almost worshipped as gods in acknowledgement of their supernatural control over the elements and because of the light they had brought from the celestial spheres to Avebury and all over Britain, long before the young earth had fully solidified. The god-men travelled here on rays from the higher spheres and dimensions, all rays converging on the Isle of Britain. Avebury and Stonehenge mark the place where the cosmic rays meet. By breath alone the Sun-priests could raise giant weights or raze buildings to the ground. White Eagle said that these circles and at other points all over Britain are the chakras of this mystic isle.

White Eagle related how the four angels of the East, West, North and South convened at the stones, accompanied by the Devic Lords. He described these cosmic energies as the higher beings who rule over the orders of nature: some beautiful, others fearful to behold, some in giant form, some winged, others cloven, others horned with pointed ears.

White Eagle declared that Britain, the Grail Chalice of the planet, was the first home of the ancient white brothers of the Hyperborea regions. Subsequently, centres of the ancient brotherhood were established in many countries. These cannot be discerned with the naked eye because they occupy a higher dimension.

Through Grace Cooke, White Eagle conveyed a very powerful message to humanity. He said that happening right now is the bringing into manifestation from the very soil of Britain the true light of spiritual brotherhood. The Brotherhood of the Great White Light is renewing its manifestation, a magical-mystical process felt in the hearts of those who are open to its divine energies. White Eagle said that Britain is the omphalos for this global renewal of divine power in which Ar-thor, the Once and Future King, will re-emerge to do final battle with the forces of darkness.

Alice

White Eagle once remarked in reference to Lewis Carroll's master work that Alice is the story of a little girl who dropped into the well and instead of drowning found herself in fairyland, a land of great beauty. In fact, observed White Eagle, Alice was inside her own soul world. Prior to her journey she had been lazing dreamily.

When one concentrates on this quiet place inside we become lost to the outer world. It is at this moment that one is able to delve deeply into one's own personal, private and special well of truth. It is there that anything is possible. One may enter a beautiful, spiritual world and walk and speak with its marvellous inhabitants.

White Eagle dwelt on the subject of the fairy folk, the nature spirits and other, higher forces that direct the etheric workers. They are created out of the finer ethers that interpenetrate the four elements. White Eagle said it is absolutely necessary for one that is intent on advancing their spiritual path to become aware of the nature spirits. This is because the Elementals' etheric life is ultimately concerned with man's spiritual evolution and his appreciation of nature's beauty and abundance.

White Eagle urged that man should seek to be aware of the vast host of angelic and etheric beings—the grand company of Nature—that are agents of the Universal Law. Seen from a higher state of consciousness, "good" and "evil" are two forces working together to produce the perfect life and the power of mastership in the individual life.

John Lennon's famous fairytale of a girl with psychedelic eyes is about Caroll's Alice. Three months before his untimely death in December 1980, Lennon confirmed this to David Sheff of *Playboy Magazine*. Lennon's timeless allegory is rich with symbolism.

Alice is "A-luce," a figure of light, a fairy-goddess. In Lennon's imagination, Alice never left the Wonderland and Looking Glass world. Perhaps the little girl that Carroll returned to the surface was a changeling. Like Arthur and Guinevere, Alice resides in a timeless, enchanting realm waiting for the time when humankind yearns once more for the loving protection of the Goddess when the surface world is sorely threatened.

In Lennon's ode to Alice he describes a man in a boat on the river. Surely, this is Charles Dodgson who with his friend, Robinson Duckworth, on a "golden afternoon" in July 1862 rowed the three Liddell sisters down the Isis to Godstow in Oxfordshire and told the siblings of Alice's adventures in Wonderland.

All at once Lennon propels the man out of space and time to a place with a sky the colour and appearance of marmalade. This is Wonderland, the grin of the Cheshire Cat filling the sunny afternoon sky. Someone calls to the man. He peers above brightly coloured cellophane flowers. For an instant he sees Alice. Her eyes assume the brightness of the sun and then she vanishes like the Cheshire Cat.

In his search for the enchanting girl the young man sees wondrous scenes. Soon, a fantastical vehicle, one he can only describe from the limitations of his subconscious frame of reference as an origami taxi fashioned from newspaper, appears on a nearby shore. He is drawn to enter this Unidentified Flying Object, which, once he is aboard, ascends rapidly. With his head in the clouds the man is taken home.

However, this was not to be the last time he makes such an incredible journey. Some time later he finds himself on a train. The rhythmic thrum of the locomotive's engine idling on the station tracks while awaiting the guard's whistle induces receptiveness and the opening of a Gateway. He looks out of the window and there at the turnstile stands the girl, her eyes filled with all the brilliant hues of the rainbow. "A-luce"—Alice—has come finally to bring him home, to his true home: Wonderland, the Otherworld...Tír Na nÓg.

Waterfalls
The child saw his mother fetch the vacuum cleaner from the cupboard under the stairs. Excited, he ducked behind an armchair in the sitting room. There he waited in breathless anticipation. Moments later she switched on the cleaner and the whirr of its powerful machinery transported the hidden observer to a place where a young boy, not long re-born from the world of spirit, once again felt timeless and free. Wrapped tight in his Otherworldly cocoon, the boy became one with the plunge and power of a distant waterfall, the cascade and he becoming indistinguishable.

The fall's complex counterpoint harmonies held him transfixed during his magical descent. Down, down he fell, all the while nourished by nature's magnificent music. Presently, his mother flicked the off-switch and the machine fell silent. Deep inside the boy, the cascade kept on falling; it would always keep falling in its breathless quest to reach the indigo pool so very far below.

Eight years passed by. He snuggled up into his sleeping bag on the first night of scout camp in the Yorkshire moors. The rhythmic timbre of nearby Hardraw Force swiftly reprised the work of his mother's old Hoover. The music of the fall, combined with the deep powerful sounds of men chanting, pulled his spirit from its canvas confines. In a higher dimension of nature, ancient teachings were made available before he passed into his teens and a new life of learning and responsibility.

He sat on a rock by Hardraw's foaming pool and observed the first signs of dawn. A cowled figure emerged from a nearby cave, briefly made a friendly glance across the pool and did obeisance to the rising sun. Suddenly, men in horned helmets rushed out of the gloom with drawn swords and converged upon the Druid priest. Instantly, the young Scout woke with a start, his vision fresh in every detail.

Eighteen years raced by. Lying in bed a little after dawn he was occupying the netherworld between sleep and wakefulness, dipping in and out of both as he fought the pull of a new day. He slipped into a new dream. He was riding on the top deck of a bus. His was the next stop. He scurried down the stairs and jumped from the bus. Set back from the road in front of him was a 1960s style redbrick, glass-fronted, two-storey building. He went inside. He had a feeling it was a small college of some kind. It appeared to be deserted. He came back outside and this time he saw that to the right of the building was an alleyway with a long wooden fence bordering a row of domestic rear gardens.

He walked down the alley, which veered to the left after a hundred yards. He took the turn and found himself standing on the bank of a canal.

Suddenly, the dreamer and the dreamed changed places. For the longest moment he was *actually standing on the canal bank*. He could feel the grass beneath his feet, hear the moving current upon the water and feel the autumn breeze on his face. The experience was real and genuine in every possible aspect.

He said out loud, "This is no dream." These words of realisation brought him back as swiftly as he had been despatched. He woke with a tremendous jolt as if struck by lightning.

Twelve years later, 1993, the dreamer, now a married man of forty-two with a seven-year old son of his own, parked his rented VW Golf in a picnic area in the Pyrenean foothills by Pont d'Espagne. He and his two female companions had just driven from Lourdes. They were members of a study group who had arrived from Europe, U.S.A. and Australia to visit places of ancient mystical power. Tomorrow they would be travelling to Montségur, a scene of mass sacrifice and, hence, a very special place of forgiveness.

"The disguised knights were placed at different levels in the encampment as cooks, herdsmen, chicken keepers and servants. Alain had been posing as a smithy, a trade he had learned from his father. These concealments allowed the knights to see, hear and feel the pulse of proceedings as the mountain community began to fall.

"Alain watched as the first to be manhandled down the mountain were pushed roughly into the meadow and tied to a stake. These were the bishops and the priests, the formal members of the Order who had undergone the Consolamentum, the sacred initiatory rite of baptism of the Cathars. Consequently, they neither felt pain from the flames nor cried out. This absence of yells and screams caused fury among the watching troops and papal clergy.

"But as the executioners gradually worked their way through to the uninitiated: the faidit and wives and children in whom the understanding and dedication were not deeply instilled within their souls, the pain was recognisable. They had no protection against the agony of the flames. Intervention was necessary. Through a sign from one of the dressed Templars all those that were incognito stepped into the shadows, drew their crossbows and killed the vulnerable as the flames began to leap high. Time and again, Alain and his companions, unseen, took aim and brought a swift death to a woman or child in pain and distress. These merciful acts doubly infuriated those who were responsible for the executions because they wanted to hear the moans, groans and death gasps.

"The dead were taken down and new ones put up. Another concealed group euthanized the young and infirm. A great furore began to develop and the only thing that kept the proceedings from degenerating into a state of complete imbalance were the five Templars who stood very strong, steadfast and still. The observers were able to cover for Alain and his disguised companions who, hiding in the shadows within the tents and behind animals, brought peace to those younger ones that were dying."[104]

Today was clear, mild and dry. The plan was to eat a light picnic and then take a walk in the nearby wild flower meadows. Each person filled a paper plate with cold chicken and salad bought earlier from Les Halles de Lourdes.

Sipping from a bottle of Perrier, he slipped a CD of Ray Lynch's "Sky of Mind" album into the player. On the first strike of the bell in the opening bar of "Quandra," the clear mountain weather turned instantly to thick fog.

At the same time the Perrier bottle, the paper plate and its contents, the picnic bag by his side and, finally, the car itself vanished. His companions would report sharing the same experience. The surrounding mountains shook with the power of an invisible fall. His body disintegrated into billions of tumbling droplets, each a soaring voice in an infinitely large choir of celebrants.

He saw dancing lights, felt every pore and nerve fill with the energy of renewal and, finally, he drifted back to earth during the closing bars of Quandra.

In celebration of this and of my earlier journeys in the higher reaches of Nature, I composed these lines:

---

[104] Finlay, G., *The Looking Glass Ripper*, CreateSpace Independent Publishing Platform, 2015

250

At nine, like little Gavroche, I would swagger in the kerbs,
An urchin shuffling nature's dross, his stockings clung with
dirt.

At thirteen I would chuck for chestnuts high on autumn's scents,
Of cinnamon and clove and musk that prick the nasal vents.

At twenty four an autumn drive 'neath titian boughs o'erarched
Would fix my soul as nature's leafed cathedral housed my path.

Today I am that Arab kid, that priest along the road,
And autumn's charms are multiplied with each new change of
clothes.

For, truth, I am the Emperor, as naked as at birth,
Whose time-spun robes enrich the soul's perceptions of the
earth.

A young boy's remarkable twentieth century Christmas journey
I conclude this book with one of the most remarkable stories that ever came my way. I heard it from a penpal who, while on holiday in a small Tuscan village just before Christmas in the late 1970s, was told it by a close friend of "Luigi." Later that same day my friend was introduced to Luigi, a Prince of the Church visiting his family for Christmas who affirmed the truth of his extraordinary experience. He showed my friend one of the magical white roses that he had been gifted fifty years earlier.

Luigi was born in Tuscany a few years after the end of the First World War, a conflict that had claimed his father's life. This story takes place when he was seven years old. The time of year is three days before Christmas.

Money was tight for Luigi and his mother and the boy was sad because he could not buy his mother a Christmas present. He poured his heart out to a friendly neighbour who told him that it was a time of year to rejoice and to *believe*, not to believe *in* something specific (because that rules out so many possibilities) but just to embrace the simple power of total, unconditional belief that all is good and that anything is possible. She urged Luigi to keep saying to himself, "I am happy and I believe." In this way, if he believed in what he was saying with all his heart, he would have a Christmas gift for his mother.

With this advice ringing in his ears, Luigi went out into the village to peer into the shop windows. He entered a quiet street and saw an unfamiliar shop that had the words "Objets d'Art" carved on its sign. The window display was magical. It was full of pictures from past Christmases and statues of gnomes and fairies making toys. Its centrepiece was a magnificent Christmas tree that twinkled and dazzled with jewels, candles and crystals.

Just then it began to rain. Luigi lingered for a few moments in the open doorway but eventually found the courage to step inside. An old gentleman wearing pince-nez and smoking a pipe put down the large book he was reading and welcomed Luigi enthusiastically.

"Come in, Luigi, and feel free to browse until the rain stops. In my shop you can touch and handle anything you like. Nothing will ever break!"

The shop was a veritable wonderland, a cornucopia of all manner of treasures to delight a small boy. A music box on the shop counter was playing a beautiful melody that he recognised was one of his mother's Christmas favourites, "Silent Night! Holy Night! All is Calm…"

Luigi was admiring a suit of armour when he was drawn to a large freestanding, oval pivot-mirror. It was the height of a man and its frame was adorned with intricate carvings of gnomes, elves and fairies. He examined it for a few minutes and was about to move on to other delights when two small men appeared in the mirror and beckoned him to come with them. Startled, Luigi looked behind him. The shopkeeper was nowhere to be seen. He turned around and was amazed to see the two little men standing on his side of the mirror. Beaming from ear to ear, each held out a hand and said, "Come, Luigi, we have been

waiting for you." At this point, three small steps appeared and descended to the spot where Luigi was standing. Unafraid, Luigi allowed the gentle gnomes to each take a hand and, together, they climbed the steps into the mirror. Luigi found himself in a beautiful garden surrounded by a high wall. The garden was filled with exquisite blooms. The gnomes invited Luigi to sit at a small toadstool-shaped stone table and partake of sweet tea and tiny almond cakes. Luigi sipped and chewed, discovering that the tea and cakes were the best he had ever tasted.

After a few minutes Luigi heard the screech of an eagle and a growing rumble. Excitedly, the gnomes told Luigi his ride was coming and that they must first pick some flowers. It was then that Luigi realised that the garden was filled only with magnificent white roses. He picked the most appealing of the beautiful flowers and was then led by the gnomes out of a gate into a meadow.

Waiting there was a large chariot pulled by five white stallions. The charioteers were two men in gladiator tunics and a very small old woman. With a speed and strength belying her advanced years, the woman jumped from the chariot, pulled Luigi aboard and fastened around his waist a gold-braided rope. She explained that this would keep him from falling out during the journey ahead. She held Luigi's arm firmly but caringly and the chariot surged forward. Within moments it was hurtling along a road of multicoloured lights.

After what seemed like hours, the chariot arrived on a mountaintop where a tall man wearing a floppy hat greeted him. The woman introduced the man as the Master of the Solstice. Smiling warmly, this timeless man bent down and gently shook Luigi's outstretched hand.

Luigi asked the man, "What is a Solstice?"

Patiently, the man explained that the word comes from the Latin and literally translates as "sun stands still." He said that the Solstice occurs twice a year, one such occurring at this time in December. Being a devout Catholic lad, Luigi took exception to this statement insisting that in his village this time of year is called Christmas, the celebration of the birth of Jesus. At this Luigi grew sad and told the man that although for most people this was a happy time he was sad because he didn't have a present for his mother. The man in the floppy hat asked Luigi if he had heeded his neighbour's advice and had been repeating, "I am happy and I believe." Luigi nodded.

Over the next two hours the Master of the Solstice patiently explained to Luigi why the three days before Christmas have always been deemed special. He explained that the key to understanding its power and beauty is to consider nature. The man told him that in addition to nature providing sunshine, rain, the wind, the oceans, flowers, animals, trees and, conversely, earthquakes, tornadoes, hurricanes, lightning, floods and storms, it has within it a powerful, universal energy. Some call it God. Others use different descriptions according to their individual faith, philosophy or belief. He explained that this power shows itself through nature and talks to man through nature. Nature is this Power's body. Bewildered at first, Luigi asked a torrent of questions as he sought to understand the meaning of this gentle man's words. The Master of the Solstice explained that the destructive parts of nature only bring calamity to man because he does not take the time to listen to what nature has to say to him.

In response to Luigi asking how to talk to nature, the man said that one does so in the way Luigi had been doing by talking joyfully to oneself and rejoicing that one truly and deeply believes. In this way, said the Master of the Solstice, one talks to nature and, in response, people like him who are special gardeners for this universal power hear these conversations and help give special strength to those who are happy and who believe.

He explained that during the three days of the Solstice there is a special universal heavenly calm. He said that however one acts during these three days, so will go the rest of their year. The solstice reflects and amplifies how one feels about oneself and those around them. He said that the power of "I believe" is a state of mind: an energy of hope, joy, love, giving and all the beautiful things in life.

The Master of the Solstice asked Luigi what he wanted to be when he was older.

"A priest," Luigi said emphatically.

The man told Luigi that to be a priest was a grand goal, especially to help people to be happy and to believe.

A deep rumble signified the approach of the chariot. In his closing remarks the Master of the Solstice re-emphasised what he had taught the boy who had made a remarkable journey through space and time from a small Tuscan village to a special mountaintop. He told Luigi that if he became a priest he should be happy and believe. In this way, he would always have a unique connection to the special power that lies behind Christmas.

Just before Luigi boarded the chariot for his journey home the Master of the Solstice gave a special blessing to the roses that the lad had brought with him from the gnomes' garden, saying. "Luigi, these are for your mother."

In what seemed like a blink of an eye the chariot brought Luigi to the garden behind the mirror. The two gnomes looked at the bouquet of roses in Luigi's hands and let out a whistle. "Those are now very special roses, Luigi," they said bowing their heads in reverence.

Luigi stepped through the mirror into the Objects d'Art shop and bade farewell to the elderly proprietor. As if in a dream, he walked slowly down the little backstreet that housed the shop. He turned around to look at it one last time and was amazed to see that it had disappeared.

Luigi made for home but as he walked the village streets he met village folk who expressed amazement that he should be carrying such beautiful flowers so long out of season. Filled with the joy of the Solstice and with the words of the man in the floppy hat fresh in his ears, Luigi made gifts of the blooms wishing his delighted recipients, "Buon Natale." By the time he got home he had just one white rose left from the bouquet. No matter.

Excitedly, Luigi gave the rose to his mother with a big kiss and wished her "Buon Natale." Suddenly, music could be heard from outside the kitchen door. On stepping outside to investigate, Luigi and his mother saw a heap of beautiful gifts, one of which was the music box from the Objets d'Art shop. Luigi's mother opened the lid and a haunting melody filled the air:

> *"Silent Night! Holy night!*
> *All is Calm…"*

Oh, Luigi," his mother exclaimed. "The rose, the white rose has brought all of this to us!" Luigi became a priest and made rapid advancement in the Church. From time to time, he would open the music box and gaze upon his most treasured possession, a dried white rose, saying, "I am happy and I believe…"

Luigi's story, passed down to family and friends, has many of the ingredients we have been examining in these pages.

It reveals that a Gateway to a higher dimension can appear in any form. On this occasion, it materialised as an Objets d'Art shop. There have been reports that similar thresholds have appeared as a gas station, a café in Montmartre, an Indian burial ground and a Gothic Cathedral labyrinth. They emerge so that individuals drawn to them may learn more about themselves and their life's pathway, and, above all, about the principle and beauty of "things are never what they seem," and "I am happy and I believe."

Luigi was guided through the magical mirror and across the temporary threshold by Elemental energies in the form of cheery gnomes. At no time during his unique adventure did he feel afraid or threatened by the otherworldy characters he encountered. He was collected by a mighty chariot heralded by a golden eagle, and steered by a kindly goddess figure and two powerful men dressed as Luigi's favourite historical gladiator heroes.

Just as in so many reports of Biblical marvels and UFO appearances, the chariot shot off at great speed in a blaze of light and colour. It opened a corridor to a higher dimension of nature where a timeless representative of the Universal Powers taught Luigi of the true power underlying Christmas.

Nonsense? Impossible? Hallucination? Just couldn't happen?

Luigi believed in every part of it. And perhaps those whose personal nature is to be happy and to believe may believe it also.

"There are more things in heaven and earth, Horatio,
Than are dreamt of in your philosophy."

William Shakespeare, *Hamlet*

Bulgarian hikers capturing a photo of a grey NHE in Yundola
forest, 2 December 2013

Bibliography

Anderson, Douglas, and Verlyn Flieger (eds). *Tolkien on Fairy-stories*, London. HarperCollins*Publishers*, 2014.

Bender, Albert. *Flying Saucers and the Three Men*, Clarksburg, West Virginia. Saucerian Books,1963.

Bloecher, Ted. *The Report on the UFO Wave of 1947*, Washington, D.C., 1947.

Bohm, David. *Wholeness and the Implicate Order*, Great Britain. Routledge, 1980.

Bord, Janet. *Real Encounters with Little People*, London. Michael O'Mara Books Limited, 1997.

—, and Colin Bord. *Mysterious Britain*, St. Albans. Granada Publishing Limited, 1974.

—, *The Secret Country*, St. Albans. Granada Publishing Limited, 1974.

Briggs, Katherine. *A Dictionary of Fairies*, London. Penguin Books, 1977.

Bulwer-Lytton, Sir Edward. *Vril: the Power of the Coming Race*, Whitefish, Montana. Kessinger Publishing LLC (first published 1871).

Campbell, John. *The Gaelic Otherworld*, Glasgow. James Maclehose and Sons, 1900.

Casteneda, Carlos. *Tales of Power*, New York. Simon & Schuster, 1974.

Cathie, B., *The Energy Grid*, Illinois. Adventures Unlimited Press, 1990.

—, *The Harmonic Conquest of Space*, Illinois. Adventures Unlimited Press, 1998.

Conan Doyle, Arthur. *The Coming of the Fairies*, London. Hodder & Stoughton, 1922.

Cook, Nick. *Hunt for Zero Point*, London. Arrow, 2002.

Cooke, Grace. *Sun-Men of the Americas*, Liss, Hampshire. The White Eagle Trust, 1983.

—, and Cooke, Ivan. *The Light in Britain*, Liss. The White Eagle Publishing Trust, 1971.

Corso, Philip, *The Day After Roswell*, London. Pocket Books, Simon and Schuster, 1997.

Dalton, J.J. *The Cattle Mutilators*, New York. Manor Books, Inc., 1980.

Denham, Michael. *The Denham Tracts,* London. The Folklore Society, 1895.

Devereux, Paul. *Earth Lights*, Wellingborough. Turnstone Press Limited, 1982.

—, *Places of Power*, London. Blandford Press, 1990.

—, *Spirit Roads*, London. Collins & Brown, 2003.

—, *Symbolic Landscapes*, Glastonbury. Gothic Image Publications, 1992.

Eason, Cassandra. *A Complete Guide to Fairies & Magical Beings*, London. Judy Piatkus (Publishers) Limited, 2001.

Evans-Wentz, Walter, Y. *The Fairy Faith in Celtic Countries*, Glastonbury. The Lost Library, 2010.

Finkelstein, David. *The Space-Time Code*, Physical Review, 5D, no.12 [15 June 1972]: 2922.

Gardner, Edward. *Fairies: A Book of Real Fairies*, London. The Theosophical Publishing House, 1945.

Godwin, Joscelyn. *Atlantis and the Cycles of Time*, Raoulster, Vermont. Inner Traditions, 2011.

Good, Timothy. *Earth: an Alien Enterprise*, London: Pegasus Books, 2013.

Graddon, Nigel. *Otto Rahn and the Quest for the Grail,* Kempton, Illinois. Adventures Unlimited Press, 2008.

Grosso, Michael. *UFOs and the Myth of the New Age*, in *Cyberbiological Studies of the Imaginal Component in the UFO Contact Experience*, ed. Dennis Stillings, St. Paul, Minnesota. Archaeus Project, 1989.

Hall, Manley. *The Secret Teachings of All Ages*, Los Angeles. The Philosophical Research Society, Inc., 1928.

—, *Unseen Forces*, Los Angeles. Philosophical Research Society, Inc., 1978.

Hartland, Edwin. *The Science of Fairytales*, Indo-European Publishing, 2016.

Helsing, Jan. *Secret Societies and their Power in the 20th Century*, Gran Canaria, Spain. Ewertverlag S.L., 1995.

Hesemann, Michael. *UFOs: the Secret History*, New York: Marlowe and Company, 1998.

—, *The Cosmic Connection: Worldwide Crop Formations and ET Contacts*, Bath. Gateway Books, 1996.

—, *The Fatima Secret*, New York. Dell Publishing, 2000.

Hesemann, Michael, and Philip Mantle. *Beyond Roswell*, London. Michael O'Mara Books Limited, 1997.

Howe, Linda Moulton. *An Alien Harvest*, Huntingdon Valley, PA. Linda Moulton Howe Productions, 1989.

—, *Glimpses of Other Realities, Volume II: High Strangeness*, New Orleans. Paper Chase Press, 1998.

—, *Mysterious Lights and Crop Circles*, New Orleans, Paper Chase Press, 2000.

Jeans, James. *The Mysterious Universe*, New York. E.P. Dutton, 1932.

Jung, Carl. *Flying Saucers: A Modern Myth of Things Seen in the Sky*, London. Ark Paperbacks edition, 1987.

Keel, John. *Operation Trojan Horse*, San Antonio. Anomalist Books, 1970.

—, *Haunted Planet*, West Virginia. New Saucerian Books, 2014.

—, *The Endles Procession*, Pursuit Magazine, Third Quarter, 1982.

Keightley, Thomas. *Fairy Mythology, volume 2*, Amsterdam. VAMzzz Publishing, 2015.

Kirk, Robert. *The Secret Commonwealth of Elves, Fauns and Fairies*, New York. Dover Publications, Inc. edition, 2008.

Layne, Meade. *The Coming of the Guardians*, San Diego. Inner Circle Press, 2009.

LeShan, Lawrence. *The Medium, The Mystic and the Physicist*, New York. Viking Press, 1974.

Lovecraft, H.P., *The Call of Cthulhu*, Weird Tales Magazine, 1928.

MacManus, Dermot. *The Middle Kingdom: the faerie world of Ireland*, Buckinghamshire. Colin Smythe Limited, 1973.

Michell, John. *The Flying Saucer Vision*, London. Abacus, 1974.

—, *The New View Over Atlantis*, London. Thames and Hudson, 1983.

Monroe, Robert. *Journeys Out Of the Body*, New York. Anchor Press, 1973.

Paget, Peter. *The Welsh Triangle*, St. Albans. Granada Publishing Limited, 1979.

Pope, Nick. *The Uninvited: An Exposé of the Alien Abduction Phenomenon*, London. Thistle Publishing, 2015.

Pugh, Randall, and Frederick Holiday. *The Dyfed Enigma*, London. Faber and Faber, 1979.

Randles, Jenny. & Warrington, Peter. *UFOs-A British Viewpoint*, London. Robert Hale Limited, 1979.

Redfern, Nick. *A Covert Agenda*, London. Simon & Schuster UK, 1998.

—, *Cosmic Crashes*, London. Simon & Schuster UK, 2000.

Roberts, Anthony, and Geoff Gilbertson. *The Dark Gods*, London, Granada Publishing, Ltd, 1985.

Rux, Bruce. *Architects of the Underworld*, Berkeley: Frog, Ltd, 1996.

Sarfatti, J., *Implications of Meta-Physics for Psychoenergetic Systems, in Psychoenergetic Systems*, Vol. 1, London. Gordon and Breach, 1974.

Sikes, Wirt. *British Goblins: Welsh Folk-Lore, Fairy Mythology, Legends and Traditions*, London. Low, Marston, Searle and Rivington, 1880.

Spence, Lewis. *The Mysteries of Britain*. London. Senate, 1994.

Steinman, William. *UFO Crash at Aztec*, UFO archives, 1987.

Stillings, D., (Ed). *Cyberbiological Studies of the Imaginal Component in the UFO Contact Experience*, Archaeus Project, 1989.

Strieber, William. *Communion: A True Story*, New York. Harper, 2008.

Talbot, Michael. *Mysticism and the New Physics*, London. Arkana, 1993.

—, *The Holographic Universe*, London. HarperCollins*Publishers*, 1996.

Vallée, Jacques. *Passport to Magonia*, Brisbane. Daily Grail Publishing, 2014.

—, *UFOs: The Psychic Solution*, St. Albans. Panther Books Ltd, 1977.

Walker, Evan. *The Nature of Consciousness*, Mathematical Biosciences 7, 1970.

Wegener, Franz. *Heinrich Himmler: German Spiritualism, French Occultism and the Reichsführer-SS*, CreateSpace Independent Publishing Platform, 2013.

Zipes, Andrea, ed. *The Original Folk & Fairytales of the Brothers Grimm*, Princeton. Princeton University Press, 2014.

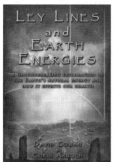

LEY LINE & EARTH ENERGIES
An Extraordinary Journey into the Earth's Natural Energy System
By David Cowan & Chris Arnold

The mysterious standing stones, burial grounds and stone circles that lace Europe, the British Isles and other areas have intrigued scientists, writers, artists and travellers through the centuries. How do ley lines work? How did our ancestors use Earth energy to map their sacred sites and burial grounds? How do ghosts and poltergeists interact with Earth energy? How can Earth spirals and black spots affect our health? This exploration shows how natural forces affect our behavior, how they can be used to enhance our health and well being.

368 PAGES. 6x9 PAPERBACK. ILLUSTRATED. $18.95. CODE: LLEE

ANCIENT ALIENS & SECRET SOCIETIES
By Mike Bara

Did ancient "visitors"—of extraterrestrial origin—come to Earth long, long ago and fashion man in their own image? Were the science and secrets that they taught the ancients intended to be a guide for all humanity to the present era? Bara establishes the reality of the catastrophe that jolted the human race, and traces the history of secret societies from the priesthood of Amun in Egypt to the Templars in Jerusalem and the Scottish Rite Freemasons. Bara also reveals the true origins of NASA and exposes the bizarre triad of secret societies in control of that agency since its inception. Chapters include: Out of the Ashes; From the Sky Down; Ancient Aliens?; The Dawn of the Secret Societies; The Fractures of Time; Into the 20th Century; The Wink of an Eye; more.

288 Pages. 6x9 Paperback. Illustrated. $19.95. Code: AASS

HESS AND THE PENGUINS
The Holocaust, Antarctica and the Strange Case of Rudolf Hess
By Joseph P. Farrell

Farrell looks at Hess' mission to make peace with Britain and get rid of Hitler—even a plot to fly Hitler to Britain for capture! How much did Göring and Hitler know of Rudolf Hess' subversive plot, and what happened to Hess? Why was a doppelganger put in Spandau Prison and then "suicided"? Did the British use an early form of mind control on Hess' double? John Foster Dulles of the OSS and CIA suspected as much. Farrell also uncovers the strange death of Admiral Richard Byrd's son in 1988, about the same time of the death of Hess.

288 Pages. 6x9 Paperback. Illustrated. $19.95. Code: HAPG

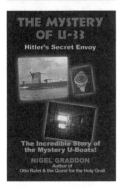

THE MYSTERY OF U-33
By Nigel Graddon

The incredible story of the mystery U-Boats of WWII! Graddon first chronicles the story of the mysterious U-33 that landed in Scotland in 1940 and involved the top-secret Enigma device. He then looks at U-Boat special missions during and after WWII, including U-Boat trips to Antarctica; U-Boats with the curious cargos of liquid mercury; the journey of the Spear of Destiny via U-Boat; the "Black Subs" and more. Chapters and topics include: U-33: The Official Story; The First Questions; Survivors and Deceased; August 1985—the Story Breaks; The Carradale U-boat; The Tale of the Bank Event; In the Wake of U-33; Wrecks; The Greenock Lairs; The Mystery Men; "Brass Bounders at the Admiralty"; Captain's Log; Max Schiller through the Lens; Rudolf Hess; Otto Rahn; U-Boat Special Missions; Neu-Schwabenland; more.

351 Pages. 6x9 Paperback. Illustrated. $19.95. Code: MU33

ANCIENT ALIENS ON THE MOON
By Mike Bara
What did NASA find in their explorations of the solar system that they may have kept from the general public? How ancient really are these ruins on the Moon? Using official NASA and Russian photos of the Moon, Bara looks at vast cityscapes and domes in the Sinus Medii region as well as glass domes in the Crisium region. Bara also takes a detailed look at the mission of Apollo 17 and the case that this was a salvage mission, primarily concerned with investigating an opening into a massive hexagonal ruin near the landing site. Chapters include: The History of Lunar Anomalies; The Early 20th Century; Sinus Medii; To the Moon Alice!; Mare Crisium; Yes, Virginia, We Really Went to the Moon; Apollo 17; more. Tons of photos of the Moon examined for possible structures and other anomalies.
248 Pages. 6x9 Paperback. Illustrated.. $19.95. Code: AAOM

ANCIENT ALIENS ON MARS
By Mike Bara
Bara brings us this lavishly illustrated volume on alien structures on Mars. Was there once a vast, technologically advanced civilization on Mars, and did it leave evidence of its existence behind for humans to find eons later? Did these advanced extraterrestrial visitors vanish in a solar system wide cataclysm of their own making, only to make their way to Earth and start anew? Was Mars once as lush and green as the Earth, and teeming with life? Chapters include: War of the Worlds; The Mars Tidal Model; The Death of Mars; Cydonia and the Face on Mars; The Monuments of Mars; The Search for Life on Mars; The True Colors of Mars and The Pathfinder Sphinx; more. Color section.
252 Pages. 6x9 Paperback. Illustrated. $19.95. Code: AMAR

ANCIENT ALIENS ON MARS II
By Mike Bara
Using data acquired from sophisticated new scientific instruments like the Mars Odyssey THEMIS infrared imager, Bara shows that the region of Cydonia overlays a vast underground city full of enormous structures and devices that may still be operating. He peels back the layers of mystery to show images of tunnel systems, temples and ruins, and exposes the sophisticated NASA conspiracy designed to hide them. Bara also tackles the enigma of Mars' hollowed out moon Phobos, and exposes evidence that it is artificial. Long-held myths about Mars, including claims that it is protected by a sophisticated UFO defense system, are examined. Data from the Mars rovers Spirit, Opportunity and Curiosity are examined; everything from fossilized plants to mechanical debris is exposed in images taken directly from NASA's own archives.
294 Pages. 6x9 Paperback. Illustrated. $19.95. Code: AAM2

ANCIENT TECHNOLOGY IN PERU & BOLIVIA
By David Hatcher Childress
Childress speculates on the existence of a sunken city in Lake Titicaca and reveals new evidence that the Sumerians may have arrived in South America 4,000 years ago. He demonstrates that the use of "keystone cuts" with metal clamps poured into them to secure megalithic construction was an advanced technology used all over the world, from the Andes to Egypt, Greece and Southeast Asia. He maintains that only power tools could have made the intricate articulation and drill holes found in extremely hard granite and basalt blocks in Bolivia and Peru, and that the megalith builders had to have had advanced methods for moving and stacking gigantic blocks of stone, some weighing over 100 tons.
340 Pages. 6x9 Paperback. Illustrated.. $19.95 Code: ATP

TECHNOLOGY OF THE GODS
The Incredible Sciences of the Ancients
by David Hatcher Childress

Childress looks at the technology that was allegedly used in Atlantis and the theory that the Great Pyramid of Egypt was originally a gigantic power station. He examines tales of ancient flight and the technology that it involved; how the ancients used electricity; megalithic building techniques; the use of crystal lenses and the fire from the gods; evidence of various high tech weapons in the past, including atomic weapons; ancient metallurgy and heavy machinery; the role of modern inventors such as Nikola Tesla in bringing ancient technology back into modern use; impossible artifacts; and more.

356 PAGES. 6x9 PAPERBACK. ILLUSTRATED. $16.95. CODE: TGOD

COVERT WARS AND BREAKAWAY CIVILIZATIONS
By Joseph P. Farrell

Farrell delves into the creation of breakaway civilizations by the Nazis in South America and other parts of the world. He discusses the advanced technology that they took with them at the end of the war and the psychological war that they waged for decades on America and NATO. He investigates the secret space programs currently sponsored by the breakaway civilizations and the current militaries in control of planet Earth. Plenty of astounding accounts, documents and speculation on the incredible alternative history of hidden conflicts and secret space programs that began when World War II officially "ended."

292 Pages. 6x9 Paperback. Illustrated. $19.95. Code: BCCW

THE ENIGMA OF CRANIAL DEFORMATION
Elongated Skulls of the Ancients
By David Hatcher Childress and Brien Foerster

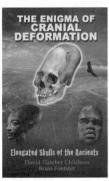

In a book filled with over a hundred astonishing photos and a color photo section, Childress and Foerster take us to Peru, Bolivia, Egypt, Malta, China, Mexico and other places in search of strange elongated skulls and other cranial deformation. The puzzle of why diverse ancient people—even on remote Pacific Islands—would use head-binding to create elongated heads is mystifying. Where did they even get this idea? Did some people naturally look this way—with long narrow heads? Were they some alien race? Were they an elite race that roamed the entire planet? Why do anthropologists rarely talk about cranial deformation and know so little about it? Color Section.

250 Pages. 6x9 Paperback. Illustrated. $19.95. Code: ECD

ARK OF GOD
The Incredible Power of the Ark of the Covenant
By David Hatcher Childress

Childress takes us on an incredible journey in search of the truth about (and science behind) the fantastic biblical artifact known as the Ark of the Covenant. This object made by Moses at Mount Sinai—part wooden-metal box and part golden statue—had the power to create "lightning" to kill people, and also to fly and lead people through the wilderness. The Ark of the Covenant suddenly disappears from the Bible record and what happened to it is not mentioned. Was it hidden in the underground passages of King Solomon's temple and later discovered by the Knights Templar? Was it taken through Egypt to Ethiopia as many Coptic Christians believe? Childress looks into hidden history, astonishing ancient technology, and a 3,000-year-old mystery that continues to fascinate millions of people today. Color section.

420 Pages. 6x9 Paperback. Illustrated. $22.00 Code: AOG

ORDER FORM

**10% Discount
When You Order
3 or More Items!**

One Adventure Place
P.O. Box 74
Kempton, Illinois 60946
United States of America
Tel.: 815-253-6390 • Fax: 815-253-6300
Email: auphq@frontiernet.net
http://www.adventuresunlimitedpress.com

ORDERING INSTRUCTIONS

✓ Remit by USD$ Check, Money Order or Credit Card

✓ Visa, Master Card, Discover & AmEx Accepted

✓ Paypal Payments Can Be Made To:
   info@wexclub.com

✓ Prices May Change Without Notice

✓ 10% Discount for 3 or more Items

SHIPPING CHARGES

United States

✓ Postal Book Rate { $4.00 First Item / 50¢ Each Additional Item

✓ POSTAL BOOK RATE Cannot Be Tracked!

✓ Priority Mail { $5.00 First Item / $2.00 Each Additional Item

✓ UPS { $6.00 First Item / $1.50 Each Additional Item

   NOTE: UPS Delivery Available to Mainland USA Only

Canada

✓ Postal Air Mail { $10.00 First Item / $2.50 Each Additional Item

✓ Personal Checks or Bank Drafts MUST BE
   US$ and Drawn on a US Bank

✓ Canadian Postal Money Orders OK

✓ Payment MUST BE US$

All Other Countries

✓ Sorry, No Surface Delivery!

✓ Postal Air Mail { $16.00 First Item / $6.00 Each Additional Item

✓ Checks and Money Orders MUST BE US$
   and Drawn on a US Bank or branch.

✓ Paypal Payments Can Be Made in US$ To:
   info@wexclub.com

SPECIAL NOTES

✓ RETAILERS: Standard Discounts Available

✓ BACKORDERS: We Backorder all Out-of-
   Stock Items Unless Otherwise Requested

✓ PRO FORMA INVOICES: Available on Request

ORDER ONLINE AT: www.adventuresunlimitedpress.com

Please check: ✓

☐ This is my first order   ☐ I have ordered before

Name _____
Address _____
City _____
State/Province _____ Postal Code _____
Country _____
Phone day _____ Evening _____
Fax _____ Email _____

Item Code	Item Description	Qty	Total

Please check: ✓

Subtotal ▶ _____
Less Discount-10% for 3 or more items ▶ _____

☐ Postal-Surface — Balance ▶ _____

☐ Postal-Air Mail — Illinois Residents 6.25% Sales Tax ▶ _____
   (Priority in USA) — Previous Credit ▶ _____

☐ UPS — Shipping ▶ _____
   (Mainland USA only) Total (check/MO in USD$ only) ▶ _____

☐ Visa/MasterCard/Discover/American Express

Card Number _____

Expiration Date _____

10% Discount When You Order 3 or More Items!